The Ultimate Kauai Guidebook
Kauai Revealed

4th Edition

Andrew Doughty & Harriett Friedman

WIZARD
PUBLICATIONS
INC

The Ultimate Kauai Guidebook
Kauai Revealed; 4th Edition

Published by Wizard Publications, Inc.
Post Office Box 991
Lihu'e, Hawai'i 96766–0991

ISBN 0–9639429–8–0   4/4q
Library of Congress Control Number 2001088660
Printed in China

Cataloging-in-Publication Data
Doughty, Andrew
      The Ultimate Kauai guidebook : Kauai revealed / Andrew Doughty and Harriett
Friedman. -- 4th ed. Lihue, HI : Wizard Publications, Inc., 2003
      248 p. : col. illus., col. photos, col. maps ; 21 cm.
      Includes index.
      Summary: A complete traveler's reference to the Hawaiian island of Kauai, with
full color illustrations, maps, directions and candid advice by authors who reside in Hawaii.
      ISBN 0-9639429-8-0
      LCCN 2001088660

      1. Kaua'i (Hawaii) - Guidebooks I. Friedman, Harriett II. Title

    DU628.K3   919.69'41_dc21

All photographs (except the cover) taken by Andrew Doughty. (And he *wishes* he
had been able to take that one.)
Cover imagery courtesy of NASA.
Cartography by Andrew Doughty.
All artwork and illustrations by Andrew Doughty and Harriett Friedman.

Pages 2–3: Wai'ale'ale Crater, with its 3,000-foot waterfall-etched walls, was the
spiritual center of the ancient Hawaiian universe.

We welcome any comments, questions, criticisms or contributions you may have,
and have incorporated some of your suggestions into this edition. Please send to
the address above or e-mail us at **aloha@wizardpub.com**

Check out our Web site at **www.wizardpub.com** for up-to-the-minute changes.

Dedicated to Sammie Dollar, who soars on the wind with the white-tailed tropic birds.

CONTENTS

CONTENTS

In a sense, this is not a guidebook, it's more of a love story. We first came to Kaua'i as tourists and were immediately smitten. We had no idea that a place like this could exist anywhere in the world. Now as residents, we marvel at its beauty every day.

Longtime locals have been stunned at some of the items in our book. We've found many special places that people born and raised here never knew about. Visitors will find this book as valuable as having a friend living on the island.

Kaua'i is a unique place. People who visit here recognize this immediately. There are plenty of places in the world featuring sun and sea, but no other place offers the incomparable beauty, lushness and serenity as Kaua'i. Living here, we get to see first-time visitors driving around with their jaws open, shaking their heads in disbelief at what they see. Without a doubt, you will never see more smiles than during your visit to Kaua'i.

Our objective in writing this book is to assist you in finding the bliss that can accompany a Kaua'i visit. We recognize the effort people go through to visit here, and our goal is to expose you to every option imaginable so you can decide what you want to see and do.

We took great pains to structure this book in such a way that it will be fun, easy reading and loaded with useful information. This book is not a bland regurgitation of facts arranged in textbook fashion. We feel strongly that guidebooks should present information so that you don't have to read through every page every time you want to find something. If you're here on vacation, your time is extremely precious. You worked all year to get here, and you don't want to spend all your time flipping through a book looking for something. You want to be able to locate what

you want, when you want it. You want to be able to access a comprehensive index, a thorough table of contents and refer to high-quality maps that were designed with *you* in mind. You want to know which helicopter, SCUBA, boat tour or lu'au is the best on the island. You want to be shown those things that will make this vacation the best of your life.

A quick look at this book will reveal features never before used in a guidebook. Let's start with the maps. They are more detailed than any other maps you will find, yet they omit extraneous information that can sometimes make a chore of reading a map. We know that people often have a hard time determining where they are on a map, especially here, so we have included landmarks. Most notable among these are mile markers. At every mile on main roads, the government has erected numbered markers to tell you where you are. We are the first to put these markers on a map so you can use them as reference points. We also made every effort to place north at the top of the page. It can be confusing when you see a map with south pointing up or to the right. Only a couple of trail maps deviate from this rule. Additionally, we repeatedly drove every inch of every road on the maps. This is important because *many* of the roads represented on existing maps have been shifted, moved or eliminated. You could become very frustrated trying to find certain beaches or other scenic spots using other maps. We personally check every place and often use aerial photography and a GPS to determine the best methods for getting to certain places.

Early on we spent three days trying to find a certain secluded beach using existing maps. When we checked aerial shots, we discovered that *every single*

map was wrong. Getting to the beach was a snap—if you knew where to go. Where needed, we've drawn legal public beach access in yellow, so you'll know when you are legally entitled to cross someone's land. Lastly, all the maps are 3-D. We've found that *accurate* shaded relief maps easily convey much more information to the map reader.

One of the things unique to this book is the acceptance of change. We produce brand new editions of our books every two years or so, but in the intervening time we are constantly incorporating changes into the text nearly every time we do a new printing. We also post these changes on our Web site. This allows us to make some modifications throughout the life of each edition. We don't have the luxury of making every change that happens on a weekly basis, but it does give us more flexibility than if we only acknowledged changes every two years.

Slick (and not so slick) free magazines and publications are strewn throughout the island. Most claim to point you to assorted wonders. There's nothing wrong with that. But the adage, "You get what you pay for," applies. Let's put it this way. If all the companies in this book were companies that we had to solicit for advertising, how much candor do you think we could provide? That's why *you* pay for the book, not the companies we describe. We're free to be as brutally honest as we want to be. Since we accept no advertisements, our allegiance is to our readers, not advertisers. Nonetheless, these free publications can be useful for the coupons that advertisers put inside.

As you read this book, you will notice that we are very candid in assessing businesses. Unlike some other guidebooks that send out questionnaires asking a business if they are any good (gee, they

all say they're good), we've had *personal* contact with the businesses listed in this book. We accept no payment for our reviews, we make no deals with businesses for saying nice things, and again, there are *no advertisements* in our book. If we gush over a certain company, it comes from personal experience with the company. If we rail against a business, it is for the same reason. All businesses mentioned in this book are here by *our* choice. None have had any input into what we say, and we have not received a single cent from any of them for their inclusion. (In fact, some would probably pay to be left out of this book, given our comments.) We always approach businesses as *anonymous travelers* and later as guidebook writers only if we need more information. This ensures that we are treated the same as you. (We were once *anonymously* reviewing a restaurant when a writer from another guidebook walked in, told the manager their identity and asked for food. Not surprisingly, the food was "great." But ours was lousy!) What you get here is our unbiased opinion on how companies operate—nothing more, nothing less.

This book is intended to bring you independence in exploring Kaua'i. We don't want to waste your precious time by giving you bad advice or bad directions. We want you to experience the best that the island has to offer. In the end, it's probably fair to say that our ultimate objective is to have you leave Kaua'i shaking your head saying, "I never knew a place like this existed."

We hope we succeed.

Andrew Doughty
Harriett Friedman

Kapa'a, Hawai'i

The walls of Wai'ale'ale Crater, from which the island of Kaua'i burst forth in a fiery cataclysm, are now home to innumerable waterfalls. This part of the crater is called the Weeping Wall.

INTRODUCTION

As with people, volcanic islands have a life cycle. They emerge from their sea floor womb to be greeted by the warmth of the sun. They grow and mature and eventually die before sinking forever beneath the sea.

How It Began

The Hawaiian Islands were born of fire thousands of feet below the surface in the icy cold waters on the Pacific Ocean floor. A rupture in the earth's crust caused a vent to spew hot magma that built upon itself as it reached upward. When it began, no one knows exactly, but the first of the still existing islands to boil to the surface was Kure. Nothing remains of that island today but its fringing coral reef, called an atoll.

As the Pacific plate shifted over the opening of the vent like steel over a cutting torch, more islands were created.

Midway, French Frigate Shoals, Necker, Nihoa—all of these once-great islands were born and then mostly consumed by the angry ocean. What we call Hawai'i is just the last in a series of islands created by this vent. Someday these, too, will be nothing more than atolls, footnotes in the geologic history of the earth. But this vent isn't finished yet. The Big Island of Hawai'i is still expanding as lava from its active volcano continues even now to create additional real estate on that island. As we sit here, the future island of Lo'ihi is being created 20 miles southeast of the Big Island. Although still 3,200 feet below the surface of the ocean, in but a geologic moment, the Hawaiian volcano goddess Pele will add yet another piece of paradise to her impressive domain.

These virgin islands were barren at birth. The first life forms to appreciate these new islands of volcanic rock were marine creatures. Fish, mammals and microscopic animals discovered this new underwater haven and made homes for themselves. Coral polyps attached themselves to the lava rock and succeeding generations built upon these, creating what would become a coral reef.

Meanwhile, on land, seeds carried by the winds were struggling to colonize the rocky land, eking out a living and breaking down the lava rock. Storms brought the occasional bird, hopelessly blown off course. The lucky ones found the islands. The even luckier ones arrived with mates or had fertilized eggs when they got here. Other animals, stranded on a piece of floating debris, washed ashore against all odds and went on to colonize the islands. These introductions of new species were rare events. It took an extraordinary set of circumstances for a new species to actually make it to the islands. Single specimens were destined to live out their lives in lonely solitude. On average, a new species was successfully deposited here only once every 20,000 years.

As the plants and animals lived out their lives, they broke up the rock, forming soil and organic debris. The ocean, meanwhile, was busily working to reclaim the horizon from these interruptions of land. Waves battered unmercifully against the fragile lava rock. In this battle between titans, there can be but one winner. While the creation of land eventually ceases on an individual island, the ocean never gives up. Wave after wave eventually takes its toll.

In addition to the ocean, rain carves up the islands. As the islands thrust themselves upward into the moisture-laden trade winds, their challenge to the rain clouds is accepted. As the air encounters the slopes of these tall islands, it rises and cools, causing the air to release its humidity in the form of rain. This rain forms channels that easily carve valleys in the soft lava rock.

So what is the result of all this destruction? Paradise. Absolute paradise. There are few things more beautiful than Mother Nature reclaiming that which she gave birth to. The older the island, the more beautiful the landscape. A

Each successive wave is like a sculptor's chisel, slowly shaping the island. Large storms can generate powerful waves, such as this one, which, over the eons, patiently return the island to the sea.

On rare occasions this ancient Hawaiian petroglyph is exposed in the mouth of the Wailua River.

Hawaiian island is never more lovely than in its middle age, when the scars of constant environmental battles are carved into its face. Lush landscaped valleys, razorback ridges, long, sandy beaches—those things we cherish so much are the result of this destructive battle.

Kauaʻi consists of 553 square miles of beach, rain forest, desert, mountains and plains. The island's landscape is as varied as its people. At Waiʻaleʻale in the island's center, it rains every day, making it the wettest place on earth. Just a few miles to the west, rain is rare, creating dry, almost arid conditions. The north shore is as lush as any place on the planet. The south shore is a sunny playground. The island's first inhabitants surely must have felt blessed at the discovery of this diversity.

THE FIRST SETTLERS

Sometime around the fourth or fifth century A.D., a large double-hulled voyaging canoe, held together with flexible sennit lashings and propelled by sails made of woven pandanus, slid onto the sand on the Big Island of Hawaiʻi. These first intrepid adventurers encountered an island chain of unimaginable beauty.

They had left their home in the Marquesas Islands 2,500 miles away for reasons we will never know. Some say it was because of war, overpopulation, drought or just a sense of adventure. Whatever their reasons, these initial settlers took a big chance and surely must have been highly motivated. They left their homes and searched for a new world to colonize. Doubtless, most of the first groups perished at sea. There was no way for them to know that there were islands in these waters. The Hawaiian Islands are the most isolated island chain in the world. Those who did arrive brought with them food staples from home: taro, breadfruit, pigs, dogs and several types of fowl. This was a pivotal decision. These first settlers found a land that contained almost no edible plants. With no land mammals other than the Hawaiian bat, the first settlers subsisted on fish until their crops could mature. From then on, they lived largely on fish and taro. Although we associate throw-net fishing with Hawai'i, this practice was introduced by Japanese immigrants much later. The ancient Hawaiians used fishhooks and spears for the most part or drove fish into a net already placed into the water. They also had domesticated animals that were used as ritual foods or reserved for chiefs.

As the culture evolved and flourished, it developed into a hierarchical system of order. The society was governed by chiefs, called ali'i, who established a long list of taboos called kapu. These kapu were designed to keep order, and the penalty for breaking one was usually death by strangulation, club or fire. If the violation was serious enough, the guilty party's family might also be killed. It was kapu, for instance, for your shadow to fall across the shadow of the ali'i. It was kapu to interrupt the chief if he was speaking. It was kapu to prepare men's food in the same container used for women's food. It was kapu for women to eat pork or bananas. It was kapu for men and women to eat together. It was kapu not to observe the days designated to the gods. Certain areas were kapu for fishing if they became depleted. This allowed the area to replenish itself.

While harsh by our standards today, this system kept order. Most ali'i were sensitive to the disturbance their presence caused and often ventured outside only at night, or a scout was sent ahead to warn people that an ali'i was on his way. All commoners were required to pay tribute to the ali'i in the form of food and other items.

In January 1778 an event occurred that would forever change Hawai'i. Captain James Cook, who usually had a genius for predicting where to find

Who Were the Menehune?

Although the legend of Menehune exists throughout the Hawaiian Islands, the folklore is strongest on Kaua'i. Hawaiian legend speaks of a mythical race of people living in the islands before the Polynesians. Called the Menehune, these people were always referred to as small in stature. Initially referring to their social stature, the legend evolved to mean that they were physically short and lived in the woods away from the Hawaiians. (The Hawaiians avoided the woods when possible, fearing that they held evil spirits, and instead stayed on the coastal plains.) The Menehune were purported to build fabulous structures, always in one night. Their numbers were said to be vast, as many as 500,000. Today, archeologists speculate that a second wave of colonists, probably from Tahiti, may have subdued these initial inhabitants, forcing them to live in the woods. It is interesting to note that in a census taken of Kaua'i around 1800, 65 people from the upper region of the Wainiha Valley identified themselves as Menehune.

Today, Menehune are jokingly blamed for anything that goes wrong. If you lost your wallet, Menehune took it. If your car won't start, Menehune have been tinkering with it. Kaua'i residents greatly cherish their legends of the Menehune.

islands, stumbled upon Hawai'i. He had not expected islands to be there. He was on his way to Alaska to search for the Northwest Passage linking the Atlantic and Pacific oceans. As Cook approached the shores of Waimea, Kaua'i, on January 19, 1778, the island's inhabitants thought they were being visited by gods. Rushing aboard to greet their visitors, the Kauaians were fascinated by what they saw: pointy-headed beings (the British wore tricornered hats) breathing fire (smoking pipes) and possessing a death-dealing instrument identified as a water squirter (guns). The amount of iron on the ship was incredible. (Hawaiians had only seen iron in the form of nails on driftwood but never knew the source.) Cook left Kaua'i and briefly explored Ni'ihau before heading north for his mission on February 2, 1778. When Cook returned to the Big Island of Hawai'i after failing to find the Northwest Passage, he was killed in a petty skirmish over a stolen rowboat. The Hawaiians were horrified that they had killed a man they had earlier presumed to be a god.

Just after this, Kamehameha the Great of the Big Island began consolidating his power by conquering the other islands in the chain. Kaua'i, however, presented a unique problem. Cut off from the rest of the chain by the treacherous Kaua'i Channel, Kaua'i's King Kaumuali'i had no intention of submitting himself to Kamehameha. In the spring of 1796 Kamehameha tried to invade Kaua'i. He and his fleet of 1,200 canoes carrying 10,000 soldiers left O'ahu at midnight hoping to reach Wailua, Kaua'i, by daybreak. They were in the middle of the Kaua'i Channel when the wind and seas picked up. Many of the canoes were swamped. Reluctantly, he ordered a retreat, but too late to stop some of his advance troops who were slaughtered after they arrived at the south shore beach of Maha'ulepu.

The earliest Hawaiians built elaborate terraces to grow taro, used to make poi.
This one, in the Limahuli Garden, is estimated to be 700–1,000 years old.

Ancient Hawaiians lived off the sea. With reefs teaming with life, Hawaiian waters have always been generous to the people of Hawai'i.

In 1804 Kamehameha tried again. He gathered 7,000 men, all heavily armed, and prepared to set sail for Kaua'i. Just before they were to leave, typhoid struck, decimating his troops and advisers. Kamehameha himself contracted the disease but managed to pull through. Kaua'i's king must have seen the writing on the wall and agreed to give his kingdom of Kaua'i over to Kamehameha. When Kamehameha died, his son, in order to solidify his power on Kaua'i, arranged to kidnap Kaua'i's King Kaumuali'i and forced him to marry his step-mother, the powerful widow of Kamehameha. Kaua'i's last king never returned and was eventually buried on Maui.

During the 19th century, Hawai'i's character changed dramatically. Businessmen from all over the world came here to exploit Hawai'i's sandalwood, whales, land and people. Hawai'i's leaders, for their part, actively participated in these ventures and took a piece of the action for themselves. Workers were brought in from many parts of the world, changing the racial makeup of the islands. Government corruption became the order of the day, and everyone seemed to be profiting except the Hawaiian commoner. By the time Queen Lili'uokalani lost her throne to a group of American businessmen in 1893, Hawai'i had become directionless. It barely resembled the Hawai'i Captain Cook had encountered the previous century. The kapu system had been abolished by the Hawaiians shortly after the death of Kamehameha the Great. The "Great Mahele," begun in 1848, had changed the relationship Hawaiians had with the land. Large tracts of land were sold by the Hawaiian government to royalty, govern-

What's it Like in the Wettest Spot on Earth?

The center of the island is called Mount Wai'ale'ale, meaning "rippling waters." It is here that you will find the rainiest spot on the planet with an average of 440 inches of rain per year and a median of 432 inches. Rain around the rest of the island is a fraction of this (see chart on page 28). The ancient Hawaiians recognized the importance of this spot and built a temple on the summit, its remains visible to this day. The only way you will get to see Wai'ale'ale up close and personal is by air.

The top of Mount Wai'ale'ale is somewhat barren. While this might sound strange given its moniker as the wettest spot on Earth, remember that few plants in this world are genetically programmed to deal with that much rain at that altitude. Plus the ever-present rain clouds prevent sunshine from enriching the plants. The bogs on top of the mountain make for a less than well-defined soil base, and fungi and lichen flourish in the constant moisture. The result is few trees. Those trees that do survive are stunted by nature's over-generous gift of water.

Just below the summit—3,000 feet straight down, to be precise—exists the unimaginable lushness one would expect from abundant rain. As the clouds are forced up the walls of Wai'ale'ale Crater, they shed a portion of their moisture. With the majority of the rain falling on the summit, the crater floor is left with just the perfect amount. With volcanically rich soil left over from the fiery eruptions, the crater floor has become a haven for anything green. Ferns rule the crater. The ground shakes beneath your feet as your footsteps echo through generations of water-saturated fallen ferns which have created a soft underbelly to what once was a savage, lava-spewing giant.

There is a surprising lack of insect presence, and most that are there are endemic, appearing nowhere else on earth. Aside from mosquitoes in the stream beds, we encountered almost no insects in the dense fern growth of the crater. The only exception was a single flightless grasshopper. We found some 'o'opu fish inhabiting streams between towering waterfalls. They use their pelvic fins to actually *climb* the falls and live in these isolated pools.

Everywhere one looks, plants have taken root. Every rock has moss, every fallen tree has other plants growing on it, every crevice has growth. Surely, no other place on earth is as lush as Wai'ale'ale Crater.

The summit of Wai'ale'ale feeds the Wailua River 3,000 feet below the sheer cliffs.

ment officials, commoners and foreigners, effectively stripping many Hawaiians of land they had lived on for generations.

The United States recognized the Republic of Hawai'i in 1894 with Sanford Dole as its president. It was later annexed and then became a territory in 1900. During the 19th and 20th centuries, sugar established itself as king. Pineapple was also heavily grown in the islands, and the entire island of Lana'i was purchased for the purpose of growing pineapple. As the 20th century rolled on, Hawaiian sugar and pineapple workers found themselves in a lofty position—they became the highest paid workers for these crops in the world. As land prices rose and competition from other parts of the world increased, sugar and pineapple became less and less prof-

On Kaua'i, the first settlers found an Eden more perfect than any place they'd ever known.

itable. Today, these crops no longer hold the position they once had. In the 1990s the "Pineapple Island" of Lana'i completely shifted away from pineapple and started luring tourists. And where dozens of sugar companies once dotted the islands, today only two remain—one here and one on Maui. Former sugar workers have moved into other vocations, usually tourist-related or farming.

The story of Hawai'i is not a story of good versus evil. Nearly everyone shares in the blame of what happened to the Hawaiian people and their culture. Nevertheless, today Hawai'i is struggling to redefine its identity. The Islands are looking back to the past for guidance. During your stay you will be exposed to a place that is attempting to recapture its cultural roots. There is more interest in Hawaiian culture and language than ever before. Sometimes it is clumsy, sometimes awkward. There is no common agreement regarding how to do it, but in the end, a reinvigoration of the Hawaiian spirit will no doubt be enjoyed by all.

NI'IHAU

No man is an island, or so they say. But in Hawai'i, one family can own one. The island of Ni'ihau is a dry, somewhat barren island of 46,000 acres located 17 miles to the west of Kaua'i. When Scottish-born Eliza Sinclair was sailing in the islands with her family in 1863, they were looking for land on which to settle. Having turned down offers of several tracts on O'ahu (including Waikiki, which they dismissed as showing no promise), they were about to leave for California when King Kamehameha V offered to sell them Ni'ihau. When Eliza's sons went to look at it, they found a green, wet island with abundant grass—perfect for raising cattle. What they were unaware of at the time was that Ni'ihau had experienced a rare rainy period and was flourishing as a result. They offered $6,000, the King countered with $10,000, and they took it.

This was 1864 and, unfortunately for the Sinclairs, the residents of Ni'ihau did not respect their ownership and resisted them. They had a further setback when an old Hawaiian showed them a deed indicating ownership to a crucial 50-acre sliver of Ni'ihau deeded to the old man by King Kamehameha III. The Sinclairs were in a bind and elicited the aid of Valdemar Knudsen to negotiate the pur-

chase of the remaining 50 acres. He spoke fluent Hawaiian and was well known and respected by the islanders. Knudsen went to Ni'ihau and offered $1,000 to the old man by slowly stacking the silver coins on a table while he explained how much better off the old man would be if he sold his land and lived in comfort on Kaua'i. After repeated refusals from the man, Knudsen went to take the money away when the old Hawaiian's wife grabbed the money, and the deal was consummated on the spot.

When the Sinclairs discovered that the land was actually dry and barren, unsuitable for a cattle ranch at that time, they arranged to buy 21,000 acres of West Kaua'i. (They would continue to buy land on Kaua'i, eventually acquiring 20 percent of the island, which they own to this day.) If you take a helicopter ride, you may see their fabulous estate nestled high in the mountains near Olokele.

Today, about 200 Hawaiians live on Ni'ihau. There is one unpaved road going halfway around the island, no telephones, except for a wireless two-way to Kaua'i and no cable TV. (Some residents tell us they've unsuccessfully tried to talk the Robinsons—the descendants of Eliza Sinclair—into getting a satellite dish so they can get CNN.) Intermittent power is

So close and yet so far. This is as close as most will ever come to the "forbidden" island of Ni'ihau.

supplied by generator and solar.

Ni'ihau's one school hosts around 40 students. The sense of family on the island is strong, and only Hawaiian is spoken in most homes. (Classes, however, are taught in English.) Ni'ihau residents are a deeply religious people, and crime against one another is almost unknown. They are intensely proud of their community and feel strongly that their people, their heritage and their way of life are special and are protected by God.

They live in one village called Pu'uwai (located in the only part of Ni'ihau where you can't see Kaua'i) and receive their mail once a week—the Post Office only delivers as far as Makaweli on Kaua'i. They shop for clothes and other durable items on Kaua'i, where most have family.

Time is fluid there. If someone says they'll see you on Wednesday, it could be any time of the day. There's no such thing as being late on Ni'ihau.

With a warehouse for staples and gardens for their fruits and vegetables, Ni'ihau islanders are reasonably self-sufficient. Travel to and from the island is via old military transports (like the kind in *Saving Private Ryan*) and the rough, bumpy ride takes around 3 hours each way (during which many get seasick).

Life on Ni'ihau is certainly not without problems. No drugs or alcohol are allowed on the island, and families have been banished forever from the island for growing pakalolo (marijuana). Their mortality rate is high. When the Robinsons closed the ranch operation in the late '90s all the workers lost their minimum wage jobs. The unemployment rate on Ni'ihau is now *100%,* and virtually everyone receives welfare and/or food stamps. With no permanent streams on the island, water is sometimes scarce. Although the largest lake in the state is

on Ni'ihau, it is usually only a few feet deep, muddy and generally unpleasant.

The Robinson's land is valued at close to a *billion* dollars, but crushing tax burdens and modest revenue (from Kaua'i sugar operations) leave them relatively cash poor. Though the land has been in the family for almost a century and a half, every time a land-owning relative dies, the government takes a huge bite out of the family in massive inheritance taxes. They claim that they can only afford to go out to dinner a few times a year. (You can dry your eyes now after that one.) As a result, they have recently warmed to the idea of using some of their Kaua'i land for tourism. They currently offer tours of some of their mountain land near Waimea Canyon. They almost allowed the federal government to install (for a fee) rocket launchers on Ni'ihau as part of an expansion of the Pacific Missile Range Facility on Kaua'i's west side. The deal fell through when the government insisted on an ethnographic survey, which the secretive Robinsons feared would be used to create precedents that would allow native Hawaiians *from Kaua'i* to visit the island (for constitutionally allowed ritual or gathering purposes). Instead, they are now planning a 250-room resort called Kapalawai on some of their west Kaua'i land.

The Robinsons claim that their unique deed to the island gives them ownership of Ni'ihau's beaches—directly in conflict with state law that proclaims that *all* beaches in Hawai'i are public beaches. To date nobody has challenged them in court. If you land on a beach on Ni'ihau, you will be asked to leave. If you refuse, a truly *gargantuan* Hawaiian gentleman will be summoned, and he will ask you a bit more firmly. This request is usually sufficient to persuade all but the most determined individuals to leave.

The bird-of-paradise is a striking flower found all over the island.

In order to get to Kaua'i, you've got to fly here. This may sound painfully obvious, but many people spend time trying to find an ocean cruise to the Islands. With the advent of jets, the long span of open ocean makes regular cruises here in feasible.

GETTING HERE

When planning your trip, a travel agent can be helpful. Their commission has been paid directly by the travel industry, though that may change in the future. The Internet is quickly becoming a great source for companies selling travel packages. If you don't want to or can't go through these sources, there are several large wholesalers that can get you airfare, hotel and a rental car, often cheaper than you can get airfare on your own. **Pleasant Hawaiian Holidays** (800) 242–9244 and **Suntrips** (800) 786–8747 are two of the more well-known providers of complete package tours. They are renowned for their impossibly low rates. We've always been amazed that you can sometimes get round trip airfare from the mainland, a hotel and car for a week for as low as $700 per person, depending on where you fly from and where you stay. That's a small price to pay for your little piece of paradise. **Cheap Tickets** (800) 377–1000 usually lives up to its name.

If you arrange airline tickets and hotel reservations yourself, you can often count on paying top dollar for each facet of your trip. The prices listed in the WHERE TO STAY section reflect the RACK rates, meaning the published rates before any discounts. Rates can be significantly lower if you go through a tour company.

When you pick your travel source, shop around—the differences can be dramatic. A diligent agent can make the difference between affording a *one-week* vacation and a *two-week* vacation. They don't all check the same sources for bargains; there is an art to it. Look in the Sunday travel section of your local newspaper—the bigger the paper, the better, or check on-line versions of major papers.

Though most visitors fly into Honolulu

before arriving, there are some direct flights to Kaua'i. Not having to cool your heels while changing planes on O'ahu is a *big* plus. Otherwise, inter-island flights are like buses; you can always take the next one, and you can sit anywhere you want. If you fly to Kaua'i from Honolulu, the best views are usually on the left side (seats with an "A"). When flying to Honolulu from the mainland, sit on the left side coming in, the right going home. Inter-island flights are done by **Aloha** (800 367–5250) and **Hawaiian** (800 367–5320 from the mainland; 800 882–8811 from the islands). Many of the airlines are getting picky about what they allow as carry-on. Hawaiian, for example will often confiscate your reasonably sized carry-on, especially if it has wheels, no matter how small. (Unless you're in first class, of course. In that case, feel free to bring along your bed from home.)

If the Lihu'e airport check-in line is long when you're leaving, you can often avoid the line completely by finding a porter near the line who will check your bag and prepare your ticket for a buck a bag. They are not always easily identified, so have one person hunt them out while the other waits in line, just in case.

WHAT TO BRING

This list will be helpful in planning what to bring. Obviously you won't bring everything on the list, but it might make you think of things you may otherwise overlook.

- Waterproof sunblock (SPF 15 or higher)
- Two bathing suits
- Shoes—thongs, trashable sneakers, reef shoes, hiking or trail shoes
- Mask, snorkel and fins

- Camera with lots of film
- Mosquito repellent for some hikes (*Lotions,* not liquids, containing DEET seem to work longest.)
- Insulated water jug to keep in the car—(Coleman makes a perfect 2-quart jug for this purpose.)
- Shorts and other cool cotton clothing
- Hat or cap for sun protection
- Light windbreaker jacket (for trip to Kalalau Lookout or helicopter trip)
- Fanny pack—also called waist pack to carry all your various vacation accouterments. Waterproof packs or boxes are convenient for snorkeling.
- Cheap, simple backpack—you don't need to go backpacking to use one; a 10-minute trek down to a secluded beach is much easier if you bring a simple pack.
- Long lightweight pants for hiking if you are going through jungle country.

GETTING AROUND
Rental Cars

The rental car prices in Hawai'i *can be* (but aren't always) cheaper than almost anywhere else in the country, and the competition is ferocious. Nearly every visitor to Kaua'i gets around in a rental car, and for good reason. The island's towns are separated by distances sufficient to discourage walking. Many of Kaua'i's best sights can only be reached if you have independent transportation.

At Lihu'e Airport, rental cars can easily be obtained from the booths across the street from the main terminal. It's usually a good idea to reserve your car in advance since companies can run out of cars during peak times. If you are interested in a cell phone, some have them available for about $5 per day.

On the following page are the companies currently operating on Kaua'i:

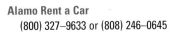

Alamo Rent a Car
(800) 327–9633 or (808) 246–0645

Avis Rent a Car
(800) 831–8000 or (808) 245–3512

Budget Rent a Car
(800) 527–0700 or (808) 245–1901

Dollar Rent a Car
(800) 800–4000 or (808) 245–3651

Hertz Rent a Car
(800) 654–3131 or (808) 245–3356

National Rent a Car
(800) 227–7368 or (808) 245–5636

Rent A Wreck
(800) 536–1391 or (808) 821–9582

Thrifty Rent a Car
(800) 847–4389 or (808) 246–6252

If you are between the ages of 21 and 25, **Alamo** and **Dollar** will rent to you, but expect to pay $15–$25 more *per day* for the crime of being young and reckless. If you're 18 to 21, **Rent A Wreck** will rent to you. Otherwise, see BUSES or bring a bike. If you don't have a credit card, **Chris The Fun Lady** at (808) 822–7759 should be able to help in advance. A cash deposit is necessary.

Below are a few tips to keep in mind when you rent your car on Kaua'i.

- The **Hanama'ulu Shell Station** (which will pump it for you) or the Shell in **Kapa'a** often have the cheapest gas on the island. Rental car company gas rates are usually high and are meant to dissuade you from returning the car empty (unless you pay for a full tank at the beginning).

- Many COLLISION DAMAGE WAIVERS will not cover vehicles on unpaved roads or beaches. Consider this when driving on dirt cane roads or at Polihale.

- Seat belt use is required by law and police will stop you for this alone.

Car break-ins can be a problem anywhere. They seem to be more frequent in the summer due to school vacations. The places usually hit are those that require you to leave your car in a secluded place for an extended period of time. Contrary to popular belief, locals are targeted nearly as often as tourists. To protect yourself, don't leave anything valuable in the car. (Well…maybe the seats can stay.) At secluded spots that have recently been robbed, savvy locals will often leave their doors unlocked and the windows partially open to prevent having their windows smashed. If you park in a secluded spot and notice several piles of glass on the ground, leave your windows rolled down a little—broken glass is evidence that some juvenile has a new hobby. Don't kid yourself into believing that trunks are safe—they are often easier to open than doors. One place thieves rarely look is under the hood. But don't put something there after you arrive at your destination since someone might be watching. We once drove up to the parking area at Secret Beach, and there was a suspicious looking guy there. Mr. Slick acted busy by spending considerable time checking the oil in his car—*but the rusted hulk had no wheels all the way around.* Be alert and you should be OK.

All of this is not meant to convey the impression that car break-ins are rampant. In fact, the opposite is true. You could probably spend your entire life here and never experience one. (We haven't.)

But if you lose you brand new $1,000 auto-everything digital camera to some juvenile dipstick because you were one of the few...well, won't *you* feel sick?

Four-Wheel Drive

With its many rugged roads, one of the best ways to see Kauaʻi is by four-wheel drive. These can be difficult to

Hey, I Recognize That Place...

When Hollywood wants to convey the impression of beauty, lushness and the exotic, it's no contest what location they choose. Kauaʻi has long been the location of choice for movie directors looking for something special. As you drive around the island, keep an eye out for the locations of scenes from some of these movies: all three *Jurassic Park*

movies, *Dragonfly, To End All Wars, 6 Days/7 Nights, Mighty Joe Young, George of the Jungle, Outbreak, North, Honeymoon in Vegas, Hook, Lord of the Flies, Flight of the Intruder, Throw Mama From the Train, The Thorn Birds, Uncommon Valor, Body Heat, Raiders of the Lost Ark, Fantasy Island, King Kong, Acapulco Gold, Islands in the Stream, The Hawaiians, Lost Flight, Hawaiʻi, Girls! Girls! Girls!, Donovan's Reef, Blue Hawaiʻi, South Pacific, Miss Sadie Thompson* and many

Harrison Ford rehearsing at Mahaʻulepu for the movie, 6 days/7 Nights.

more. Hollywood discovered Kauaʻi years ago.

Only Hollywood would use zillion-dollar cranes to construct "primitive" huts or supply rain near the wettest spot on earth as did producers of the Kevin Costner film, Dragonfly.

Even a beach with no sand can have something to offer.
Queen's Bath on the north shore is an example.

come by at times. Ask if they have disabled the 4WD mechanism. If you use a gold credit card for the automatic insurance, check with the card carrier to see if you are covered when you're on unpaved roads. Another tip is to avoid deep, soft sand. Even 4WD vehicles can get stuck in sand if they have the wrong tires. If you must drive on sand, let much of the air out of the tires to get more sand traction. (We'll leave it up to you how to get the air back in.) If you already *are* stuck in sand, try pulling the carpet from the trunk and driving on it to get out. (Oh, the car companies will love us for *that* one.) Rental car companies are always changing the vehicles to keep them new. At press time, all the companies we list had SUVs or other 4WD vehicles. Expect to pay up to $60–$90 per day for the privilege of cheating the road builders.

Exotic Cars

So ya wanna drive a fantasy car. Vipers, 'Vettes and other sexy autos can be had—for the right price. You're looking at around $300 for a Corvette, $550 for a Viper. That's *per day!* Half-day rates are available on some. Bear in mind that there are no opportunities to open them up—we have no wide open highway straightaways—but if you just want to experience the thrill of driving a fantasy car and you have a wad of money burning a hole in your pocket, give it a shot.

Call **Hawaiian Riders** (822–5409 in Kapa'a, 742–9888 in Po'ipu). They will rent to 21 year olds, and you won't need a credit card—just *lots* of cash.

Buses

Kaua'i has a bus system called the Kaua'i Bus (clever, eh?). It goes from Kekaha to Hanalei and fares are $1.50. A monthly pass is $15. There are stops all along the main highway, but they aren't always marked as well as they should be. For a bus schedule or more information, call 241–6410.

Less Than 4 Wheels

If you really want to ham it up, try renting a HOG. (*Note:* The Supreme Court recently ruled that publishers cannot be held liable for bad puns.) **Pacific Island Rentals** in Kapa'a (821–9090) rents Harley-Davidsons. Rates start at $69 for 3 hours and go up to $179 for overnight. Excellent selection of HOGS here. Overpriced? Probably. But nothing else feels like a genuine Harley. **Hawaiian Riders** (below) also rents them for about the same price but their selection isn't quite good and they're not as easy to deal with.

Scooters/Mopeds are also available. We've seen some pretty close calls and consider them too unstable to recommend. (Be *real* careful on hills.) **Hawaiian Riders** (822–5409) has them for $50 a day and you gotta be 18.

Taxis

If you want to tour the island by taxi… you have entirely too much money to burn. For those who need an occasional taxi service, you will find these available: **North Shore Cab** at 826–6189, **ABC Taxi** at 639–4310 on the east shore, or **City Cab** at 245–3227 on the south shore.

GETTING MARRIED ON KAUA'I

The beauty of Kaua'i has provided the backdrop for many engagements, weddings and vow renewals. And why not? It's in the air here. People are genuinely happy on Kaua'i, and the aroma of joy can make your life together even sweeter. Whether you choose a natural or

Large banyan trees, such as this one near the Waimea Plantation Cottages, are found throughout the islands. Note the person standing underneath. The largest banyan tree in the world takes 10 minutes to walk around. (It's in India.)

manmade waterfall, a sunset on a beach, an elegant chapel, beautiful garden or an ancient Hawaiian temple, Kaua'i can create nuptial memories that will last a lifetime.

With the advent of the Internet and e-mail you can now arrange your own wedding, no matter how far away you are. All of the legal requirements, as well as possible wedding locations, are just a click away. Everything from helicopter flights landing at private waterfalls to just the two of you on a beach at sunset with a minister is available.

Some of the more popular wedding locations are at the Princeville Hotel, Hanalei Bay Resort, Marriott, Hyatt, Sheraton and the Waimea Plantation Cottages. Many resorts have wedding coordinators and private wedding sites on property. You might also want to consider renting a private home for you and

your guests. Don't let the RACK rates and wedding package prices scare you off. Nothing's carved in stone. And remember, no beach is private, and no one can charge you to use one.

The number of details in planning a wedding is dizzying, and many couples prefer the assistance of an independent wedding coordinator. They can be tremendously helpful in navigating the complicated waters of your marriage. (Well, the ceremony, at least. After that, you're on your own.) Don't let yourself get herded into activities (for which they get a commission), and be on the lookout for add-ons that can ratchet up the price. Be especially selective of your photographer and videographer. This is a one-time event that can't be duplicated.

Some of the more reputable companies are listed below. Unlike most activities, we can't review each in depth. It's

not possible to get married a dozen times and critique the way each coordinator did their job. We have, however, anonymously contacted virtually all of the coordinators on the island (in the guise of planning a wedding) and these stood out.

Coconut Coast Weddings
   (800) 585–5595 or (808) 828–0999
Mohala Wedding Services
   (800) 800–8489 or (808) 821–8199
Garden Island Weddings (Chapel by the Sea)
   (808) 632–0505
Weddings on the Beach
   (800) 625–2824 or (808) 742–7099
Island Weddings
   (800) 998–1548 or (808) 828–1548

WEATHER

Kauaʻi doesn't have the best weather in the state, but the best weather in the state is on Kauaʻi. What do we mean by that? Well, when it's good here, it's as good as weather can get—brilliant sunshine, crystal clear air and gentle but constant breezes. That's when it's good.

Yeah, but I've heard it always rains on Kauaʻi. We heard this many times before we came here for the first time. The reality of Kauaʻi is that it gets more rain than the other Hawaiian islands. In fact, the rainiest spot on earth is smack dab in the middle of the island. Mount Waiʻaleʻale is the undisputed rain magnet, receiving an average of 440.22 inches per year (that's more than 36 *feet*) and a median of 432 inches per year. The mountain is shaped like a funnel pointing directly into the moisture-laden trade winds, which are forced to drop their precious cargo during their march up the slopes. The summit of Waiʻaleʻale is other-worldly, with plants stunted and dwarfed by the constant inundation of rain. Moss, fungi and lichen flourish in the

swamp just west of the actual peak. Alakaʻi Swamp contains flora and fauna found nowhere else in the world. On the opposite side of the mountain, the spent clouds can do no more than drift by, making the west side of the island rather arid. What rain it does get comes from the sporadic Kona winds. (Throughout the islands, Kona winds refers to winds that come from the southwest and are often associated with inclement weather.)

All that said, the odds are overwhelming that rain will *not* ruin your Kauaʻi vacation. The coast gets *far* less rain than the waterlogged central interior, and throughout Kauaʻi the lion's share of rain falls at night. When it does rain during the day, it is usually quite short-lived, often lasting a matter of a few minutes. One of the things that takes a little getting used to is the fleeting nature of the weather here. In many parts of the country, rain or sunshine are words used *by themselves* to describe the day's weather. On Kauaʻi, a warm, passing shower is to be expected and rarely signifies that a long period of rain is to follow. If you call the local telephone number for the National Weather Service (see below), you will probably hear something like this. "Today—mostly sunny, with a few passing windward and *mauka* (mountain) showers. Tonight—mostly fair with a few passing windward and *mauka* showers. Tomorrow—mostly sunny, with a few passing windward and *mauka* showers." So don't get bummed if it suddenly looks ominous in the sky. It'll probably pass within a few minutes, leaving happy plants in its wake.

If you want to know whether to take the top down on the convertible, look into the wind, and you'll be able to see the weather coming. Dark clouds drop rain—the darker the cloud, the harder the rain. It's as simple as that, and you

Median Monthly Rainfall Distribution

Waimea	Po'ipu	Mt. Wai'ale'ale	Princeville	Kapa'a
19" per year	36" per year	432" per year	85" per year	48" per year

Inches

will often see locals looking windward if they feel a drop on their heads. If you're inland, you will often be able to hear the rain approaching. When you hear the sound of a rushing river but there isn't one around, take cover until it passes. (Mango trees are ideal for this purpose and have ancillary benefits, as well.)

In planning your daily activities, a good rule of thumb is that if it is going to be a rainy day, the south shore will probably be sunny, and the west shore will almost certainly be sunny. The exception is during Kona winds when weather is the opposite of normal.

Storm systems do discover the state from time to time. Sometimes they're here for days. If one happens to hang around during your trip, don't despair. We first met Kaua'i during one of the wettest times in decades. We even had lightning, which is rare. And it was during that stay that we fell in love with the island and vowed to make it our home. Kaua'i in the rain is still Kaua'i.

As far as hurricanes are concerned, don't waste your time worrying about them. It's true, we had a real 'okole kicker back in September 1992. Hurricane 'Iniki was a category 4 storm that stripped the island bare. But after this pruning, the island recovered and is greener than ever. Hurricanes are few and far between here. The only previous hurricanes to hit the state this century were 'Iwa in 1982 and Dot in 1959. When Isabella Bird traveled here in 1873, where she penned her excellent book *Six Months in the Sandwich Isles,* she reported that "hurricanes are unknown in the islands," which

means that there hadn't been one in living memory. (Of course, if one *does* strike during your stay, kindly disregard this last statement.)

As far as **temperatures** are concerned, Kaua'i is incredibly temperate. The average *high* during January is 78°, whereas our hottest time, late August/early September, has an average *high* of 85°. With humidity percentages usually in the 60s and low 70s, Kaua'i is almost always pleasant. The exception is the extreme west side, which is about 3 degrees hotter. (That might not sound like much, but you sure do notice it.)

Kaua'i's surface **water temperatures** range from a low of 73.4° in February to a high of 80° in October. Most people find this to be an ideal water temperature range. (Ocean water near a river mouth, such as Lydgate State Park, can get colder—we've seen the ocean get as low as 70° there during unusually cold Februarys.)

To get current weather or ocean information call:

National Weather Service, Weather Forecast—245-6001
National Weather Service, Hawaiian Waters Forecast—245-3564

Where Should I Stay?

If your decision about when to visit and where to stay takes rainfall amounts into account, the graph on the facing page should be of interest. Winter is our rainiest season. (But that's also when you will see the waterfalls at their best.) The north shore is a more popular place to stay in the summer, and the south shore is more popular in the winter due to rainfall distribution and surf.

GEOGRAPHY

Kaua'i is located in the tropics at 22° latitude, meaning that it receives direct sunlight twice each year three weeks before and after the summer solstice. (No part of the mainland United States ever receives direct sunshine due to its more northern location.) The island is 553 square miles, with 50 of its 113 miles of shoreline composed of sand beaches. Compared to the other Hawaiian Islands, Kaua'i has by far the highest proportion of sand beach shoreline. You might read in brochures about "white sand beaches."

Actually, they are *golden* sand beaches, unlike the truly white sand beaches found in other parts of the world. Kaua'i is too old to have any volcanic black sand beaches since the creation of *volcanic* black sand ends when the lava flow stops. (Waimea's black sand beach is from lava flecks chipped from riverbeds and from dirt.)

Kaua'i's interior is mountainous, with deeply eroded valleys and large plains around most of the coastal areas. Its rainfall is more varied than any place in the world. The northern and eastern parts of the island (called the windward side) receive the majority of the rain, with the southern and western section (leeward side) considerably drier. (See rain graph on facing page.)

Looking at the map on the fold-out back cover, you will notice that a highway stretches *almost* all the way around the island. This means that Ke'e is as far as you can go by car on the north shore, and Polihale or the top of Waimea Canyon Road is as far as you can go on the west side. An attempt to link the two a few

years back ended with almost comic results. (See page 90 for more on that.)

The maps in this book are unique in that they show the roadside mile markers. These correspond to the little green signs you will see along the main roads of Kaua'i. This will give you a perspective regarding distances beyond the map scales. Another feature of our maps is that north always points up. We have found that many people get confused when they try to use a map where south is pointing to where east should be, etc. The only exceptions we made were a couple trail maps that benefited from using a specific elevated perspective.

In getting around, distances are usually measured in time, rather than miles. **Traffic** is sometimes a problem in Lihu'e and Kapa'a, so be prepared to wait.

See the back fold-out map for a chart of driving times. From Lihu'e, the average driving time (*barring traffic*) is:

Ha'ena	60 minutes
Hanalei	50 minutes
Kapa'a	15 minutes
Po'ipu	25 minutes
Waimea Canyon	60 minutes

HAZARDS
The Sun

Excluding the accommodations tax, the hazard that affects by far the most people is the sun. Kaua'i's latitude means we receive sunlight that's more direct than anywhere on the mainland. (The more overhead the sunlight is, the less atmosphere it is filtered through.) If you want to enjoy your *entire* vacation, make sure that you wear a strong sunblock. We recommend a waterproof sunblock with at least an SPF of 15. **Gels** work best in the ocean, **lotions** are best if you're staying dry. Try to avoid the sun between 11

a.m. and 2 p.m. since the sun's rays are particularly strong during this time. If you are fair-skinned or unaccustomed to the sun and want to lay out, 15–20 minutes per side is all you should consider the first day. You can increase it a bit each day. *Beware of the fact that Kaua'i's ever constant trade winds will hide the symptoms of a burn until it's too late.* You may find that trying to get your tan as golden as possible isn't worth it; tropical suntans are notoriously short-lived, whereas you are sure to remember a bad burn far longer.

Water Hazards

The most serious water hazard is the surf. During the winter, many beaches are not swimmable. Eastern and northern beaches are especially dangerous, and the sad fact is that more people drown in Hawai'i each year than anywhere else in the country. This isn't said to keep you from enjoying the ocean, but rather to instill in you a healthy respect for Hawaiian waters. See BEACHES for more information on this.

Ocean Critters

Hawaiian marine life, for the most part, is quite friendly. There are, however, a few notable exceptions. Below is a list of those that you should be aware of. This is not mentioned to frighten you out of the water. The odds are overwhelming that you won't have any trouble with any of the beasties listed below. But should you encounter one, this information should be of some help.

SHARKS—Kaua'i does have sharks. They are mostly white-tipped reef sharks with an occasional hammerhead or tiger shark. Contrary to what most people think, sharks are in *every* ocean and

Watch where you choose to take a nap.

don't pose the level of danger people attribute to them. In the past 25 years, there have been a total of 14 documented shark attacks off Kaua'i, mostly tigers attacking surfers. Considering the number of people who swam in our waters during that time, you are more likely to choke to death on a bone at a lu'au than be attacked by a shark. If you do happen to come upon a shark, however, swim away slowly. This kind of movement doesn't interest them. *Don't* splash about rapidly. By doing this you are imitating a fish in distress, and you don't want to do that. The one kind of ocean water you want to avoid is murky water, such as that found near river mouths. These are not interesting to swim in anyway. Most shark attacks occur in murky water at dawn or dusk since sharks are basically cowards who like to sneak up on their prey. In general, don't go around worrying about sharks. *Any* ani-

mal can be threatening. (Even President Carter was once attacked by a rabbit.)

SEA URCHINS—These are like living pin cushions. If you step on one or accidentally grab one, remove as much of the spine as possible with tweezers. See a physician if necessary.

CONE SHELLS—People tend to forget that shells are created by organisms to serve as housing. Most of these creatures are capable of protecting themselves by the use of a long stinger called a proboscis, which injects venom. You might hear that it's safer to pick up a shell by the large end. You should be aware that many shells have stingers that can reach any part of the shell and can penetrate gloves. Therefore, it is recommended that you do not pick up live shells. If you do find yourself stung, immediately apply hot water, as it breaks down the protein venom.

PORTUGUESE MAN-OF-WAR—These are related to jellyfish but are unable to swim. They are instead propelled by a small sail and are at the mercy of the wind. Though small, they are capable of

inflicting a painful sting. This occurs when the long, trailing tentacles are touched, triggering hundreds of thousands of spring-loaded stingers, called nematocysts, which inject venom. The resulting burning sensation is usually very unpleasant but not fatal. Fortunately, the Portuguese Man-of-War is not a common visitor to Kaua'i. When they *do* come ashore, usually during the summer on the east shore, they usually do so in great numbers, jostled by a strong storm offshore. If you see them on the beach, don't go in the water. If you do get stung, immediately remove the tentacles with a gloved hand, stick or whatever is handy. Rinse thoroughly with salt or fresh water to remove any adhering nematocysts. Then apply ice for pain control. If the condition worsens, see a doctor. The old treatments of vinegar or baking soda are no longer recommended. The folk cure is urine, but you might look pretty silly applying it.

CORAL—Coral skeletons are very sharp and, since the skeleton is overlain by millions of living coral polyps, a scrape can leave proteinaceous matter in the wound, causing infection. This is why coral cuts are frustratingly slow to heal. Immediate cleaning and disinfecting of coral cuts should speed up healing time. We don't have fire coral around Kaua'i.

SEA ANEMONES—Related to the jellyfish, these also have stingers and are usually found attached to rocks or coral. It's best not to touch them with your bare hands. Treatment for a sting is similar to that of a Portuguese Man-of-War.

Bugs

Though devoid of the myriad of hideous buggies found in other parts of the world, there are a few evil critters brought here from elsewhere that you should know about. The worst are **centipedes**. They can get to be six or more inches long and are aggressive predators. If you do happen to get stung, you won't die (but you might wish you had). You'll probably never see one, but if you get stung, even by a baby, the pain can range from a bad bee sting to a mild gunshot blast. Some local doctors say the only cure is to stay drunk for three days. Others say to use meat tenderizer.

Cane spiders are big, dark and look horrifying, but they're not poisonous. (But they seem to *think* they are. I've had *them* chase *me* across the room when *I* had the broom in my hand.) We *don't* have no-see-ums, those irritating sand fleas common in the South Pacific and Caribbean.

Mosquitoes were unknown in the islands until the first stowaways arrived on Maui on the *Wellington* in 1826. Since then they have thrived. A good mosquito repellent containing DEET will come in handy, especially if you plan to go hiking. *Lotions* (not thin liquids) with DEET seem to work and stick best. Forget the guidebooks that tell you to take vita-

min B12 to keep mosquitoes away; it just gives the little critters a healthier diet. If you find one dive bombing you at night in your room, turn on your overhead fan to help keep them away. Local residents and resorts often rely on genetically engineered plants such as Citrosa, which irritate mosquitoes as much as they irritate us.

Bees are more common on the drier west side of the island. Usually, the only way you'll get stung is if you run into one. If you rent a scooter, beware: One of us received his first bee sting while singing *Come Sail Away* on a motorcycle. A bee sting in the mouth can definitely ruin one of your precious vacation days.

Regarding **cockroaches**, there's good news and bad news. The bad news is that here, some are bigger than your thumb and can fly. The good news is that you probably won't see one. One of their predators is the **gecko**. This small, lizardlike creature makes a surprisingly loud chirp at night. They are cute and considered good luck in the islands (probably because they eat mosquitoes and roaches).

One thing nearly all visitors have heard is there are no **snakes** in Hawai'i. There is concern that the brown tree snake *might* have made its way onto the islands from Guam. Although mostly harmless to humans, these snakes can spell extinction to native birds. Guam has lost nearly all of its birds due to this egg-eating curse. Once they are fertilized, the snakes can reproduce for life from a single specimen. If there are any on Kaua'i (and this has not yet been confirmed), it would be a major disaster. Government officials aren't allowed to tell you this, but we will: If you ever see one anywhere in Hawai'i, please *kill it* and contact the Department of Land and Natural Resources at 274–3433. At the very least, call the DLNR immediately. The entire bird population of Hawai'i will be grateful.

Road Hazards

There are a couple things you should know about driving around Kaua'i. The speed limits here are probably slower than what you are used to, and Kaua'i police do have a few places where they regularly catch people. (That's code for speed traps.) We mention some in the tours. Also be aware that we have some-

The albatross is protected on Kaua'i.

thing on Kaua'i called CONTRA FLOW. During commute hours, colored cones are placed on the lane divisions forcing you to drive on the wrong side of the road. The area between Lihu'e and Wailua is an example of CONTRA FLOW, and it can be a bit unnerving for the uninitiated. Also, wearing seat belts is required by law, and police will pull you over for this alone. You should know that the Kaua'i Police Department regularly receives funds to enhance their seat belt violation enforcement, speeding enforcement and their sobriety checkpoints. So don't even think about violating these laws or you will likely get stung.

Lastly, even in paradise we have our traffic. Don't overlook the Kapa'a Bypass on the east shore, the Koloa Bypass on the south shore and the Puhi Bypass near Lihu'e.

Dirt

Dirt? Yes dirt. Kaua'i's infamous red dirt has ruined many new pairs of Reeboks in its time. If you are driving on a cane road on the west side and have your window rolled down, you will eat a lot of it. It's always best to bring some trashable sneakers if you plan to do any hiking. And leave your silk argyle socks at home. If you want to know how staining it can be, just ask the makers of *Red Dirt Shirts*. They use one bucket of Kaua'i mud to dye *five hundred* shirts.

Dehydration

Bring and drink lots of water when you are out and about, especially when you are hiking. Dehydration sneaks up on people. By the time you are thirsty, you're already dehydrated. It's a good idea to take an insulated water jug with you in the car or one of those 1½ liter bottles of water. Our weather is almost

certainly different than what you left behind, and you will probably find yourself thirstier than usual. Just fill it before you leave in the morning and *suck 'em up* (as we say here) all day.

Swimming in Streams

Kaua'i offers lots of opportunities to swim in streams and sometimes under waterfalls. It's a fulfillment of a fantasy for many people. But there are several hazards you need to know about.

Leptospirosis is a bacteria that is found in some of Hawai'i's fresh water. It is transmitted from animal urine and can enter the body from open cuts, eyes and by drinking. Around 100 people a year in Hawai'i are diagnosed with the bacteria, which is treated with antibiotics if caught relatively early. You should avoid swimming in streams if you have open cuts, and treat all water found in nature with treatment pills before drinking. (Simple filters are ineffective for lepto.)

Also, while swimming in freshwater streams, try to use your arms as much as possible. Kicking an unseen rock is easier than you think. Also, consider wearing reef shoes or, better yet, tabis, while in streams. (Tabis are sort of a fuzzy mitten for your feet that grab slippery rocks quite effectively. You can get them at Kmart or Wal-Mart in Lihu'e or Longs Drugs in Kapa'a.

Though rare, flash floods can occur in any freshwater stream anywhere in the world, even paradise. Be alert for them.

Lastly, remember while lingering under waterfalls that not everything that comes over the top will be as soft as water. Rocks coming down from above could definitely ruin the moment.

Grocery Stores

Definitely a hazard. Restaurants may

be expensive, but don't think you'll get off cheap in grocery stores. Though you'll certainly save money cooking your own food, a trip to the store here can be startling. Phrases like *they charge how much for milk?* echo throughout the stores. One tip: Foodland and Safeway both offer discount cards (called Maika'i Cards and Safeway Club Cards, respectively) that can bring pretty big savings off their otherwise confiscatory rates. Kapa'a's stores are easily seen along the Hwy; north shore has Foodland at Princeville Shopping Center and Big Save in Hanalei. The south shore has Big Save in Koloa on Koloa Road.

Roosters

OK, so you don't normally think of roosters as hazards. And normally they're not. These guys are wild in many parts of the island and can be charming. But our roosters have proliferated since Hurricane 'Iniki freed so many back in 1992, and they are particularly stupid here. They don't seem to know when they're supposed to crow, so they do it all day long just to cover themselves. (Probably for liability purposes.) If any of these two-legged alarm clocks are near where you're staying, you may find yourself waking up *real* early.

TRAVELING WITH CHILDREN

Perhaps we should have put this section under HAZARDS. If you are looking for baby-sitters, nearly every lodging on the island has lists of professional services, as well as employees who baby-sit. Some hotels, such as the Hyatt and the Marriott, offer rather elaborate services that can be a rug-rat's dream. If you are staying at a place that has no front desk, contact your rental agent for an up-to-date list of sitters.

If you need a crib, stroller, car seat and the like, Ready Rentals at 823–8008 or (800) 599–8008 from the mainland can help. Also try Keiki Kottage (821–1234).

As far as swimming in the ocean with your little one, Lydgate State Park in Wailua has a boulder-enclosed keiki (kid)

Though the ocean can be dangerous to keikis (kids), there are several protected pockets, called baby beaches, such as Keiki Cove pictured here, that usually offer protection for supervised young'uns.

Visitors are prohibited by law from bringing their worries to Kaua'i.

pond that is wildly popular. (See the aerial photo on the inside back cover.) There is also a playground (Kamalani), the best on the island. Overall, it's a nice place for keikis. Also check out **Salt Pond Beach Park** in Hanapepe and **Baby Beach**, both under BEACHES. **Po'ipu Beach Park** in Po'ipu is popular with local parents, as well as visitors. These are considered the best places for children except during periods of high surf. Obviously surf and keikis don't go well together.

During calm summer surf, **Kalihiwai Beach** can be a pleasant place to bring kids. While not as protected as Lydgate or Salt Pond, it's picturesque and your kids will make many new local friends.

THE PEOPLE

The people of Kaua'i are the friendliest people in the entire country. "Oh, come on!" you might say. But this is not the admittedly biased opinion of someone who lives here. This conclusion was reached by the participants in the *Condé Nast Readers' Choice Awards*. This is a sophisticated and savvy lot. *Condé Nast* is the magazine of choice for world travelers. When asked in their yearly poll, readers rate Kaua'i at or near the top of the list in friendliness nearly every year. While we're at it, in the same poll, two of Kaua'i's resorts (the Hyatt and the Princeville Hotel) are consistently rated in the top 20 tropical resorts in the world.

What does this mean? Well, you will notice that people smile here more than other places. Drivers wave at complete strangers (without any particular fingers leading the way). If you try to analyze the reason, it probably comes down to a matter of happiness. People are happy here, and happy people are friendly people. It's just that simple. Some people compare a trip to Kaua'i with a trip back in time, when smiles weren't rare, and politeness and courtesy were the order of the day.

Some Terms

If you are confused regarding terms in Hawai'i, this should help. A person of Hawaiian blood is **Hawaiian**. That is a racial term, not a geographic one, so only people of the Hawaiian race are called Hawaiian. They are also called **Kanaka Maoli**, but only another Hawaiian can use this term. Anybody who was born here, regardless of race (except whites) is called a **local**. If you were born elsewhere but have lived here a while, you are called a **kama'aina**. If you are white, you are a **haole**. It doesn't matter if you have been here a day or your family has been here for over a century, you will always be a **haole**. The term comes from the time when westerners first encountered these islands. Its precise meaning has been lost, but it is thought to refer to people with no background (since westerners could not chant the kanaenae of their ancestors).

The continental United States is called the **mainland**. If you are here and are returning, you are not "going back to the states" (we *are* a state). When somebody leaves the island, they are **off-island**.

Ethnic Breakdown

Kaua'i has an ethnic mix that is as diversified as any you will find. Here, *everyone* is a minority; there are no majorities. The last census count revealed the ethnic makeup below.

Asian	21,042
White	17,255
Hawaiian or other Pacific Islander	5,334
Other	505
American Indian or Alaska Native	212
Black	177
Mixed or didn't respond	13,938
Total	**58,463**

Hawaiian Time

One aspect of Hawaiian culture you may have heard of is Hawaiian Time. The stereotype is that everyone in Hawai'i moves just a little bit more slowly than on the mainland. We are supposed to be more laid back and don't let things get to us as easily as people on the mainland. This is the stereotype... OK, it's *not* a stereotype. It's real. During your visit, if you get in the rhythm, you'll notice that this feeling infects *you* as well. You might find yourself letting another driver cut in front of you in circumstances that would incur your wrath back home. You might find yourself willing to wait for a red light without feeling like you're going to explode. The whole reason for coming to Hawai'i is to experience beauty and a sense of peace, so let it happen. If someone else is moving a bit slower than you would like, just go with it.

THE HAWAIIAN LANGUAGE

The Hawaiian language is a beautiful, gentle and melodious language that flows smoothly off the tongue. Just the sounds of the words conjure up trees gently swaying in the breeze and the sound of the surf. Most Polynesian languages share the same roots and many have common words. Today, Hawaiian is spoken *as an everyday language* only on the privately owned island of Ni'ihau, 17 miles off the coast of Kaua'i (see INTRODUCTION). Visitors are often intimidated by Hawaiian. With a few ground rules you'll come to realize that pronunciation is not as hard as you might think.

When missionaries discovered that the Hawaiians had no written language, they sat down and created an alphabet. This Hawaiian alphabet has only 12 letters. Five vowels: A, E, I, O and U, as

well as seven consonants: H, K, L, M, N, P and W.

The consonants are pronounced just as they are in English, with the exception of W. It is often pronounced as a V. Vowels are pronounced as follows:

A—pronounced as in Ah if stressed or above if not stressed.

E—pronounced as in say if stressed or dent if not stressed.

I—pronounced as in bee.

O—pronounced as in nose.

U—pronounced as in true.

If you examine long Hawaiian words, you will see that most have repeating syllables, making them easier to remember and pronounce.

One thing you will notice in this book are glottal stops. These are represented by an upside-down apostrophe ʻ and are meant to convey a hard stop in the pronunciation (and are quite awkward to type). So if we are talking about the type of lava called ʻaʻa, it is pronounced as two separate As (AH-ah).

Another feature you will encounter are diphthongs (no, that's not a type of bathing suit), where two letters glide together. They are ae, ai, ao, au, ei, eu, oi and ou. Unlike many English diphthongs, the second vowel is always pronounced. One word you will read in this book, referring to Hawaiian temples, is heiau (HEY-ee-ow). The e and i flow together as a single sound, then the a and u flow together as a single sound. The ee sound binds the two sounds, making the whole word flow together.

Let's take a word that might seem impossible to pronounce. When you see how easy this word is, the rest will seem like a snap. The Hawaiian state fish used to be the Humuhumunukunukuapuaʻa. At first glance it seems like a nightmare. But if you read the word slowly, it is pronounced just like it looks and isn't nearly as horrifying as it appears. Try it. Humu (hoo-moo) is pronounced twice. Nuku (noo-koo) is pronounced twice. A (ah) is pronounced once. Pu (poo) is pronounced once. Aʻa (ah-ah) is the ah sound pronounced twice, the glottal stop indicating a hard stop between sounds. Now you should try it again. Humuhumunukunukuapuaʻa. Now, wasn't that easy? OK, so it's not easy, but it's not impossible either.

Below are some other words that you might hear during your visit:

ʻAina (eye-nah)—Land.

Akamai (ah-kah-MY)—Wise or shrewd.

Aliʻi (ah-LEE-ee)—A Hawaiian chief; a member of the chiefly class.

Aloha (ah-LOW-ha)—Hello, goodbye, or a feeling or the spirit of love, affection or kindness.

Hala (hah-la)—Pandanus tree.

Hale (hah-leh)—House or building.

Hana (ha-nah)—Work.

Hana hou (ha-nah-HO)—To do again.

Haole (how-leh)—Originally foreigner, now means Caucasian.

Heiau (hey-ee-ow)—Hawaiian temple.

Hui (hoo-ee)—Joint ownership, usually of land.

Hula (hoo-lah)—The storytelling dance of Hawaiʻi.

Imu (ee-moo)—An underground oven.

ʻIniki (ee-nee-key)—Sharp and piercing wind (as in Hurricane ʻIniki).

Kahuna (kah-HOO-na)—A priest or minister; someone who is an expert in a profession.

Kai (kigh)—The sea.

Kalua (KAH-loo-ah)—Cooking food underground.

Kamaʻaina (kah-ma-EYE-na)—Long-time Hawaiʻi resident.

Kane (kah-neh)—Boy or man.

Kapu (kah-poo)—Forbidden, keep out.
Keiki (kay-key)—Child.
Kokua (koh-koo-ah)—Help.
Kona (koh-NAH)—Leeward side of the island; wind blowing from the south, southwest direction.
Kuleana (koo-leh-AH-nah)—Concern, responsibility or jurisdiction.
Lanai (lah-NIGH)—Porch, veranda, patio.
Lani (lah-nee)—Sky or heaven.
Lei (lay)—Necklace of flowers, shells or feathers. The mokihana berry lei is the lei of Kaua'i.
Liliko'i (lee-lee-koi)—Passion fruit.
Limu (lee-moo)—Edible seaweed.
Lomi (low-mee)—To rub or massage; lomi salmon is raw salmon rubbed with salt and spices.
Lu'au (loo-ow)—Hawaiian feast; literally means taro leaves.
Mahalo (mah-hah-low)—Thank you.
Makai (mah-kigh)—Toward the sea.
Malihini (mah-lee-hee-nee)—A newcomer, visitor, or guest.
Mauka (mow-ka)—Toward the mountain.
Moana (moh-ah-nah)—Ocean.
Mo'o (moh-oh)—Lizard.
Nani (nah-nee)—Beautiful, pretty.
Nui (new-ee)—Big, important, great.
'Ohana (oh-hah-nah)—Family.
'Ono (oh-no)—Delicious, the best.
'Okole (oh-koh-leh)—Derrière.
Pakalolo (pah-kah-low-low)—Marijuana.
Pali (pah-lee)—A cliff.
Paniolo (pah-nee-OH-low)—Hawaiian cowboy.
Pau (pow)—Finish, end; i.e., pau hana means quitting time from work.
Poi (poy)—Pounded kalo (taro) root that forms a paste.
Pono (poh-no)—Goodness, excellence, correct, proper.
Pua (poo-ah)—Flower.
Pupu (poo-poo)—Appetizer, snacks, or finger food.

Puka (poo-ka)—hole.
Wahine (vah-hee-ney)—Woman.
Wai (why)—Fresh water.
Wikiwiki (wee-kee-wee-kee)—To hurry up, very quick.

Quick Pidgin Lesson
Hawaiian pidgin is fun to listen to. It's like ear candy. It is colorful, rhythmic and sways in the wind. Below is a list of some of the words and phrases you might hear on your visit. It's tempting to read some of these and try to use them. If you do, the odds are you will simply look foolish. These words and phrases are used in certain ways and with certain inflections. People who have spent years living in the islands still feel uncomfortable using them. Thick pidgin can be incomprehensible to the untrained ear (that's the idea). If you are someplace and hear two people engaged in a discussion in pidgin, stop and eavesdrop for a bit. You won't forget it.

Pidgin Words and Phrases
An' den—And then? So?
Any kine—Anything; any kind.
Ass right—That's right.
Ass wy—That's why.
Beef—Fight.
Brah—Bruddah; friend; brother.
Brok' da mouf—Delicious.
Buggah—That's the one; it is difficult.
Bummahs—Bummer; too bad.
Bus laugh—To laugh out loud.
Bus nose—How one reacts to a bad smell.
Chicken skin kine—Something that gives you goose bumps.
Choke—A lot.
Cockaroach—Steal; rip off.
Da kine—A noun or verb used in place of whatever the speaker wishes. Heard constantly.

Fo Days—plenty; "He got hair fo days."

Geevum—Go for it! Give 'em hell!

Grind—To eat.

Grinds—Food.

Hold ass—A close call when driving your new car.

How you figga?—How do you figure that? It makes no sense.

Howzit?—How is it going? How are you? Also, Howzit o wot?

I owe you money or wot?—What to say when someone is staring at you.

Lesgo—Let's go; let's do it.

Make house—Make yourself at home.

Make plate—Grab some food.

Mek ass—Make a fool of yourself.

Mo' bettah—This is better.

No can—Cannot; I cannot do it.

No make lidat—Stop doing that.

No, yeah?—No, or is "no" correct?

'Okole squeezer—Something that suddenly frightens you ('okole meaning derrière).

O wot?—Or what?

Poi dog—A mutt.

Shahkbait—Shark bait, meaning pale, untanned people.

Shaka—Great! All right!

Shredding—Riding a gnarly wave.

Sleepahs—Flip flops, thongs, zoris.

Stink eye—Dirty looks; facial expression denoting displeasure.

Suck rocks—Buzz off, or pound sand.

Talk story—Shooting the breeze; to rap.

Tanks eh?—Thank you.

Waddascoops?—What's the scoop? What's happening?

Yeah?—Used at the end of sentences.

MUSIC

Hawaiian music is far more diverse than most people think. Many often picture Hawaiian music as someone twanging away on an 'ukulele (pronounced OO-KOO-LAY-LAY, not YOU-KA-LAY-LEE) with his voice slipping and sliding all over the place, as though he has an ice cube down his back. In reality, the music here can be outstanding. There is the melodic sound of the more traditional music. There are young local bands putting out modern music with a Hawaiian beat. There is even Hawaiian reggae and hip hop. If you get a chance, stop by **Borders Books and Music** (246–0862) at Kukui Grove in Lihu'e. They have a good selection of Hawaiian music.

THE HULA

The hula evolved as a means of worship, later becoming a forum for telling a story with chants (called mele), hands and body movement. It can be fascinating to watch. When most people think of the hula, they picture a woman in a grass skirt swinging her hips to the strumming of an 'ukulele. But in reality there are two types of hula. The modern hula, or hula 'auana, uses musical instruments and vocals to augment the dancer. It came about after westerners first encountered the islands. Missionaries found the hula distasteful, and the old style was driven underground. The modern type came about as a form of entertainment and was practiced in places where missionaries had no influence. Ancient Hawaiians didn't even use grass skirts. They were later brought by Gilbert Islanders.

The old style of hula is called hula kahiko (also called 'olapa). It consists of chants and is accompanied only by percussion and takes years of training. It can be exciting to watch as performers work together in a synchronous harmony. Both men and women participate

with women's hula somewhat softer (though no less disciplined) and men's hula more active. This type of hula is physically demanding and requires strong concentration. Keiki (children's) hula can be charming to watch, as well.

Kaua'i was the home of the most prestigious hula school in all the islands. People came from every part of the chain to learn the hula at the Ka-ulu-a-Paoa. Great discipline was required, and the teachers could be very strict. The remains of this school are still evident at a plateau above Ke'e Beach.

The lu'aus around the island usually have entertaining hula shows, though not as "authentic" as some of the festival demonstrations seen on occasion. Some resorts and shopping centers also have hula shows at times.

BOOKS

There is an astonishing variety of books available about Hawai'i and Kaua'i. Everything from history, legends, geology, children's stories and just plain ol' novels. **Borders Books** (246–0862) near Kukui Grove in Lihu'e has a dazzling selection, and their people know their stuff. Walk in and lose yourself in Hawai'i's richness. In Kapa'a on the Hwy in Kinipopo Shopping Center just north of the Wailua River, **Tin Can Mailman** (822–3009) also has a very nice selection, as well as hard-to-find used books. Nice folks. **Waldenbooks** (822–7749) at Kaua'i Village is also a good source. Lastly, don't forget the **Kaua'i Museum** (246–2470). They, too, have interesting and hard-to-find books.

A NOTE ON PERSONAL RESPONSIBILITY

This edition, more than any book we've ever done, has included the sad task of removing places that you can no

longer visit. The reason, universally cited, is *liability*. Although Hawai'i has a statute indemnifying landowners, the mere threat is often enough to get something closed. Because we, more than any other publication, have exposed heretofore unknown attractions, we feel the need to pass this along.

Please remember that this isn't Disneyland—it's nature. Mother Nature is hard, slippery, sharp and unpredictable. If you go exploring and get into trouble, whether it's your ego that's bruised or something more tangible, please remember that neither the state, the private land owner or this publication *told* you to go. You *chose* to explore which is what life, and this book, are all about. And if you complain to, or threaten someone controlling land, they'll rarely fix the problem you identified. They'll simply close it...and it will be gone for good.

MISCELLANEOUS INFORMATION

Kaua'i has no distinct visitor season. People come here year round to enjoy the island's blessings. However, certain times of the year are more popular than others. Christmas is always a particularly busy time, and you may have trouble getting a room if you are determined to stay at a particular resort. The graph below illustrates typical visitor distribution here. The island never feels crowded the way other destinations can feel.

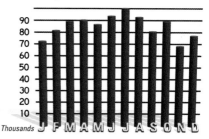

90
80
70
60
50
40
30
20
10
Thousands J F M A M J J A S O N D

The bountiful lushness of the Garden Island presents itself in many ways.

Travelers' checks are usually accepted, but you should be aware that some merchants might look at you like you just tried to offer them Mongolian money. You should also know that the American Express Card seems to be less welcome here than some destinations. A number of places will not accept it.

The area code for the entire state is 808. If you are planning to see either of the National Tropical Botanical Gardens or the Grove Farm Museum, make your reservations before you get here to assure admittance. Campers should also obtain their permits before they arrive, especially for the Na Pali Coast. See CAMPING under ACTIVITIES.

If you wear sunglasses, *polarized* lenses are highly recommended. Not only are colors more brilliant here, but the lower latitudes of Hawai'i make polarized lenses particularly effective.

This might sound surprising, given poll results. When pollsters ask people where they would like to go, Kaua'i is always in the top 10.

Photographs taken here are rarely developed properly on the mainland since they aren't familiar with our colors. We've tried every developer on the island and, for what it's worth, have found the best color matching at Photo Spectrum in Lihu'e (on Hwy across from McDonald's) at 245-7667. Kmart (245-7742) one hour service in Lihu'e on Nawiliwili Road is cheaper and does a respectable job.

If you lose your new wedding ring (or anything else metallic) while frolicking at a beach, there are people for hire on the island with metal detectors. The one we recommend is Ken at 823-6424. Ken's in his 60s and is the terror of the triathlon circuit. Good luck trying to keep up with him.

One attraction becoming more popular on Kaua'i is the "NO TRESPASSING"

sign. Sometimes these are sincere. Other times, they are a way for large land owners with deep pockets to avoid liability. It's sometimes tough to tell them apart. We've even had a representative of a large land owner tell us outright that they don't mind if people ignore their signs—the sign puts users on notice that they are on their own and not to come crying to them if they get hurt. We're not encouraging trespassing, we just want to tell you how many people feel here and leave it up to your own good judgment.

It is customary on Kaua'i for *everyone* to remove their shoes upon entering someone's house (sometimes an office). Kaua'i's red dirt can be particularly pernicious, and nobody wants to spend their day cleaning floors.

Daylight Savings isn't observed here.

If you are going to spend any time at the beach (and you really should), woven bamboo beach mats can be found all over the island for $1 or $2. Some roll up, some can be folded. The sand comes off these more easily than it comes off towels.

Cell phones are available from **Cingular** (888) 639-5001 for just over $23 per day.

If you want to arrange a **flower lei** for you or your honey as you arrive at the airport on a direct flight (no inter-island flights), call **Greeters of Hawai'i** at (800) 366-8559 before you arrive. For $21, it's a pretty romantic way to start your trip, huh? While on island, **Flowers and Joys** (822-1569) in Kapa'a has nice leis for reasonable prices. A plumeria lei is $7. (Not bad!)

THE INTERNET

Our Web site, **www.wizardpub.com**, has recent changes, links to cool sites, the latest satellite weather shots and more. We've posted our own aerial photos of nearly every resort on the island—so you'll *know* if oceanfront *really* means oceanfront. The site also has links to every company listed in the book that has a site—including those we like and those we recommend against. For the record we don't charge a cent for links (it would be a conflict of interest), and there are no advertisements on the site. (Well...except for our own books, of course.) Some books and magazines print all of the URL addresses, but it seems pretty mean to make you type in all of those long, clumsy URLs. Besides, they change too often and too quickly. Posting them as links from our site allows us to keep those Internet addresses current. (And they look downright ugly in print, anyway.)

In earlier editions we had a **Calendar of Events** mentioning festivals, island celebrations and special events. Waste of time! Organizers make changes so often (including days before scheduled events) that it wasn't reliable enough to continue printing it in advance. But the Internet is perfect for that. So the Web site has updated listings of island events.

If you're on-island and need Web access (to check your mail, etc.), most of the big resorts have business services available for around $20 an hour. Many other places have Web access, usually for around $10 per hour. On the north shore try **Akamai** (826-1042), on east shore try **Computer Hospital** (822-2667) or **Business Support Services** (822-5504), south shore has **Koloa Country Store** (742-1255) and **Na Pali Explorer** (338-9999). The various libraries around the island sometimes offer free surfing from their computers if you purchase a $10 library card. Try the Lihu'e library first at 241-3222.

A father swims with his daughter in Queen's Bath, a north shore gem.

NORTH SHORE SIGHTS

Kaua'i's north shore, where lushness takes on a whole new meaning. Every shade of green imaginable is represented in the myriad of plant life. Its beaches are exquisite and its mountains unmatched in their sheer majesty. After a heavy rain, you will literally be unable to count the number of waterfalls etched into the sides of north shore mountains.

For the sake of clarity, we will identify the north shore as everything north of Kapa'a. (Look at the fold-out back cover map to orient yourself.) While this description includes Anahola (which some may consider east shore), it is easier to remember it this way, and anyone driving north of Kapa'a is usually going to the north shore anyway. The main highway, which stretches around the island, occasionally changing its name, has mile markers every mile. These little green signs can be a big help in knowing where you are at any given time. Therefore, we have placed them on the maps represented as a number inside a small box . We will often describe a certain feature or unmarked road as being "⁴⁄₁₀ miles past the 22 mile marker." We hope this helps.

Everything is either on the *mauka* side of the highway (toward the mountains) or *makai* (toward the ocean). Since people get these confused, we'll refer to them as *mauka side* and *ocean side*.

All beaches we mention are described in detail in the section on BEACHES.

Driving north of Kapa'a, you'll see Kealia Beach on your right, just past the 10 mile marker. This is a popular boogie boarding beach. At this beach you can often see water spitting into the air from the collision of an incoming and outgoing wave, called *clapotis* for the trivia-minded. (Doesn't that sound more like something a sailor might pick up while on shore leave?)

ANAHOLA

Next, comes the town of Anahola. This area is designated Hawaiian Homelands, meaning it is available to persons of Hawaiian descent. The spike-shaped mountain you see on the *mauka* side is Kalalea Mountain, also called King Kong's Profile. As you drive north of Anahola, look back, and you will see the striking resemblance to King Kong (fitting, since the remake was filmed here in 1976). To the right of the profile is a small hole in the mountain called (this is clever) Hole-in-the-Mountain. It used to be bigger, but a landslide in the early 1980s closed off most of it. You can see it best between the 15 and 16 mile markers. One legend says that a supernatural bird named Hulu pecked the hole in order to see Anahola on the other side. Geologists say that there was once a long lava tube stretching from Wai'ale'ale to the sea. The mountain mass on either side of the ridge has been removed by ceaseless erosion, leaving only the ridge and its ghost of a lava tube.

Duane's Ono-Char Burger is in Anahola. This is a good place for burgers and shakes if you're hungry.

There are several secluded beaches north of Anahola that require walks of various lengths. See map on following page and the BEACHES section.

At the 20 mile marker is Hawaiian Hardwood. They do some interesting things with wood, including turning giant slabs into tables.

KILAUEA

The former plantation town of Kilauea is just past the 23 mile marker and is accessible off Kolo Road. It is known for the Kilauea Lighthouse (828–1413). This is a postcard-perfect landmark perched on a bluff and represents the northernmost point of the main Hawaiian Islands. When it was built in 1913, it had the largest clamshell lens in

Perched on a bluff overlooking the vast Pacific Ocean, the Kilauea Lighthouse stands as a silent sentry.

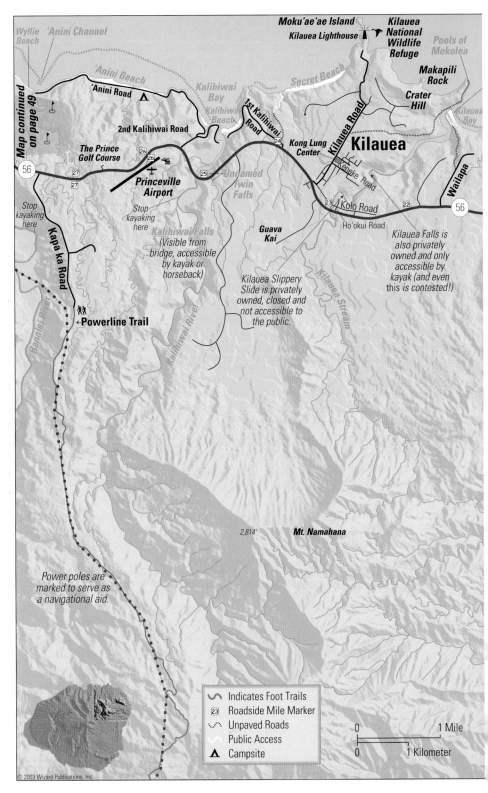

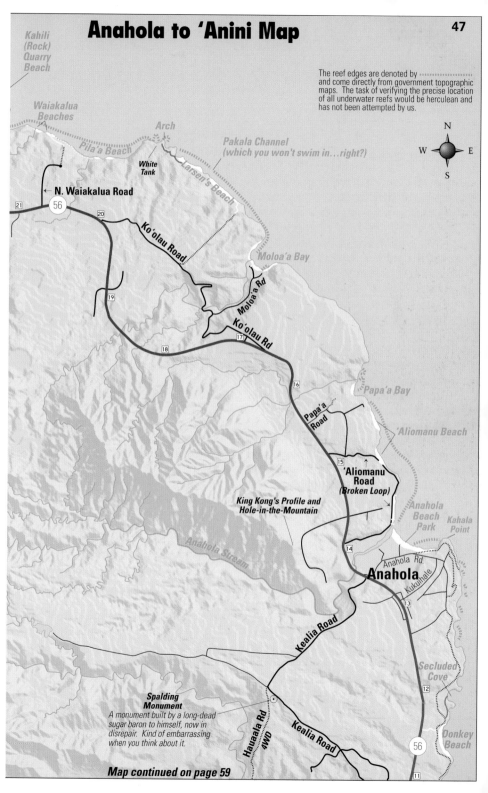

The reef edges are denoted by ·············
and come directly from government topographic
maps. The task of verifying the precise location
of all underwater reefs would be herculean and
has not been attempted by us.

Kahili
(Rock)
Quarry
Beach

Waiakalua
Beaches

Pila'a Beach

Arch

White
Tank

Larsen's Beach

Pakala Channel
(which you won't swim in...right?)

N
W E
S

N. Waiakalua Road

21
56
20

Ko'olau Road

19

Moloa'a Bay

Moloa'a Rd

Ko'olau Rd

18
17

16

Papa'a Bay

Papa'a
Road

'Aliomanu Beach

15

'Aliomanu
Road
(Broken Loop)

King Kong's Profile and
Hole-in-the-Mountain

Anahola
Beach
Park

Kahala
Point

Anahola Stream

14

Anahola Rd.

Anahola

Kukuihale

13

Kealia Road

Secluded
Cove

12

**Spalding
Monument**
A monument built by a long-dead
sugar baron to himself, now in
disrepair. Kind of embarrassing
when you think about it.

Hauaala Rd
4WD

Kealia Road

56

Donkey
Beach

Map continued on page 59

11

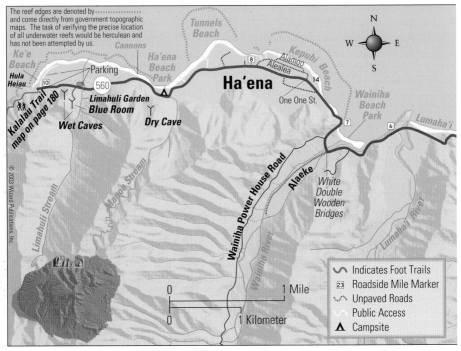

The reef edges are denoted by ············· and come directly from government topographic maps. The task of verifying the precise location of all underwater reefs would be herculean and has not been attempted by us.

Ke'e Beach
Hula Heiau
Parking
560
Limahuli Garden
Blue Room
Wet Caves
Kalalau Trail map on page 180
© 2003 Wizard Publications, Inc.
Limahuli Stream
Manoa Stream

Tunnels Beach
Cannons
Ha'ena Beach Park
Dry Cave

Ha'ena
One One St.
8 Alamoo Alealea
14
Kepuhi Beach
Wainiha Beach Park
Lumaha'i

Wainiha Power House Road
Alaeke
White Double Wooden Bridges
Wainiha River
Lumahai River

N
W — E
S

7
6

0 ———— 1 Mile
0 ———— 1 Kilometer

⌃	Indicates Foot Trails
23	Roadside Mile Marker
⋰	Unpaved Roads
	Public Access
▲	Campsite

existence and was used until the mid '70s when it was replaced by a beacon. Directly offshore is Moku'ae'ae Island, a bird sanctuary. Self-guided tours of the lighthouse area are available, though you can't go upstairs and visit the light itself. The view from the bluff is smashing and worth your time. Open 10–4. Take Kilauea Road. There are also guided hikes of nearby Crater Hill at 10 a.m. M–Th. Reserve in advance at 828–0168.

Kilauea has also become a high-priced refuge for dot.com millionaires (at least, those who survived the market bloodbath). Many exotic compounds are sprinkled about the area, just beyond sight.

Just north of Kilauea, Banana Joe's on the *mauka* side is one of the better places on the island to get fresh fruit and smoothies. (Much better than the nearby Mango Mamas.) Joe and Cindy have been here since 1986 and grow much of the fruit themselves, and the selection is usually excellent. Try something totally exotic. They also carry numerous locally made products. The frosties are excellent.

KALIHIWAI

After Kilauea you will notice two Kalihiwai Roads on the map. It used to be a loop connected at the bottom via a bridge. The bridge was erased by a tsunami in 1957, and the state hasn't replaced it yet. (Give 'em time, they're still trying to decide if computers will be just another passing fad.) The first Kalihiwai Road leads to a beautiful little bay, Kalihiwai Bay. This is a good place to stretch your legs and enjoy the scenery.

Back on the highway, there's a small pull-out ½ mile past the 24 mile marker. It's the only place you can park to walk to an unnamed falls 320 yards ahead on the left. (The falls are sometimes used by people to rinse off saltwater after they've been to Secret Beach.) The

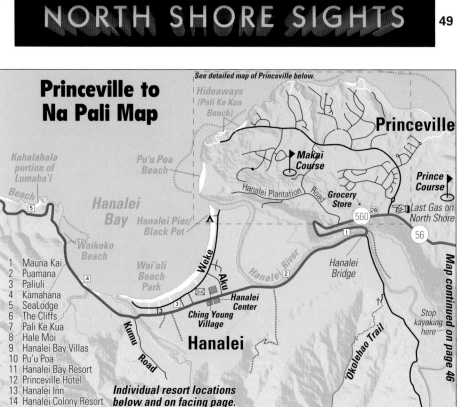

Princeville to Na Pali Map

See detailed map of Princeville below.

Hideaways (Pali Ke Kua Beach)

Princeville

Kahalahala portion of Lumaha'i Beach

Pu'u Poa Beach

Makai Course

Prince Course

Hanalei Plantation Road

Grocery Store

Last Gas on North Shore

Hanalei Bay

Hanalei Pier/ Black Pot

560 · 28 · 56

1

Waikoko Beach

Wai'oli Beach Park

Weke

Aku

Hanalei Center

Ching Young Village

Hanalei River

2

Hanalei Bridge

Map continued on page 46

1 Mauna Kai
2 Puamana
3 Paliuli
4 Kamahana
5 SeaLodge
6 The Cliffs
7 Pali Ke Kua
8 Hale Moi
9 Hanalei Bay Villas
10 Pu'u Poa
11 Hanalei Bay Resort
12 Princeville Hotel
13 Hanalei Inn
14 Hanalei Colony Resort

4

3

Kumu Road

Hanalei

Okolehao Trail

Stop kayaking here

Individual resort locations below and on facing page.

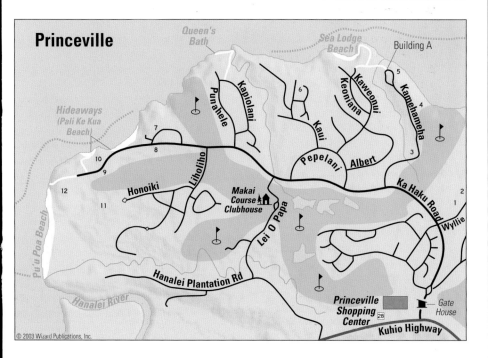

Princeville

Queen's Bath

Sea Lodge Beach

Building A

Hideaways (Pali Ke Kua Beach)

Kapiolani

Punahele

Keoniana

Kaweonui

Kamehameha

5

6

7

8

Kaui

9

10

Liholiho

Pepelani

Albert

Ka Haku Road

4

3

12

11

Honoiki

Makai Course Clubhouse

Lei O Papa

Wylie

2

1

Pu'u Poa Beach

Hanalei Plantation Rd

Princeville Shopping Center

28

Gate House

Hanalei River

Kuhio Highway

The Hanalei Lookout is a postcard waiting to happen...

stream flows under the road and falls again into the valley. The long bridge past the falls has a narrow walkway. Visible on the *mauka* side is Kalihiwai Falls, a gorgeous, two-tiered falls. The cars on this bridge *seem* to go by at 110 mph, so be careful. There used to be a closer turnout, but the state closed it because of our old buddy, *liability.*

As you continue, the second Kalihiwai Road leads to 'Anini Beach, where many of the rich and famous choose to build their homes. This is one of the safest places on the north shore to swim and is protected by a long, fringing reef.

PRINCEVILLE

Continuing on Highway 56, the resort area of Princeville beckons. It was named after Prince Albert, the 2-year-old son of King Kamehameha IV. Although the young lad died two years later, the name stuck. The resort is renowned for its ocean bluff condominiums and its golf. In fact, the best course

on the island (some say the best in all Hawai'i) is The Prince Course located on your right after the 26 mile marker. This is the sort of course that makes the non-golfer want to learn.

Past the 27 mile marker is Kapa Ka Road. The end of this road is one end of the Powerline Trail—10¼ miles of outstanding views. See HIKING on page 152.

Princeville's cliffs lead many to think that it has no beaches to offer. *Au contraire*, beaches don't get much better than Hideaways, a very pleasant little pocket of coarse sand. The catch is that you need to hike down about 5–10 minutes to it. Another gem is Queen's Bath. This is a natural pool located on a lava bench. See BEACHES. The Princeville Hotel is a good place to dine, shop or just gawk. If you are staying in Princeville, you may choke over the prices at Foodland or Big Save in Hanalei. Consider stocking up on food in

A REAL GEM

Kapa'a where it's *somewhat* cheaper.

As you leave Princeville, note that the highway changes names again and the mile markers start at 0. The gas station here is the last place to get gas on the north shore (and they have the prices to prove it!). Across the street is the Hanalei Lookout. Many postcards have been sold featuring this view. This valley is where most of the taro in Hawai'i is grown. Taro corm (the root portion) is pounded to make poi. This is the stuff everyone told you not to eat when you came to Hawai'i. If you go to a lu'au, try it anyway. Then you can badmouth it with authority.

HANALEI

Going down the road, you come to the rickety looking Hanalei Bridge. (The chicken wire on the main beams is to keep rust chunks from falling on your car.) Its wood planks are slippery when wet. This is a good time to tell you about Kaua'i's one-lane bridge etiquette. *All* vehicles on one side proceed, so if the car directly in front of you goes, you go. Otherwise, stop and wait for the other side to go first. All bridges from here on have one lane. Hanalei Bridge has a 15-ton weight limit, so you won't see big tour buses past this point. One bridge, called the Waipa Bridge, was built in 1912 for $4,000. It's so sturdy that it has *never* needed a major repair. The state found this intolerable and planned to replace it with a $5 million bridge that would hopefully require *lots* of maintenance. Local residents banded together in the late '90s and successfully fought 'em off.

The area around Hanalei (meaning wreath-shaped or crescent-shaped) Bay is a pretty little community. The surfing here is famous throughout the islands for its challenging nature during the winter. The entire bay is ringed by beach. A wide assortment of people live in Hanalei, including long time locals, itinerant surfers, new age types, celebrities and every other type of individual you can imagine. You're as likely to see locals driving a Mercedes or Hummer as you are a car held together with bungee cords and duct tape.

You can pick up some good Mexican

Shave Ice: An Island Delicacy

One treat everyone should try is shave ice. Lest you be confused, shave ice is not a snow cone. Snow cones are made from crushed ice with a little fruit syrup sprinkled on. True shave ice (that's *shave*, not *shaved*) uses a sharp blade to literally "shave" a large block of ice, creating an infinitely fine powder. (Keeping the blade sharp is vital.) Add to this copious amounts of exotic fruit flavors, put it all on top of a big scoop of ice cream, and you have an island delight that is truly *broke da mouf*. In our constant quest to provide as thorough a review as possible, we have unselfishly tried nearly every combination of shave ice. The result: We recommend the rainbow shave ice with macadamia nut ice cream. But by all means, engage in research of your own to see if you can come up with a better combination. The best shave ice on the island is at *Jo-Jo's Clubhouse* in Waimea. Other places include *Wishing Well Shave Ice* and *Paradise Shave Ice,* both in Hanalei and *Halo Halo Shave Ice* in Lihu'e. These can be found in the DINING section.

food from Tropical Taco in the Halele'a Building on the ocean side of the highway. Near Tropical Taco, stop by the Wishing Well Shave Ice for some world-class shave ice (though they are sometimes a bit abrasive there.)

After Hanalei, you ascend the road to a turnout overlooking Lumaha'i Beach (if it's not overgrown). This is a fantastic looking beach made famous when Mitzi Gaynor washed that man right out of her hair in *South Pacific* in 1957. The eastern portion is the best but requires a hike down. Otherwise, you can walk right onto it just before the Lumaha'i Stream.

Notice how lush everything looks from here on? This part of the island gets the perfect amount of rain and sunshine, making anything green very happy.

HA'ENA

Wainiha Beach Park, past the 6 mile marker, is often a great place to beachcomb, but the swimming is not good.

One of the best snorkel and shore SCUBA spots on the island, Tunnels Beach, is past the 8 mile marker. See BEACHES. Before you get to the 9 mile marker, the road dips at Manoa Stream. The stream flows over the road and is always creating potholes. It often creates a hole big and deep enough to pop your tire, so look for it as you cross. You are now at Ha'ena Beach Park. Camping is allowed with a county permit, and the beach is lovely year round (but the *swimming* isn't always lovely; see BEACHES). Across the street is the Manini-holo Dry Cave. Manini-holo was said to be the chief fisherman for the Menehune. He and other Menehune dug the cave looking for supernatural beasts called akua who had been stealing their fish.

Past the 9 mile marker you will come to Limahuli Stream. Many people (including us) use this stream to rinse off

saltwater after their day at Ke'e Beach, which is still ahead.

Above Limahuli Stream is the Limahuli Garden at (808) 826–1053. It is part of the National Tropical Botanical Gardens. The garden is run by a delightful fellow named Charles "Chipper" Wichman. His grandmother, Juliet Rice Wichman, was a powerful presence on Kaua'i who donated it to NTBG in 1976. They have guided tours (by reservation only) of the gardens for $15, self guided tours for $10. The garden is beautiful and features native Hawaiian plants, an area for plants brought by the first settlers and several others. A real treat is the ancient terrace system, crafted by some of the earliest Hawaiians, estimated to be 700–1,000 years old and in fantastic condition.

Just past the Limahuli Stream are the Wet Caves, called Waikapala'e Cave (reachable by a short trail) and Waikanaloa Cave (right there on the road). The upper Waikapala'e Cave contains a hidden phenomenon called the Blue Room, reachable only by swimming in the cold water. See ADVENTURES. The wet and dry caves are former sea caves, gouged by waves when the sea level was higher than it is today. We were silly enough to SCUBA dive the upper cave and can report that there is not much to see, but it was kind of fun anyway. Hawaiian legend has it these caves were dug by the fire goddess Pele. She dug them for her lover but left them when they became filled with water.

At the 10 mile marker, you have gone as far as you can go by car. This is Ke'e Beach, marked by a fabulous lagoon that offers great swimming and snorkeling when it's calm. The well-known Kalalau Trail begins here. Eleven miles of hills and switch-

A REAL GEM

The eastern portion of Lumaha'i is the best.

backs culminate in a glorious beach setting, complete with a waterfall. The first leg of the hike leads to Hanakapi'ai Beach with a side trip to Hanakapi'ai Falls. For more on the Kalalau Trail, see ADVENTURES on page 180.

Ke'e is where Na Pali Coast begins. You can see its edges from here. Part of *The Thorn Birds* and numerous other movies have been filmed at this location. If you walk past Ke'e Beach on the shoreline trail beside the rocks, you'll get an enticing look at the rugged Na Pali coastline. Look up toward the mountains and you'll see Bali Hai (Hawaiian name Makana Peak). Clever photography turned the peak into the mystical island of Bali Hai in the movie *South Pacific*. As you stare at this peak with its incredibly steep sides, picture the following scene that took place in ancient times.

Men would climb the 1,600-foot peak carrying special spears made of hau and papala. The trail was so difficult in spots that they had to cling to the side of the mountain for dear life. When it got dark, they would light the spears and hurl them toward the ocean below. The spears were designed to leave a fire trail behind, and the light show was immensely popular.

From the end of Ke'e Beach, a trail cuts through the jungle up to the Ka-ulu-Paoa Heiau, still visible by the pavement of stones outlining its foundations next to a lava cliff. Other trails to the heiau may be on private property, but the shoreline trail from the beach is public. For over 1,000 years this heiau served as the most important and prestigious school for hula in the islands. Would-be students came from around the island chain to learn from the *kumu hula,* or hula master. Please don't disturb any rocks lying about. Just past the heiau a short trail leads to a small waterfall (which is merely a trickle during dry times). *Fifty* generations of hot, thirsty students came to this tiny waterfall, sat on these very rocks and talked about their lives, hopes, fears and dreams. It's humbling to share these rocks with their spirits. It's as if you can still hear the echo of their lives in the sound of the gurgling water.

Just east of Ke'e is where the infamous Taylor Camp used to be. This is where Howard Taylor, brother of Elizabeth Taylor, owned a piece of land in the 1960s and encouraged other "hippies" to come and live off the land. The camp swelled to more than 100 people who mostly ended up living off residents or the government. Before the state condemned the property in 1977, camp residents began what would become the national *puka shell* craze when one of the residents fashioned a necklace of shells and gave it to Howard, who in turn gave it to his famous sister Liz.

If you want to park at Ke'e and find the lot full, take the dirt road next to the restrooms and stay to the left. There are many places to park along here, and it's usually less noticed.

NORTH SHORE SHOPPING

OK, so maybe you're not interested in the designer Gucci snorkel fins for $320, (with matching mask for $195) or the Dolce & Gabbana flip-flops at *$420*. (Oh, sure, the $2 ones at the ABC store work just as well but hey, you won't be as *stylin'*.) We've hit all the places for you. Here's some ideas for items to remember your visit to Kaua'i when there's 30 feet of snow outside your window.

In Kilauea, Kong Lung is a long-time favorite for upscale casual clothing and gifts. Next door is the Kilauea Farmer's Market (actually a small grocery store), which has a good selection of gourmet and organic foods.

In the Princeville Shopping Center, Kaua'i Kite & Hobby (for sale at press time) offers many options such as games, books, etc. to keep your little one entertained. We especially like their bird and shell identification cards. Good to have for reference in the car and indestructible

Walk a bit past Ke'e Beach for a great view of Na Pali.

Kaua'i's north shore is where the majority of the state's taro is grown. This field, in the Hanalei Valley, was planted with rice to look like Vietnam in the movie Uncommon Valor.

by kids (if anything is!). You can drop off your film here at Hanalei Photo.

As you drive into Hanalei there's some good shops at the Hanalei Dolphin Center at the water's edge of the Hanalei River. Ola's has some unique gift items, and Overboard offers a decent selection of island-style clothing. (Watch for the aggressive sales staff.)

At the green Halele'a Building on the makai side, Kai Kane is a good place for surf wear and island-style clothing.

At the Hanalei Center try Sand People, Tropical Tantrum, or Hanalei Surf Co. for clothing. For the kids there's Rainbow Ducks and Koconuts for Kids across the street. If you like vintage Hawaiiana, stop at Yellowfish Trading Co.; they have an excellent selection. At Ching Young Village look for Hula Moon for gifts to take back home, and watch surfboard shaping through the window at HSC Backdoor. Need to purchase or rent outdoor gear? Pedal 'n Paddle has

an excellent selection.

The north shore outdoor markets are the Waipa Market on Tuesday mornings and in Kilauea it's Thursdays at 4:30 p.m. and Saturday mornings.

NORTH SHORE BEST BETS

Best Beach—Ke'e or Hideaways
Best Snorkeling—Tunnels, Hideaways or Ke'e
Best Treat—Chocolate Suicide Cake at Zelo's, Apple Cobbler at Village Snack
Best Fast Food—Tropical Taco
Best Mexican Food—Neide's
Best Lava Swimming Pool—Queen's Bath
Best View from a Treadmill—Prince Health Club
Best Secluded Beach—Waiakalua
Best Swimming When Calm—Ke'e
Best Shore SCUBA Dive—Tunnels Beach
Best Beachcombing—Wainiha Beach
Best Golf—The Prince Course
Best View—Sunset from Ke'e overlooking Na Pali, or from Kalalau Trail

Wailua is known as the coconut coast—can you guess why?

EAST SHORE SIGHTS

Kaua'i's east shore is where the majority of the population resides. The kings of yesteryear chose the Wailua River area to live, making it forever royal ground. All members of Kaua'i royalty were born in this area. Kuamo'o Road, designated as 580 on the maps, is also called the King's Highway. In ancient times only the king could walk along the spine of this ridge. (Kuamo'o means the lizard's spine.)

Today, the east shore is often referred to as the Coconut Coast. One drive through Wailua and it's obvious why: thousands of coconut trees planted over a century ago by an idealistic young German immigrant who dreamed of overseeing a giant copra (dried coconut) empire. Unfortunately, nobody told him how long coconut trees took to mature and the plantation was not economically successful, but his legacy lives on in the form of a gigantic coconut grove.

For our description, the east shore means the Wailua/Kapa'a area to Lihu'e. (Take a look at the fold-out back cover map to orient yourself.) Both areas are heavily populated. (This is a relative term; together they have about 15,000 residents.)

The same descriptive ground rules that we discussed at the beginning of NORTH SHORE SIGHTS apply here.

Unlike other areas of the island where a single road dominates your tour, this area has many significant sights located off the main road. Therefore, we will describe them in a more scattershot manner and generally work our way from north to south.

WAILUA/KAPA'A

In the extreme northern part of Kapa'a is a delightful waterfall called Ho'opi'i Falls, which you can hike to. See HIKING on page 151.

While we are up the road off the main highway, there are several hikes in this area that provide excellent views. The Nounou Mountain Trail (also called the Sleeping Giant), the Kuilau Ridge Trail, the Jungle Hike and the Secret

Tunnel to the North Shore Hike all are located inland and all are worthy of consideration. (See HIKING under ACTIVITIES for more information.)

One aspect of ancient Hawaiian culture that can be seen to this day is the heiau, a structure carefully built from lava rocks and used for religious purposes. There are **seven heiaus** stretching from the mouth of the **Wailua River** to the top of **Mount Wai'ale'ale**. All except the Wai'ale'ale heiau are marked on the map on the next page. The mouth of the Wailua River was well known, not only throughout the Hawaiian Islands, but also in parts of central Polynesia as well. Ancient Polynesians are thought to have come all the way from Tahiti to visit it.

Wailua also means ghosts or spirits. It was thought that during a certain phase of the moon, spirits of those who died recently would paddle down the river in large numbers and work their way around the island to a cliff at Polihale (described on page 86) where they would leap to the next life. Known as **night marchers**, these ghosts are still believed to exist by many Hawaiians, and sightings are most prevalent along the highway between Wailua and Lihu'e. Interestingly, this stretch of road has also been responsible for many bad car accidents. Of course, police blame the wrecks on another type of spirit—the kind that comes in a bottle.

The first heiau, near the mouth of the Wailua River on the southern side, is called **Hauola, City of Refuge**. It is part of what was a larger structure called **Hikina A Ka La, the Rising Sun**. If a person committed an offense worthy of execution (such as allowing his shadow to touch the shadow of a chief or interrupting an important person), he would attempt to elude his executioners by coming here. By staying at the site and performing certain rites prescribed by the priest, he would earn the right to leave without harm.

The second temple is on the *mauka* side of the highway between the north end of Leho Road and the road to **Smith's Tropical Paradise**. This is called **Malae** and at 273 x 324 feet, it is the largest heiau on Kaua'i. Legend states that it was built by Menehune. Although there is not a lot to see, the view from there is interesting. If you decide to visit it, be wary of your footing.

The third heiau is just up Kuamo'o Road (580) on the left side. This area had several names and several functions. The first portion that you see is called **Holoholo-ku**. Some archeologists say that this area was used for human sacrifice. Most of the time those sacrificed were prisoners of war. If none could be found, however, the Kahuna would select a commoner and have the executioner strangle him secretly at night. Some archaeologists find this interpretation of Hawaiian history in spiritual bad taste, given its very close proximity to the **Birthstones**, described below, and assume that the area was used for animal sacrifices. The heiau was later purposely desecrated and used as a pigpen by the wife of the last king of Kaua'i, who did so as a signal that the ancient religious ways should be abandoned in favor of Christianity.

Please do not disturb offerings at heiaus.

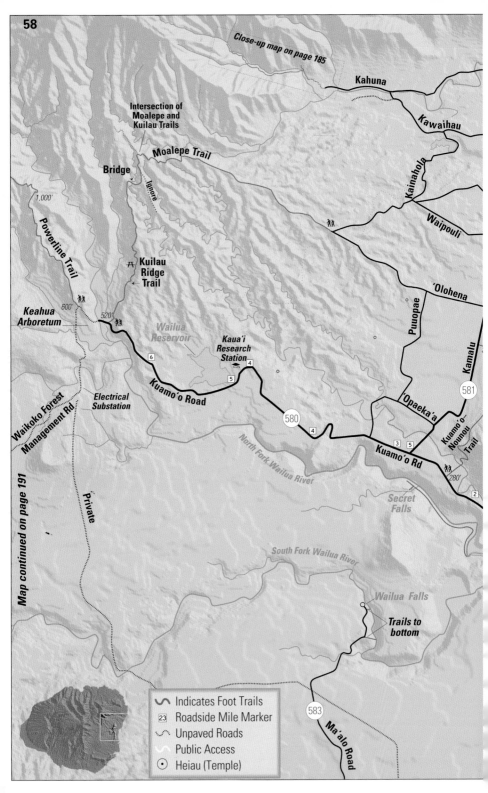

Close-up map on page 185

Kahuna

Kawaihau

Intersection of
Moalepe and
Kuilau Trails

Moalepe Trail

Bridge

Ignore

Kainahola

Waipouli

1,000'

Powerline Trail

Kuilau
Ridge
Trail

'Olohena

Keahua
Arboretum

600'

520'

Wailua
Reservoir

Puuopae

6

Kaua'i
Research
Station

Kamalu

581

5

4

Waikoko Forest
Management Rd

Electrical
Substation

Kuamo'o Road

'Opaeka'a

580

4

Kuamo'o-
Nounou
Trail

Private

North Fork Wailua River

3

5

Kuamo'o Rd

280'

2

Map continued on page 191

Secret
Falls

South Fork Wailua River

Wailua Falls

Trails to
bottom

583

Ma'alo Road

〰 Indicates Foot Trails
23 Roadside Mile Marker
⋯ Unpaved Roads
〰 Public Access
⊙ Heiau (Temple)

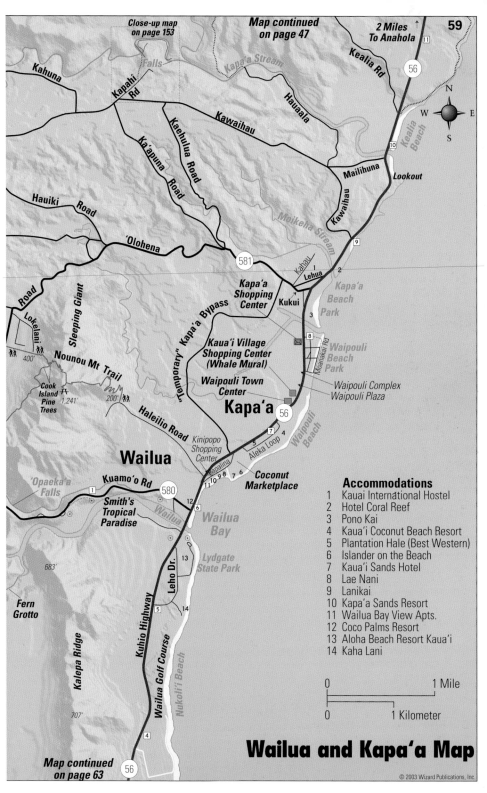

Close-up map on page 153

Map continued on page 47

2 Miles ↑
To Anahola

Kahuna

Kapahi Rd

Falls

Kapa'a Stream

Kealia Rd

Kealia Beach

56

Kawaihau

Hauaala

Kaehulua Road

Ka'apuna Road

Hauiki Road

'Olohena

N
W E
S

10

Mailihuna

Lookout

Kawaihau

Moikeha Stream

581

9

Road

Sleeping Giant

Lokelani

400'

Nounou Mt Trail

Cook Island Pine Trees

1,241'

200'

Haleilio Road

Kahau

Lehua

Kukui

1

2

Kapa'a
Shopping
Center

Kapa'a Beach Park

3

Kaua'i Village
Shopping Center
(Whale Mural)

8

Waipouli Beach Park

Moanakai Rd

Waipouli Town
Center

Kapa'a

56

Waipouli Complex
Waipouli Plaza

Kinipopo
Shopping
Center

Aleka Loop

7

5

4

Waipouli Beach

Wailua

'Opaeka'a
Falls

Kuamo'o Rd

1

580

Napalina

11 10 9 8

7 6

**Coconut
Marketplace**

Smith's
Tropical
Paradise

12

6

Wailua

Wailua
Bay

683'

Leho Dr.

13

Lydgate
State Park

Fern
Grotto

Kuhio Highway

5

14

Kalepa Ridge

707'

Wailua Golf Course

Nukoli'i Beach

Accommodations
1 Kauai International Hostel
2 Hotel Coral Reef
3 Pono Kai
4 Kaua'i Coconut Beach Resort
5 Plantation Hale (Best Western)
6 Islander on the Beach
7 Kaua'i Sands Hotel
8 Lae Nani
9 Lanikai
10 Kapa'a Sands Resort
11 Wailua Bay View Apts.
12 Coco Palms Resort
13 Aloha Beach Resort Kaua'i
14 Kaha Lani

0 _____ 1 Mile

0 _____ 1 Kilometer

Map continued on page 63

4

56

Wailua and Kapa'a Map

Just a few dozen feet up the road from **Holoholo-ku** is the **Birthstone**. It was essential that all kings of Kaua'i be born here, even if they were not of chiefly origin. One of the two stones supported the back of the mother-to-be while the other was where she placed her legs while giving birth. The outline of stones near here was where a grass shack once stood where the pregnant mother stayed until it was time to give birth. The flat slab of sandstone that you see on the ground covered the remains of a sacrificed dog, indicating that the place was kapu, or forbidden to commoners. The giant crack in the rock wall was where the umbilical cord of the newborn was placed. If a rat came and took the cord, it was a sign that the child would grow up to be a thief (or worse, a tax collector); otherwise, all was well.

Continuing up 580, a short way past the 1 mile marker, there's a dirt road angling back toward the ocean. Located at the end of the road are two large boulders. Though few residents are aware of it, the rocks' position is no accident and dates back over 1,000 years.

The ancient Hawaiians didn't live in a world of well-defined seasons. They didn't even measure their own lives in years, but rather stages of life. But they did need to keep track of the passage of the sun for planting and religious reasons. These two multi-ton rounded and shaped boulders are perfectly offset so that if you align yourself with them so they appear to touch with the right one closer to you, the sun will rise from the intersection on the summer solstice. (Winter solstice involves aligning the right side of the left boulder with the thumb-like hill on Sleeping Giant behind you.) Imagine the importance they must have attributed to this task by considering the difficulty of hauling these boulders up from the Wailua River, per-

haps one boulder from each fork for symmetry. (Hawaiians *loved* symmetry.)

If you walk down the path about 100 feet past the guard-rail, you will see several large stones. One of them was known as the **Bellstone** and, if thwacked properly, can produce a metallic clank (not the gong we have come to expect from metal bells). This sound supposedly carried throughout the entire Wailua Valley. The stone was struck in ancient times to signal the birth of what would be a new chief.

Still on 580 just before you get to the **'Opaeka'a Falls** turnout is the last heiau you will see. Called **Poli'ahu**, this is a rather mysterious heiau. Legend states that it was built by Menehune, the legendary people of small stature, and was devoted to the interests and activities of the gods, demigods and high ali'i. Look for lots of native and Polynesian-introduced plant species in the area. There is also a nice **Wailua River Lookout** here.

The actual final heiau in this chain rests atop the rain-soaked plateau of **Wai'ale'ale**. The remnants of this most sacred heiau are still visible today. Called **Ka'awako**, the altar itself stood 2 feet high, 5 feet wide and 7 feet long. Toward the rear, standing on one end was a phallic stone. It is located on the wettest spot in the entire world. According to the USGS, this spot receives 440.22 inches of rain per year. (You read a lot of numbers about the annual rainfall on **Wai'ale'ale**—this number comes straight from the people who read the rain gauges. The original gauge is in the Kaua'i Museum.)

The ancient Hawaiians were bothered that the small, sacred pool on top of Wai'ale'ale didn't feed their most sacred river, the Wailua. Not to worry. In a project that would make the Army Corps of Engineers proud, they cut a trench at the top of the mountain from the small pool

to the edge of the cliff so the water would add to the waterfalls that feed the Wailua River. Then they could say the most sacred pool fed the most sacred river.

While on Kuamo'o Road *(a well-known speed trap)*, stop by the '**Opaeka'a Falls Lookout**. These lacy falls flow year round. Late morning light is best, around 10:30 a.m. Driving past the falls, there is a crude trail between the end

of the guard-rail and the 2 mile marker (near a fire hydrant) leading to a spot several hundred feet upstream of the falls. One could walk in the stream to the edge of the falls if one wished. Needless to say, the top of 151-foot high waterfall can be very dangerous, so use your best judgment. To get to the *bottom* of 'Opaeka'a Falls see ADVENTURES on page 182.

There is another **Wailua River Lookout** across from the '**Opaeka'a Lookout**.

Continuing several miles up Kuamo'o Road, the road eventually crosses *under* a stream and becomes unpaved. It occasionally flows too heavily over the road to cross in your car. See the detailed map of this area on page 191. A 4WD is a dream back here but cars are often OK, depending on the maintenance cycle of the road and the weather. Large puddles are usually lined with small rocks, not mud. Several trailheads are in this region. The **Keahua Arboretum** is located near here, but it's been rather unkempt for years, so don't knock yourself out to see it.

The unpaved section of this road is Waikoko Forest Management Rd. The area feels like a giant oxygen factory. Take a big whiff and you'll almost get a buzz from the purity of the air. The **Jungle Hike** on page 150 and the **Secret Tunnel to the North**

Lacy 'Opaeka'a Falls is a Wailua landmark.

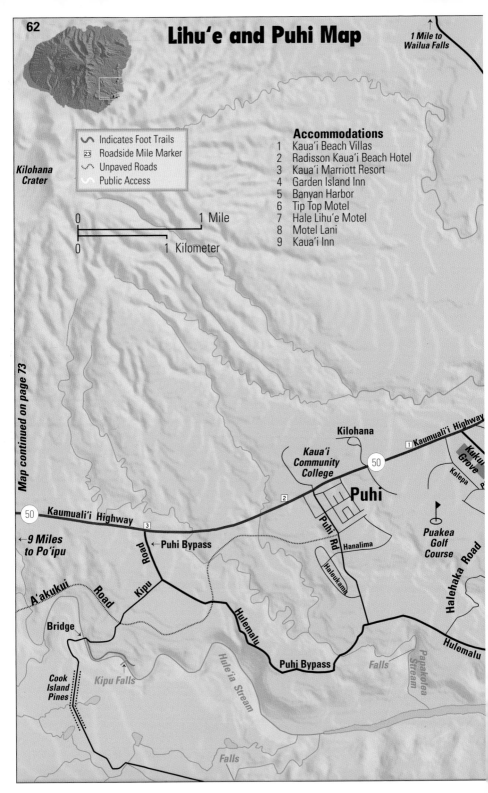

Lihu'e and Puhi Map

1 Mile to Wailua Falls

Kilohana Crater

Indicates Foot Trails
23 Roadside Mile Marker
Unpaved Roads
Public Access

0 ————————— 1 Mile
0 ————————— 1 Kilometer

Accommodations
1 Kaua'i Beach Villas
2 Radisson Kaua'i Beach Hotel
3 Kaua'i Marriott Resort
4 Garden Island Inn
5 Banyan Harbor
6 Tip Top Motel
7 Hale Lihu'e Motel
8 Motel Lani
9 Kaua'i Inn

Map continued on page 73

Kilohana

Kaua'i Community College

Kaumuali'i Highway

1

50

Kukui Grove

Kalepa

Puhi

2

Puhi Rd

Hanalima

Puakea Golf Course

Halehaka Road

50 Kaumuali'i Highway

3

← Puhi Bypass

Haleukama

← **9 Miles to Po'ipu**

A'akukui Road

Kipu Road

Hulemalu

Puhi Bypass

Hulemalu

Bridge

Falls

Papakolea Stream

Cook Island Pines

↑ *Kipu Falls*

Hule'ia Stream

Falls

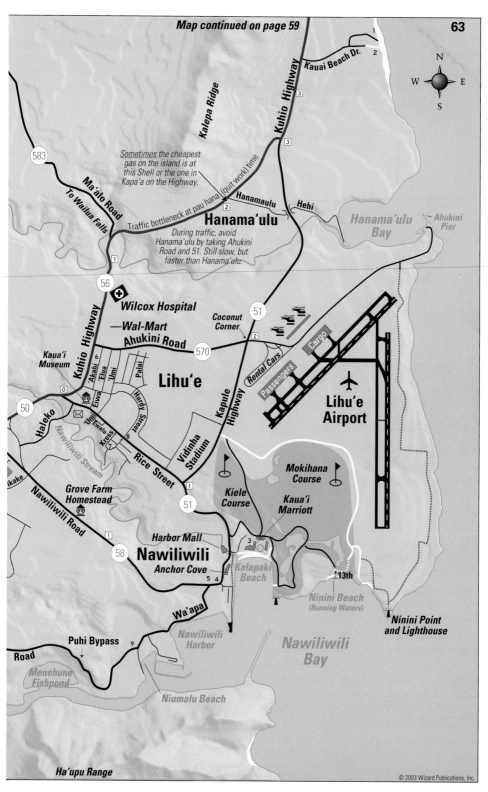

N
W · E
S

1
Kauai Beach Dr.
2

Kalepa Ridge

Kuhio Highway
3
3

Sometimes the cheapest gas on the island is at this Shell or the one in Kapa'a on the Highway.

583

Ma'alo Road

To Wailua Falls

Traffic bottleneck at pau hana (quit work) time

2 Hanamaulu
Hehi

Hanama'ulu

Hanamaulu

Hanama'ulu Bay

Ahukini Pier

During traffic, avoid Hanama'ulu by taking Ahukini Road and 51. Still slow, but faster than Hanama'ulu.

1

56
✚ Wilcox Hospital

Kuhio Highway

51

Coconut Corner
2

—Wal-Mart
Ahukini Road
570

Kaua'i Museum

'Akahi 6
'Elua
'Umi
Palai

Lihu'e

Rental Cars

Cargo

Passengers

✈
Lihu'e Airport

0
Eiwa
Ewalu
Kress
8

Hardy Street

Kapule Highway

50

Haleko

Nawiliwili Stream

Rice Street

Vidinha Stadium

1

Mokihana Course

51

Grove Farm Homestead

Nawiliwili Road

1

Kiele Course

Kaua'i Marriott

58

Nawiliwili

Harbor Mall

Anchor Cove
5 4

3

Kalapaki Beach

13th

Ninini Beach *(Running Waters)*

Ninini Point and Lighthouse

Wa'apa

Nawiliwili Harbor

Nawiliwili Bay

Puhi Bypass
9

Road

Menehune Fishpond

Niumalu Beach

Ha'upu Range

These petroglyphs are usually submerged in the mouth of the Wailua River, but can appear after heavy rains.

planted bananas in his footsteps. One day the chief ordered a heiau to be built. Villagers were too busy, so the giant volunteered. It took two weeks and he did a great job. Villagers threw a party to celebrate, and the giant ate a bit too much. (If you've been to a lu'au you can relate.) He fell asleep and has not been roused since, but is expected to wake up any time (maybe during your visit).

Shore in ADVENTURES are back here, as well as stunning forests. This area is excellent for mountain biking.

Back on the main highway, you'll find that traffic in downtown Kapa'a (on the highway) can get congested at times. The county opened up a "temporary" bypass road. (See map.) The "permanent" bypass road is scheduled to be completed sometime during the next ice age. All the land around the bypass area was for sale a few years ago. Kaua'i residents were worried that someone would buy the 1,400 acres and develop it, connecting Kapa'a to Wailua and creating a big-city feel. Entertainer Bette Midler (a part-time resident) bought it instead and promised never to put anything other than trees on it.

One of Kapa'a's notable views is the Sleeping Giant. The best angle is from the small turnout kitty-corner from the Chevron Station (on the main highway). Look *mauka* and you will see the outline of a giant. (This is your *ink blot* test for the day.) According to legend, the giant you see (you *do* see it, don't you?) was a friendly sort who flattened areas where he sat. Local villagers liked this and also

Local folklore says that if Kaua'i's people learned of an attempt to invade their island, they would light fires behind the Sleeping Giant in order to illuminate his profile at night. This would frighten invading warriors into thinking that Kaua'i had some really big dudes and that they should rethink their invasion plans.

While you are in Wailua, riverboat trips up the Wailua River can take you to the Fern Grotto for $15 per person. This is a natural amphitheater filled with ferns and is a popular place to hold weddings. See RIVER TRIPS under ACTIVITIES. The Wailua River is usually called the only navigable river in all Hawai'i, but that depends on your definition of navigable. The mouth of the river has several stones with ancient petroglyphs carved in them. After heavy rains, the river sometimes washes away large amounts of sand, revealing these stones for a short period of time. The mouth itself is always changing, and watching it wash over its banks after a heavy rain can be wild. The river can go from not flowing at all to carving up the mouth in a matter of hours.

There is a paved beachside walking path behind the Kaua'i Coconut Beach

Hotel, which makes for a pleasant stroll. A good place to take a *sandy* beach walk is from **Lydgate State Park** south as far as the Radisson Hotel. The sand is continuous almost the whole way.

Lydgate State Park is the best place on the island to learn snorkeling. It has a boulder-enclosed pond that allows water and fish in, but keeps out the ocean's force. See SNORKELING on page 171 and BEACHES on page 107. There is even a keiki (kid) pond, which is shallower. Add to this showers, restrooms and a large playground, and you have a nice little park for a day at the beach.

On the southern side of the Wailua River is **Smith's Tropical Paradise**. Here you will find a lovely garden (though it's been looking a bit faded lately) in which to stroll, filled with tropical plants and wailing peacocks (which sound like cats being tortured). Entrance is $5 per person. They also hold a pretty good lu'au here. See DINING for more information.

As you pass the **Wailua Golf Course** going south toward Lihu'e, realize that the entire coast fronting the course is a sandy beach. Called **Nukoli'i Beach**, there's rarely more than a few people on it.

LIHU'E

Coming from Kapa'a and just before you enter Lihu'e from Highway 56, you see Ma'alo Road (583). This leads to **Wailua Falls**. In an-cient (and occasionally modern) times, men would jump off the top of the falls to prove their manhood (which was often left on the rocks below). This test was often fatal. Government maps list the falls height at 80 feet. It always bothered us because it

NOT TO BE MISSED!

sure *looks* taller. So, recently we [...] a fishing line and sinker to the bottom from the lip of the falls (boy, did *we* look stupid) and measured it. To our amazement, it was 173 feet of solid drop. (We measured it *twice* to be sure.)

You might see people splashing about in the pool below the falls. It's a wonderful scene and lots of fun. They either took the steep trail (if it's dry) next to the beginning of the metal guard-rail near the viewing spot or the less steep trail ³/₁₀ mile back down the road from the end of the turn-around. (See map.) The latter requires a longer walk, but it's pretty and, when muddy, it's the easier of the two trails. Neither are professionally maintained and both can be slippery when wet. The state, in their paranoia about liability, has erected signs telling you not to take the trails to the bottom. They even cut the ropes that had been strung to make it safer and easier. (Making it *less* safe apparently makes *someone* feel safer.) We see people ignoring the signs, for what it's worth, and we don't know if you aren't *allowed* to hike down or are simply not *advised* to go.

The falls plunge into a pool that's 33 feet deep. Why so exact? Because in one of those *just because* moods awhile back, we hiked down with some friends, hauling SCUBA gear (gee, those now-confiscated ropes sure did help), and SCUBA-dived the pool. There we found 14-inch long small-mouthed bass and some giant shrimp (isn't that an oxymoron?) with bodies over 8 inches long, plus arms. Lingering beneath the falls, the scene is like an upside-down battlefield with explosions of white that will cause percussive waves to sweep through your entire body, your air-filled chest shuddering from the blasts. We also found rental car keys (perhaps tossed by an irate but shortsighted spouse), bolt cutters, a cane

If you ever saw the TV show Fantasy Island, *you'll remember Wailua Falls.*

knife and other odds and ends.

Back on the highway, if we're just trying to get *through* Lihu'e during traffic, we usually take 51 to 570 (Ahukini Road) to Highway 56. (See map on page 63 for this to make sense.) It bypasses Hanama'ulu and much of Lihu'e.

In Lihu'e, one place worth stopping for is the **Kaua'i Museum** (245–6931) on Rice Street. They have an interesting display of Hawaiian artifacts and a permanent display called *The Story of Kaua'i* and other rotating displays. Their gift shop is well stocked with books, maps and assorted items. If you are looking for topographic maps of the various areas (serious hikers prefer these as traveling companions) or just an obscure book on Kaua'i or Hawai'i, this is a good place to stop. Admission is $5 per person unless you are going to the gift shop, which is free.

If you need camping permits or other county or state items, their buildings are behind the Museum on Eiwa Street.

While you are in the area, there is a dumpy little place on Kress Street called **Halo Halo Shave Ice** inside Hamura Saimin that serves good shave ice (when they feel like serving it). Have them put ice cream on the bottom for a real treat.

Taking Rice Street east leads you to Nawiliwili Harbor. There are two shopping centers here called **Harbor Mall** and **Anchor Cove Shopping Center**. **Kalapaki Beach**, behind Anchor Cove, is a good place to watch sailboats, outrigger canoes and cruise ships, in addition to the beach's other attributes.

On Rice Street, you will pass the main entrance to the **Kaua'i Marriott**. Its other entrance is off Kapule Highway (51) and leads through **Kaua'i Lagoons** to either **Running Waters Beach** or the **Ninini Lighthouse**. If there is a maintenance volunteer at the lighthouse, ask if you can go to the top. The view from the 100-foot lighthouse (which uses a 4,700,000 can-

dlepower light) is superb. If you happen to be on top when a jet comes in for a landing, you'd swear you could reach up and touch it. To get to the lighthouse, you pass by two golf courses. **The Kiele** is definitely the better of the two.

Rice Street loops around and becomes Nawiliwili Road. It is here that you will find **Grove Farm Homestead Museum** at (808) 245–3202. This was the private home of George N. Wilcox and his nieces. It was turned into a museum by Mabel Wilcox shortly before her death in 1978. With 80 acres and several buildings to browse through, it is quite popular. (And they make an awesome sugar cookie here.) Groups of about six are escorted around the grounds and house for 2 hours for $5 per person. Even if this isn't normally your cup of tea, you will probably find it interesting. It's the story of an incredible family's rise to prominence in the old, sugar-dominated Kaua'i. It's best to make reservations before you arrive on Kaua'i, or you might not be admitted.

Off Nawiliwili Road is Wa'apa Road. Take this road to Hulemalu Road and you will come to an overlook for the **Menehune (Alekoko) Fishpond**. This is a large, impressive fishpond adjacent to the **Hule'ia Stream**. According to legend, it was built in one night by the Menehune as a gift for a princess and her brother. Estimates of its age range as high as 1,000 years. Today, it is privately owned and has fallen into disrepair as a fishpond. Nonetheless, it is a remarkable landmark that is worth a look.

Back on the main highway (which has changed its name to Hwy 50, the Kaumuali'i Hwy), we find ourselves heading south. Before the 1 mile marker is **Kukui Grove Shopping Center**, one of the biggest shopping centers on the island. It's been a bit lonely in the

mall itself recently due to competition elsewhere, but there are still some good stores there.

Past the 1 mile marker you will see **Kilohana** (245–5608) on your right. This was the home of Gaylord and Ethel Wilcox and has been lovingly restored to its former glory. Gaylord Wilcox was manager of the Grove Farm Plantation. Walk through the door of this 16,000-square-foot mansion and you get a sense of Kaua'i in days past. The furniture, fittings and motif all hearken back to a simpler day when sugar was king. Inside is **Gaylord's Restaurant** as well as several shops, galleries and a lu'au. Kilohana also offers carriage rides around the grounds pulled by Clydesdale horses at a cost of $10. They also have sugar cane field carriage rides for $24 per person, where you'll learn everything you ever wanted to know about sugar but were afraid to ask. For these latter rides, call 246–9529 for reservations.

Across from the 3 mile marker on the main highway is Kipu Road, which also acts as a bypass road. Located off this road is a glorious little hidden place you might find enchanting. If you go, do it during the week, and you *may* have it all to yourself. It is a small waterfall called **Kipu Falls** pouring into a deep pool. It is ringed half-way by a 20-foot cliff. On the far side is a rope swing with a ladder leading up the side of a tree. Get out of the pond via thick tree roots. The entire setting is wonderful. Obviously, you need to evaluate the condition of the rope, pond and ladder yourself to determine if it's safe. People use the rope all the time (including us), but we won't vouch for its safety. To get to the falls, walk the dirt road on your left just before the bridge on Kipu Road (see map). The land was formerly used for growing sugar. Although the land company has posted No

Enchanting Kipu Falls and pool—part of Kaua'i's hidden charm.

TRESPASSING signs on their land, it hasn't stopped locals—who have visited this waterfall for generations—from walking

A REAL GEM

to it. Regardless, we'll just tell you where it is and leave the rest to you. Maybe you can call Grove Farm and ask if you can use the trail to their waterfall. They've certainly been gracious about letting people use their private road to Maha'ulepu Beach in Po'ipu for years. You should know that the stream itself and the falls (though not the rope swing) are on *state land* and not owned by or leased to anyone. Only the surrounding land is private. As long as you're between the stream banks, you're not trespassing, according to county personnel we spoke with. Anyway, just before the dirt road/trail you're walking on begins to ascend, there is a very short (but sometimes slippery) trail down to the top of the falls on your right. (The sugar

cane on the main trail gets a little intrusive at times.) The entire walk takes about 5 minutes. You're on your own from here. The alternative is to walk in the stream from the bridge the whole way. That way is perfectly legal, according to the county. Remember not to leave valuables in your car, break-ins are not uncomon here.

If you were to continue on Kipu Rd., you would quickly come to a magnificent strand of Cook Island pines. These trees were highly valued as ship's masts in the Age of Discovery. This entire area is called **Kipu** and is currently leased to the Rice family and the Waterhouse Trust. William Hyde Rice was a cattle rancher, and a monument to him was erected here by his Japanese workers. Behind Ha'upu mountain is the fabulous beach called **Kipu Kai**. This long crescent of sand is a beachgoer's dream. Unfortunately, the only way to reach it is by boat or over the private road owned by Kipu Ranch and the Waterhouse Trust. This road is closed

to the public, though you can get a glimpse of Kipu Kai from the ATV tour on page 117. John Waterhouse ordered that the 1,096 acres of leased state land revert to the state at the time of death of the last of his four nieces and one nephew. So if you want to see it, put the year 2030 on your calendar of things to do. We've tried walking to Kipu Kai from Ha'ula Beach. The horse path up and over the tall mountain is riddled with evil plants with thorns that turned our exposed legs to hamburger.

EAST SHORE SHOPPING

Starting in northern Kapa'a, there's the **Kaua'i Products Fair** on weekends, next door to the **Red Dirt Store**, featuring locally made craft items and fresh produce. If you miss this one, go to the 3 p.m. (Wednesdays) **Sunshine Market** on Kahau Street in Kapa'a. (Arrive early.)

A good health food store is **Poppy's Market** in the yellow building just after the Moikeha Bridge. (Maneuvering into the parking lot in the back of the store is tricky.) We like the fresh produce, the Gorilla Vanilla coffee and the chai mix. Closed Mondays.

In downtown Kapa'a, try **Island Hemp & Cotton** and **Hula Girl** for clothing and gifts and **Kebanu** for some amazing art works, especially the wood works both locally made and from the mainland. The sound of water in the shop is very relaxing. The **Pono Market** is a good stop for manju, plate lunches and other local foods.

Continuing south just before the whale mural, the **Lemongrass Gallery** behind the Lemongrass Restaurant offers some unique items to check out.

Across the street from the Foodland is **Marta's Boat**, offering interesting items for women and kids. Plan to shop here in the afternoons to be sure they're open.

At **Coconut Marketplace** you'll find many shopping options in all price ranges. There is some beautiful non-traditional Kaua'i-designed and created

Throw-net fishing was introduced to Hawai'i by Japanese immigrants. The native Hawaiians quickly embraced this method, and today it is considered an island tradition.

...der work at **Ye Olde Ship Store**. The designs on the fossilized walrus ivory created by one of the Kaua'i artisans are especially noteworthy. There are many other stores to visit here, including **Jungle Rain**, which offers a good selection of island-style clothing and gifts. (Their stuffed roosters only *look* like the ones that woke you up this morning at 4 a.m.)

If you truly love books like we do and want to add some rare, out-of-print Hawaii-related titles to your personal collection, stop at the **Tin Can Mailman** at Kinipopo Shopping Village across from Haleilio Road. If he doesn't have it, he'll get it and let you know by e-mail.

Before or after your visit to Wailua Falls, stop by **Kapaia Stitchery**. In addition to the *unrivaled* Hawaiian print fabric selection (some of which they can make into clothing for you), they also have beautiful Japanese kimonos and everything any quilter could need. Gentlemen can relax on the lanai while their quiltress (hey, is that a real word?) checks things out.

In Lihu'e, many visitors stop at **Wal-Mart** or **Hilo Hattie's** before that last rush to the airport. Always something here for everyone. Wal-Mart is also a good first stop on the island for tabis, water shoes and all kinds of outdoor gear. (Even a nice flower lei.)

Kukui Grove Shopping Center at the corner of Hwy 50 and Nawiliwili Road is a sprawling mall in two large sections. One section contains **Borders Books**, **Kmart** and several other shops and restaurants. The other portion has some good places to grab a treat or a sandwich while shopping. You may want to browse the stores here while attending the Monday afternoon (3 p.m.) open air **Sunshine Market** or taking the little ones to **Paradise Fun**.

Heading south on the highway you'll come to **Kilohana**, a former plantation manager's private home. The jewelry at **Grande's Gems** upstairs is definitely worth a look.

Puhi Village Plaza at the stoplight in Puhi offers the chance to purchase reasonably priced fruit (go for the lychee, pineapples or apple bananas) from the **People's Market**, some baked goods from **Hanalima Baking** or some smoked marlin from **Puhi Fish & Catering**. The marlin's pricey, but hey...*it's marlin*.

In addition to the Monday market, there's also a second **Sunshine Market** on Fridays at 3 p.m. at Vidinha Stadium.

If you'd like to arrange a shipment of tropical flowers or a dwarf tree grown on lava rock, **Kaua'i Nursery & Landscape** (245–7747) on the left side as you head toward Po'ipu can arrange this for you.

EAST SHORE BEST BETS

Best Beach Walk—Lydgate State Park to Radisson Hotel

Best Place to Fulfill the U.S. RDA for Ostrich Meat—Kalapaki Beach Hut

Best View—From the top of Sleeping Giant for hikers; sunrise over Lydgate for non-hikers

Best Place for Novice Snorkelers, Fish Feeding or to Let Children Swim—Lydgate State Park

Best Treat—Apple turnover at Kaua'i Bakery

Best Hidden Gem—Kipu Falls or Ho'opi'i Falls

Best Uncrowded Beach—In front of Wailua Golf Course

Best Boogie Boarding—Kealia Beach

Best Evening Stroll—Paved beach path beginning behind Kaua'i Coconut Beach Resort (interrupted in parts)

Best Lu'au—Smith's Tropical Paradise

Best Place to Enjoy a Cocktail—Center table (near waterfall) at Duke's

Semi-protected Po'ipu Beach Park is one of the many beaches that bless the south shore.

SOUTH SHORE SIGHTS

The sunny south shore. Here, rainfall is less frequent and sunshine is abundant. Many people prefer the sunnier quality of the south shore to the lushness of the north shore. Fortunately, you can have it all.

For the sake of this discussion, we will consider the south shore everything past Puhi to Kalaheo. (Look at the fold-out back cover map to orient yourself.) Past Kalaheo, the character of the island changes again, and we will cover that under WEST SHORE SIGHTS.

The same descriptive ground rules that we discussed at the beginning of NORTH SHORE SIGHTS apply here.

All beaches we mention are described in detail in the section on BEACHES.

Driving to Po'ipu from Lihu'e along the main highway, you will pass through the Knudsen Gap between the 6 and 8 mile markers. A century ago this was the scariest part of

the island. The small gap between the mountains was the only route you could take and was a perfect place for an ambush. Even the local sheriff always dreaded going through the Knudsen Gap.

Past the 6 mile marker you will come to 520, or Maluhia Road. This road to Koloa and Po'ipu is called the Tree Tunnel. When Walter Duncan McBryde was landscaping his home in the early 1900s, he found that he had over 500 eucalyptus trees *left over*. He donated these trees, called swamp mahogany, to the county. Many residents showed up to help plant the trees. The result is the Tree Tunnel. (Part of it was torn down in the '50s when they rerouted the highway.) Today it should more aptly be called the "tree corridor." Though still beautiful, the trees don't intertwine at the top the way they did before either Hurricane 'Iwa in 1982 or 'Iniki in 1992.

KOLOA

Driving down 520 you come to the town of Koloa, sometimes called Old Koloa Town. This was the first sugar plantation town in all the

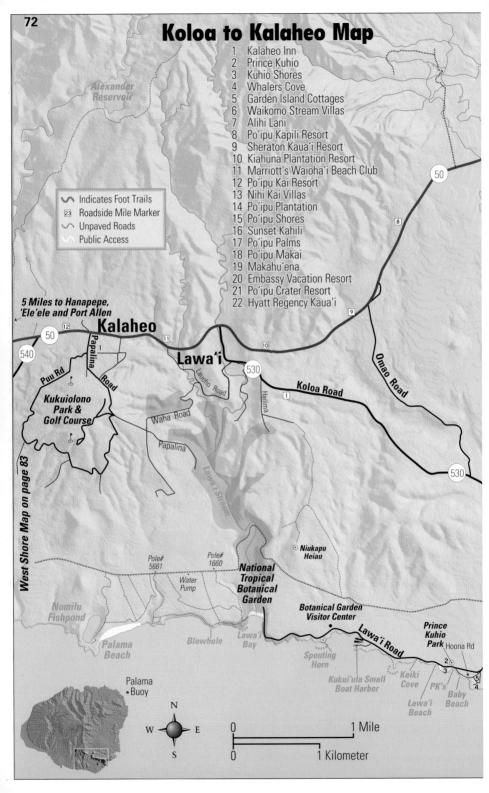

Koloa to Kalaheo Map

1 Kalaheo Inn
2 Prince Kuhio
3 Kuhio Shores
4 Whalers Cove
5 Garden Island Cottages
6 Waikomo Stream Villas
7 Alihi Lani
8 Po'ipu Kapili Resort
9 Sheraton Kaua'i Resort
10 Kiahuna Plantation Resort
11 Marriott's Waioha'i Beach Club
12 Po'ipu Kai Resort
13 Nihi Kai Villas
14 Po'ipu Plantation
15 Po'ipu Shores
16 Sunset Kahili
17 Po'ipu Palms
18 Po'ipu Makai
19 Makahu'ena
20 Embassy Vacation Resort
21 Po'ipu Crater Resort
22 Hyatt Regency Kaua'i

Indicates Foot Trails
23 Roadside Mile Marker
Unpaved Roads
Public Access

Alexander Reservoir

50

8

9

10

50

540

12

Kalaheo

5 Miles to Hanapepe, 'Ele'ele and Port Allen

11

Papalina Road

Puu Rd

Kukuiolono Park & Golf Course

Lawa'i

530

Lawho Road

Koloa Road

1

Omao Road

Halima

Waha Road

Papalina

Lawa'i Stream

530

West Shore Map on page 83

Pole# 5661

Pole# 1660

Water Pump

Niukapu Heiau

National Tropical Botanical Garden

Botanical Garden Visitor Center

Nomilu Fishpond

Blowhole

Lawa'i Bay

Lawa'i Road

Prince Kuhio Park

Hoona Rd

Palama Beach

Spouting Horn

Kukui'ula Small Boat Harbor

Keiki Cove

PK's

Lawa'i Beach

2
3
4
5

Baby Beach

Palama • Buoy

N
W E
S

0   1 Mile
0   1 Kilometer

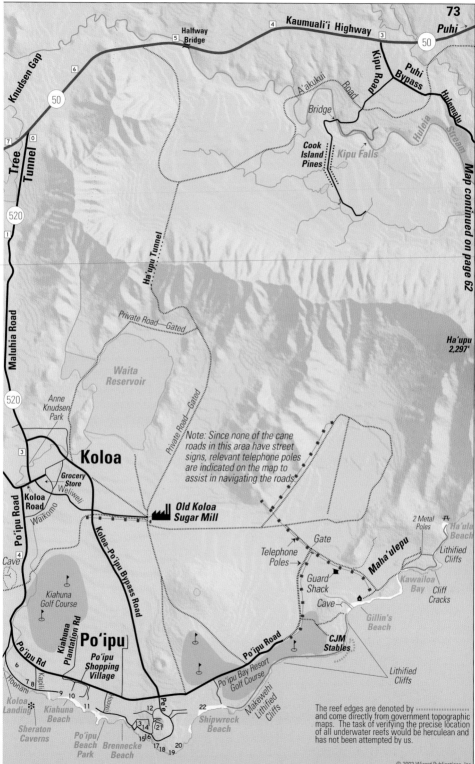

Puhi

Kaumuali'i Highway

Halfway Bridge

Knudsen Gap

Tree Tunnel

A'akukui Bridge

Kipu Road

Puhi Bypass

Huleia

Cook Island Pines

Kipu Falls

Huleia Stream

Map continued on page 62

Ha'upu Tunnel

Maluhia Road

Private Road—Gated

Waita Reservoir

Anne Knudsen Park

Ha'upu 2,297'

Koloa

Grocery Store

Weliweli

Koloa Road

Waikomo

Note: Since none of the cane roads in this area have street signs, relevant telephone poles are indicated on the map to assist in navigating the roads.

Old Koloa Sugar Mill

Private Road—Gated

2 Metal Poles

Ha'ula Beach

Lithified Cliffs

Gate

Telephone Poles

Maha'ulepu

Guard Shack

Kawailoa Bay

Cliff Cracks

Cave

Gillin's Beach

CJM Stables

Cave

Po'ipu Road

Po'ipu Bay Resort Golf Course

Lithified Cliffs

Po'ipu Road

Kiahuna Golf Course

Koloa–Po'ipu Bypass Road

Cave

Po'ipu

Kiahuna Plantation Rd

Po'ipu Shopping Village

Po'ipu Rd

Ho'onani

Kapili

Makewehi Lithified Cliffs

Koloa Landing

Kiahuna Beach

Sheraton Caverns

Po'ipu Beach Park

Brennecke Beach

Ho'owili

Pe'e

Shipwreck Beach

The reef edges are denoted by ·········· and come directly from government topographic maps. The task of verifying the precise location of all underwater reefs would be herculean and has not been attempted by us.

© 2003 Wizard Publications, Inc.

islands when Kamehameha III leased the land to Ladd and Company in 1835. The town has much charm and is worth a stop. Next to Crazy Shirts Store there is a marvelous monkeypod tree whose branches seem to meander forever. In Koloa you'll find Lappert's Ice Cream, which is made here on Kaua'i. It's still good but has been slipping lately. It's also getting pretty darned expensive. Two people can easily spend $6-$7 for one scoop each with cone. (The scoops should be bigger for that.) They also have locally roasted coffee, but it's unremarkable.

Across the street (kitty-corner) from the shops are the remnants of an old sugar mill built 150 years ago. There you will also find a plaque dedicated to the sugar plantation workers and a good (if somewhat dated) synopsis of sugar history on the island.

Looking at the map, you will see a dirt road leading to Waita Reservoir and Ha'upu Range Tunnel. They are gated and not available to visit anymore. We used to think these gates were a relatively modern annoyance until we stumbled across an old local newspaper from 1934. In a letter to the editor the writer warned people not to accept an invitation from a well-known plantation manager when he said he "wanted to show you something interesting." Apparently the crafty manager did this whenever he had a long way to drive and wanted to have somebody along to open and close all the gates.

Po'IPU

Continuing to Po'ipu on 520 and doglegging onto Po'ipu Road, watch your speed. This is a notorious speed trap and sobriety checkpoint area, and the limit is 25 mph, 15 mph near the school. (The Po'ipu Bypass shown on the map is an even more effective speed trap because you are easily lulled into

Move over sugar—coffee is the new cash crop of the south shore.

going over 35 mph.) Past the 4 mile marker is a wide dirt road. Off this road is another dirt loop road that circles a cave. The cave is an old lava tube and can be difficult to find. If you are determined, it's roughly in the center of the dirt loop road, 110 yards from the road, near a low-lying bushy tree and some large cactus plants. The land surrounding the cave is ringed by an old fence, broken in several places. This hole in the ground has a tunnel that goes back a hundred or so yards. Inside are some old civil defense water drums. A '60s bomb shelter or a never-used Y2K survival bunker? Hard to tell. There is a ladder leading down into the cave; trust it at your own risk.

Past the 4 mile marker as you approach Po'ipu, the road forks. If you take the right fork, you come to Prince Kuhio Park. There

Spouting Horn is often more dramatic at high tide.

you will find a monument to Prince Kuhio, the last royally designated heir to the Hawaiian throne. He went on to become a delegate to Congress until the early 1920s. In this park you will also find the Ho'ai Heiau, impressive in its perfection and almost chiseled appearance. The entrance is toward the rear on the left side.

Continuing along Lawa'i Road, you will come to Spouting Horn Beach Park. This wonderful delight is a small lava shelf

NOT TO BE MISSED!

where water from waves is thrust through an opening, causing water and air to squirt out a blowhole. This particular site distinguishes itself from other blowholes around Hawai'i in that it has an additional hole that blows only air, causing a loud moaning and gasping sound. Legend has it that the entire coastline in this area was once guarded by a giant female lizard called a mo'o. She would eat anyone who tried to swim or fish in the area. One day a man named Liko went fishing. The mo'o went to attack Liko, who threw a spear into the mo'o's mouth. The angry mo'o chased Liko into the lava tube. Liko escaped, but the mo'o became trapped in what we now call Spouting Horn, where its cries of hunger and pain can be heard to this day.

The Spouting Horn was formerly dwarfed by an adjacent blowhole called the Kukui'ula seaplume. That seaplume would shoot much higher—as high as 200 feet into the air. But on an early Sunday morning back in the 1920s a sugar company manager ordered one of his workers to drop blasting powder into the hole in order to widen it so the plume wouldn't shoot into the air. The reason? The salt spray from the geyser was stunting the growth of 10 acres of cane (among the company's many thousands of acres), and the manager would not stand for that. From down on the lava shelf you can see its remains in the form of a large rectangular aperture to the left of the current blowhole opening.

The view from the guard-rail is quite interesting. Many people walk down and view the Horn and some of the other delightful offerings from the lava area itself. The power and forces in this area can only be experienced from this vantage point. Be forewarned, however, that while the experience is far more rewarding than the view from the guardrails, it can be dangerous. There have been incidents where people have been swept to their deaths into the Horn. Unexpectedly large waves can even wash over the entire shelf, dragging you into the hole or over the edge into the open ocean.

There may be signs suggesting that you not go down, although county personnel we spoke with said it wasn't illegal. Use caution and common sense. If you go onto the bench, you do so at your own risk. (For some odd reason, tour bus drivers sometimes authoritative-

Watch your step around these ficus roots at the National Tropical Botanical Garden in Lawa'i. This tree is where they found the dinosaur eggs in the movie Jurassic Park.

ly yell at people on the bench, but hey…they're just tour bus drivers.) In any event, *never* stand between the hole and the ocean. A very large wave would have no difficulty dragging you in. In 1993, two visitors from San Francisco were knocked in while they stood between the hole and the ocean. One was *on crutches* at the time. They were lucky—rather than being crushed inside the hole, they were immediately sucked out of the blowhole and into the open ocean where they were rescued by some phone workers on their break.

Just before Spouting Horn is the entrance to the National Tropical Botanical Gardens. This incredibly beautiful garden consists of 186 acres called the La`wa`i Gardens and 100 acres called the Allerton Gardens. Even if you normally wouldn't visit a garden, you'll probably like this one. Rich and lush with remarkably varied plants and abundant birds, tours here are guided and last about two hours. The fee for the tour is $30 per person. Reservations are required; call 742–2623.

Going back the way you came just before the fork is a road leading to Koloa Landing. This is a popular SCUBA shore dive. Until the 1900s this was Kaua'i's main port. Whaling ships used to winter here, and all goods brought to Kaua'i came through either Koloa Landing or Waimea.

Going to the fork again, take the left (eastern) fork. (Or, as Yogi Berra used to say, "If you come to a fork in the road, *take it*.") All along Po'ipu is turtle country. Look out at the water for any reasonable length of time, and you will see green sea turtles swimming nearby. This area was developed in the '70s and '80s and has become a much sought-after visitor destination. Swanky hotels and con-

These lithified sand dunes of Maha'ulepu are a stunning testament to the power of the ocean.

dominium resorts line the road. (See WHERE TO STAY for more information.) The beaches in this area are fantastic,

A REAL GEM

with the best of the best located past the resorts at a place called Maha'ulepu. This beach (see BEACHES) sports lots of places to walk and some incredible sandstone cliffs. The dirt roads around here can be good places to ride mountain bikes. Horseback riding, windsurfing, snorkeling, fishing and more are all available in this area. The lithified cliffs from Maha'ulepu to Shipwreck Beach offer delicious shoreline hikes. See HIKING for more information.

There's lots of cactus around here. It was imported in the 1800s because it made a perfect natural cattle fence—and you don't even need to repair it.

On your way back to the main highway (50), you will pass by one of the best bargains on the island as far as food is concerned. A little hole-in-the-wall called Taqueria Norteños (see DINING) serves good and very inexpensive Mexican food in gigantic proportions.

KALAHEO

After Lawa'i comes Kalaheo (which has the best pizza on the island—see DINING). One of Kalaheo's lesser known gems is the Kukuiolono Park and Golf Course (see GOLF). This is the private course and garden donated by Walter D. McBryde to the people of Kaua'i. If you want to try your hand at golf, this is the place to learn. The price is $7 *per day*. The small Japanese garden located on the course was Mr. McBryde's pride and joy. This is where he chose to be buried, near the 8th tee.

Although it was sugar that drove the economy along here for over a century,

The alien landscape of the tortured sandstone cliffs between Maha'ulepu and the Hyatt.

it was phased out in the 1990s to grow coffee, on the assumption it would be more profitable. (So far it hasn't been.) The company, Kaua'i Coffee, has over 4,000 acres under cultivation. To be honest, it's not very good coffee. Most of the trees are an unimpressive breed called *yellow catuai*. Don't confuse it with the *far* superior coffee grown on the Kona coast of the Big Island where the coffee-growing environment is ideal. Also, Kaua'i coffee is machine picked, so that beans slightly under and over their peak get picked in the process. Kaua'i Coffee has smaller fields of *red catuai* and *blue mountain,* which is better, but it's expensive and we've only found those coffees at their visitor center located on Hwy 540 just past the 12 mile marker on Hwy 50. That 4-mile-long road, sometimes called the Coffee Highway, cuts through much of the coffee plantation. The visitor center is popular with tour buses but is only marginally interesting, and their museum is particularly scant. Only for the hard-core coffee groupies.

Incidentally, any fixed-wing pilot on the island will tell you they *love* coffee trees. Their leaves are dark and dense, which capture the sun and heat the air around them. This makes them exceptional generators of thermal currents, providing free lift when the heated air rises.

Just after the 14 mile marker you will come to the Hanapepe Valley Lookout. As you gaze over the peaceful vista, it's hard to believe that this was the scene of the bloodiest and most savage battle known to have taken place on Kaua'i. The embittered son of Kaua'i's last king started a revolt against government rule. Remember that Kaua'i had never been conquered by Kamehameha

the Great. Both of his invasion attempts had been costly in terms of men, and neither had even reached Kaua'i in large numbers. Even though Kaua'i's last king voluntarily accepted Kamehameha's rule, it forever stuck in the royal craw that Kaua'i had not been *forced* into submission. So when this revolt occurred, it was a perfect excuse to send Hawai'i troops over to show those Kauaians who was boss. Government troops sent to put down the revolt were unimaginably brutal, and their methods were reviled even among their supporters. Men, women and children were needlessly slaughtered, and the wanton killing continued for 10 days.

Everything past here is covered under West Shore Sights.

SOUTH SHORE SHOPPING

As you enter Koloa, there are several stores with good browsing potential. The wonderful scents emanating from Island Soap & Candle at the west end of Koloa will draw you in for a look. Behind their store is Discount Variety, which has a good assortment of reasonably priced items from sunglasses to beach towels. The Koloa Country Store & Cafe, down the street in the courtyard behind Crazy Shirts, offers some excellent coffee drinks, baked goods and rental of high-speed Web access. Around the corner and down Po'ipu Road is Pohaku Tees, which offers a good selection of souvenir T-shirts and other locally made items. The best place for fresh produce is the noon Monday Sunshine Market at the Koloa (Ann Knudsen) Ball Park just before you enter Koloa.

Continuing down Po'ipu Road and veering toward Po'ipu, you'll see the largest shopping center in the area, Po'ipu Shopping Village. Try the

Ni'ihau Shell Leis

The women of Ni'ihau carry on a tradition dating back centuries. With indescribable patience, they collect tiny Ni'ihau shells, then clean, drill, string and pack them with fiber, creating fabulous leis. This is no easy task. An entire day's labor often reaps only four or five useable shells. And it requires thousands of shells to make a lei. Some women only search for shells at night, believing that the sunlight dulls the shell's luster. While costing from several hundred to several thousand dollars each, this is a relative bargain given the amount of labor that goes into one. It can take several years to complete the more ornate leis. The result is a perfect, hand–crafted and tightly packed lei representing one of the last truly Hawaiian art forms. There are fewer and fewer people on Ni'ihau who are willing to participate in this process, and many consider it a matter of time before this art form will be lost.

If you purchase one, the best selection on the island is at the Hawaiian Trading Post on the corner of Highways 50 and 530 (Koloa Road) in Lawa'i. Make sure it was actually made on Ni'ihau, not a copy-cat made on Kaua'i.

One last caveat; if you buy one, do it for yourself. It would be crushing to spend all that money only to show your lei to someone and have 'em say, "Oh, yeah, I got one for free at Hilo Hattie's." While Ni'ihau shell leis are infinitely more beautiful, some might not appreciate the difference.

Tropical Dreams Ice Cream at Shipwreck Subs while you shop the variety of stores here. Stop in Hale Mana Clothing & Gifts for some unusual Asian-inspired items.

Traveling west up Koloa Road (another speed trap, so watch your speed!) at the intersection with Highway 50 is the Hawaiian Trading Post. They offer the largest display of authentic Ni'ihau shell leis on Kaua'i as well as many other types of jewelry. They also have some lovely gardens and shade trees with picnic tables for you to enjoy.

SOUTH SHORE BEST BETS

Best Strolling Beach—Maha'ulepu
Best Short Cliff Stroll—To the left of Shipwreck Beach near Hyatt
Best Snorkeling—Around the tombolo at Po'ipu Beach Park
Best Sunset View—At Spouting Horn
Best Fast Food—Taqueria Norteños
Best Ice Cream—Tropical Dreams at Shipwreck Sub, Po'ipu Shopping Village
Best Treat—Baked Chocolate Soufflé at Roy's Po'ipu Bar & Grill
Best Place To Watch Fools Jump Off A Cliff—Shipwreck Beach in front of the Hyatt Po'ipu
Best Secluded Beach—Ha'ula Beach
Best Swimming—Po'ipu Beach Park
Best Pizza—Brick Oven Pizza
Best Beachcombing—Kawailoa Bay
Best Golf—Po'ipu Bay Resort
Best Hotel Grounds—Hyatt
Best Seafood Selection—House of Seafood
Best Lasagna—Pomodoro
Best Romantic Restaurant—Tidepools at Hyatt or Beach House at Sunset.
Best Place for a Sunset Cocktail—The Point at the Sheraton

Polihale is where the Na Pali coastline gives way to seventeen miles of uninterrupted sand beach.

WEST SHORE SIGHTS

If the south shore is called the sunny south shore, western Kaua'i should be called the *very* sunny west shore. That's because rain is very scant indeed, and the temperature is 3 to 4 degrees hotter than most of the rest of the island. The first two things visitors notice on this side of the island are the relative aridity of the land and the deep red color of the soil. Trade winds coming from the northeast lose the bulk of their rain on Mount Wai'ale'ale, creating a rain shadow on the west side. Unless there are Kona winds (meaning from the south or west), you can pretty much be assured that it will be dry and sunny on the west side.

This part of the island is dominated by two attractions: the 17-mile-long sand beach stretching from Waimea to Polihale and the incredible Waimea Canyon in the interior.

HANAPEPE

As you drive along the main highway leaving Kalaheo, you will come to the **Hanapepe Valley Lookout**, described under SOUTH SHORE SIGHTS. After you go through 'Ele'ele, you come to Hanapepe. Called Kaua'i's "Biggest Little Town," Hanapepe is but a shadow of its former self. It was founded by Chinese rice farmers in the mid to late 1800s. They were opium smoking bachelors, and underground opium shops could be found there as recently as the 1930s. Hanapepe was the only non-plantation town on the island, and it gained a reputation as Kaua'i's wildest spot. In 1924 they had a riot that killed 16 Filipino workers and four police officers. This was a violent and flamboyant town that had as many bars as churches. It began to decline in the late '70s. The 1982 opening of Kukui Grove Shopping Center in Lihu'e marked the end of an era for Hanapepe's business community.

A good analogy for Hanapepe today is that of an old chair. Whereas some people look at an old stick of furniture and see a priceless antique, others see it as an old, used item to be replaced by a newer one. Depending on your outlook,

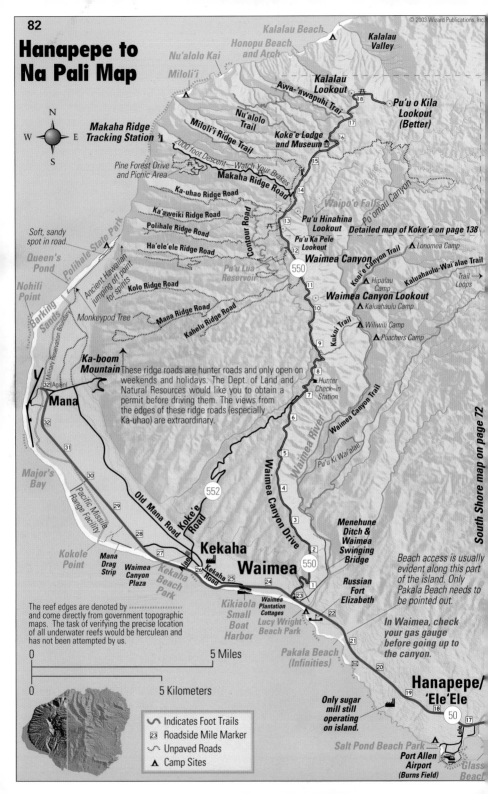

Hanapepe to Na Pali Map

© 2003 Wizard Publications, Inc.

N
W — E
S

Kalalau Beach
Honopu Beach and Arch
Nu'alolo Kai
Kalalau Valley
Miloli'i
Kalalau Lookout
Awa-'awapuhi Trail
Pu'u o Kila Lookout (Better)

Makaha Ridge Tracking Station
Nu'alolo Trail
Miloli'i Ridge Trail
Koke'e Lodge and Museum

2000 foot Descent — Watch Your Brakes
Pine Forest Drive and Picnic Area
Makaha Ridge Road

Ka-uhao Ridge Road
Ka'aweiki Ridge Road
Polihale Ridge Road
Ha'ele'ele Ridge Road

Contour Road

Waipo'o Falls
Po'omau Canyon

Pu'u Hinahina Lookout
Detailed map of Koke'e on page 138
Pu'u Ka Pele Lookout

Waimea Canyon
550

Koai'e Canyon Trail
Lonomea Camp
Hipalau Camp
Kaluahaulu-Wai'alae Trail
Trail Loops

Waimea Canyon Lookout
Kaluahaulu Camp

Soft, sandy spot in road.
Queen's Pond
Polihale State Park
Pu'u Lua Reservoir

Nohili Point
Barking Sands
Ancient Hawaiian jumping off point for spirits

Kolo Ridge Road
Mana Ridge Road
Kahelu Ridge Road

Monkeypod Tree
Military Reservation Boundary

Ka-boom Mountain
Mana
32 (Again)
32

Kukui Trail
Wiliwili Camp
Poachers Camp

Hunter Check-in Station

These ridge roads are hunter roads and only open on weekends and holidays. The Dept. of Land and Natural Resources would like you to obtain a permit before driving them. The views from the edges of these ridge roads (especially Ka-uhao) are extraordinary.

31

Major's Bay

Waimea River
Waimea Canyon Trail
Pu'u Ki Wai'alae

Old Mana Road
Pacific Missile Range Facility

30
29
552
Koke'e Road

28
Mana Drag Strip
27
Waimea Canyon Plaza
Kekaha

Waimea Canyon Drive

Kokole Point

Kekaha Beach Park
Kekaha Road
26
25
24
Waimea
550

Menehune Ditch & Waimea Swinging Bridge

South Shore map on page 72

Beach access is usually evident along this part of the island. Only Pakala Beach needs to be pointed out.

Kikiaola Small Boat Harbor
Waimea Plantation Cottages
23
22
Russian Fort Elizabeth

Lucy Wright Beach Park
21

In Waimea, check your gas gauge before going up to the canyon.

The reef edges are denoted by ············· and come directly from government topographic maps. The task of verifying the precise location of all underwater reefs would be herculean and has not been attempted by us.

Pakala Beach (Infinities)
20

Hanapepe/ 'Ele'Ele
50

0 ————————— 5 Miles
0 ————————— 5 Kilometers

19
18
17
'Ele'Ele

Only sugar mill still operating on island.

Salt Pond Beach Park

Port Allen Airport (Burns Field)

Glass Beach

Indicates Foot Trails
23 Roadside Mile Marker
··· Unpaved Roads
▲ Camp Sites

you will either find downtown Hanapepe charming or run down. Although we probably side with the run-down crowd, improvements *are* taking place and a certain amount of rehabilitation is occurring, so Hanapepe is sort of a moving target. If you have a couple minutes to spare, you might want to blow through downtown just to decide for yourself. There *are* several shops and galleries that might be worth exploring, especially Friday nights, which is art night. There's a swinging footbridge over the Hanapepe River. It replaced the old bridge that swung off during the 1992 hurricane.

This area is where most of our power is generated. People assume that, living on a tropical island, we must have some exotic way of making our electricity. Sorry to burst your bubble, but we burn oil—it's just that simple—and we have the electricity bills to prove it! In a few years we hope to burn wood chips from local tree farms to help supplement that.

If you take Lele Road (543), you will come to **Salt Pond Beach Park**. This is where they continue to make salt out of seawater (see Beaches). This park usually offers very safe swimming.

Before you get to Waimea, you will see a road to **Fort Elizabeth** just past the 22 mile marker. (The sign is misspelled.) Here are the vague remains of a Russian fort built in 1816 by George Scheffer.

Scheffer was a German-born doctor working for a Russian company. A difficult,

quarrelsome and conceited man, he had a habit of eventually alienating most people he met. (Know the type?) He did make a good first impression, however, and managed to sufficiently impress a Russian official, who sent Scheffer to Hawai'i to ingratiate himself to King Kamehameha and recover a lost ship's cargo. When Kamehameha eventually became suspicious of Scheffer, the German moved on to Kaua'i. There he found a receptive King Kaumuali'i who, although he had officially given his kingdom to Kamehameha, still resisted offshore rule. Kaua'i's king-in-name-only saw a chance to get the Russians involved and perhaps restore his power. The two men realized how much they could help each other and soon hatched plans to conquer the other islands using Russian ships. By this time Scheffer had become intoxicated by his status on Kaua'i and lost sight of the fact that he could not deliver on any of the promises he was making to Kaua'i's king. He even

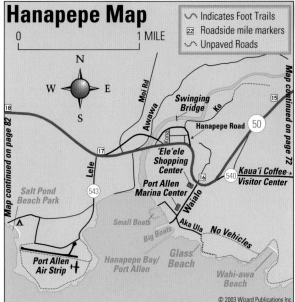

Hanapepe Map

0 ——————— 1 MILE

Indicates Foot Trails
Roadside mile markers
Unpaved Roads

Map continued on page 82
Map continued on page 72

N
W · E
S

Moi Rd
Awawa
Swinging Bridge
Hanapepe Road 50
15
18
17
Lele
'Ele'ele Shopping Center
Port Allen Marina Center
16
540
Kaua'i Coffee
Visitor Center
543
Salt Pond Beach Park
Waialo
Small Boats
Aka Ula
No Vehicles
Big Boats
Port Allen Air Strip
Hanapepe Bay/ Port Allen
Glass Beach
Wahi-awa Beach

© 2003 Wizard Publications Inc.

renamed Hanalei Valley, calling it Schefferthal, with the king's blessing.

As Scheffer began building the Russian Fort in honor of Elizabeth, a Russian consort, his sponsors back in Russia were beginning to get a hint of Scheffer's tactics. They sent a ship to Hawai'i to tell Scheffer that he was to pack and leave the island. Scheffer ignored the message and continued building the fort. By this time Kaua'i's king was becoming suspicious, and a group of American businessmen saw an opportunity to rid the island of Scheffer and Russia. They started the rumor that Russia and America were at war. Kaua'i's king abandoned Scheffer, who fled the island in a leaky old ship and set sail for O'ahu. Once there, Scheffer was told he would be taken prisoner. He fled to Brazil where he changed his name to Count von Frankenthal and tried to lure colonists to his estate of the same name.

Why are we telling you all this? Because the story's more interesting than the actual site—little more than a perimeter of rocks from the foundation. (By the way, there are lots of bees here.)

If you drive through Fort Elizabeth and take the dirt road, you'll come to the **mouth of the Waimea River**. This can be a beautiful area to linger and watch the interaction of the ocean with the river, especially when the river flow is low. The dark, rich sand separating the ocean from the river is saturated with water from the river. White waves sometimes gently lap up and down the sand without sinking in, creating a delicate show of contrasts. You'll notice an olive green tint to the sand here. This is from a semi-precious gem called olivine, which the Waimea River tirelessly mines from its lava bed along with black flecks of lava, making the floor of the Waimea Canyon lower and lower in the process.

WAIMEA

Back on the main highway you come to the town of Waimea. This part of the island usually looks best (and greenest) in the winter. Off to your right you will see the **Captain Cook Monument**. It was in Waimea that the great explorer first set foot in Hawai'i in January 1778. (He was later killed on the Big Island in a petty dispute over a stolen rowboat.)

Travel 1⅓ mile up Menehune Road on the *mauka* side of the highway to see the **Menehune Ditch**, a smooth, lined irrigation ditch designed to bring water from the Waimea River to the taro fields. Only 50 or 60 feet are now visible. It's impressive to think that the rocks used for its construction came from a quarry more than six miles away. This is one of the few Hawaiian relics that almost certainly wasn't created by the current race of Hawaiians who came from Tahiti around 1,000 A.D. *That* group didn't cut and dress stones—as is the case at Menehune Ditch—they simply stacked them. This irrigation ditch is much older and was probably built by the initial inhabitants—the original "native Hawaiians"—who came from the Marquesas Islands around 300 A.D. These first settlers lived a peaceful though less structured life until the Tahitian invaders displaced them and their culture 700 years later, establishing the Hawaiian culture we know today.

Across from the ditch is the **Waimea Swinging Bridge**. Like the one in Hanapepe, it, too, is a replacement for the old one blown away in 1992.

The **Waimea** (meaning red water) **River** is full of sediment that dyes the water red. All the beaches in the vicinity of the river are murky due to river runoff, and the swimming is correspondingly poor. (In fact, you can see the runoff from the Space Shuttle photo on the cover.)

According to legend, there was a beautiful chief's daughter named Komali'u who was sought after by many men in the village. One day a man named Mano asked her to marry him. When she refused, he killed her at a waterfall where her blood ran into the river. The chief named the village, canyon and river Waimea in memory of his daughter.

While in Waimea, **Jo-Jo's Clubhouse** (across from the 23 mile marker) serves the best shave ice on the island. (Yes—we've tried it everywhere else. It's our duty.) They offer a staggering 60 flavors and big portions at a cheap price.

KEKAHA

From Waimea, most people go up the road to the Waimea Canyon, but we will get to that later. Assuming you are continuing along the coast, you arrive in Kekaha. This is the last town on this side of the island. Past the 25 mile marker the highway hugs the beach for two miles.

It's a nice place to stop and enjoy views of Ni'ihau past the 26 mile marker and beach access here is accomplished by simply falling out of your car onto the sand.

Waimea Canyon Plaza is the last area with food along here. The **Menehune Food Mart** has sandwiches, hot dogs and very good bread pudding. Things aren't as hideously expensive there as you'd expect given the remoteness of the location.

While driving along the west side past Waimea take note of the cliffs to your right. Those are former sea cliffs cut off from the sea. The land you are driving on is different than most other land in the island chain. It's not technically volcanic. When the massive Waimea Canyon (described later) was formed, the river carried the rock and soil out of the canyon where the ocean's current drove it along the shore to the northwest (as it still does today). Much of it washed up

The dark sand of the Waimea River mouth beautifully contrasts the ocean foam slithering into the river.

on shore, forming the large plain you see today. It's an odd cocktail of fine sediment, the remains of a gigantic, now drained fringing marshy lagoon, sand, the shells of countless sea creatures and plant remains. The result is one kickin' place to grow sugar—just ask the Robinsons, who grow tens of thousands of acres of it here. (Oddly, tour guides around the island—who apparently need to get out more—are constantly telling visitors that no sugar is grown on Kaua'i anymore.)

Many maps list a town farther north called **Mana**. It was once a thriving little community until the middle of this century. This area was formerly marshy and famous for its mirages. Now the town of **Mana** is a mirage, nothing more than two mango trees and a mule. Some of its homes were moved and are now part of Waimea Plantation Cottages Resort. You can tell a former Mana cottage because it always had a door facing north and one facing south so passing spirits wouldn't get stuck inside.

From here on the coastline is pure sand. There's a great opportunity to have a huge stretch of sand to yourself along here. See Kokole Point on page 114.

You will pass the **Pacific Missile Range Facility** where they do Star Wars missile tests on occasion. Offshore, submarine hunting exercises take place almost continuously. This is a repository for some of the most sophisticated sensing equipment in the world, and they are capable of detecting a bottle bobbing up and down in the choppy water. (But for some reason, when a fishing boat is missing in the area they seem incapable of finding it.) Fronting part of the base is **Barking Sands Beach**. The sand grains at this beach have a thin coating of silica and are supposed to make a barking sound if you walk on them when condi-

tions are right (see BEACHES). Access has been awkward since the 9/11/2001 attacks. See BEACHES for more.

A well-known surf site here is **Major's Bay**, so called because it's off the old commanding officer's quarters. *Hey, wait a minute. This is a navy base. Isn't major an army rank?* True, but it *used* to be an army base and the name stuck.

POLIHALE

Looking at the map, you'll notice that the highway ends after the first 32 mile marker. Follow the map, and the first dirt road will take you to **Polihale**. (It's a public access, misleading signs notwithstanding.) On the very rare occasions that it rains heavily here, the road to Polihale can get pretty sloppy. (It also gets potholed at times.) From the extreme northern end of the beach, the magnificent cliffs of **Na Pali** beckon you with their sheer majesty. The **dunes of Polihale** are up to 100 feet high. The BEACHES section provides more information on **Polihale**.

As soon as you leave Hwy 50 on your way to Polihale, look at the mountain in front of you. It's a **military restricted area**. They've bored caves into the mountain where they store ammunition such as bombs and bullets. With so much explosives, you're about as welcome there as a pack of matches.

If it's summer, you might see kayaks coming (or rolling) in for a surf landing. From here you could walk 17 miles in the sand in one direction. Winds are usually calm here. There are facilities, including showers, restrooms and drinking water.

The Hawaiians believed that the cliffs at the end of Polihale Beach, called **Ha'ele'ele**, were the jumping off point for spirits or 'uhane leaving this world. There they would leave this life and join their ancestors forever. If there was no 'aumakua, or family of spirits, to receive

With Niʻihau and Lehua Rock in the background, a lone boat cruises Polihale from a trip down Na Pali.

them, they would wander around the area, attaching themselves to rocks and generally causing mischief. That's why it's considered unwise to take anything, such as stones, from this area. You may bring back a wayward spirit itching to get back home.

WAIMEA CANYON

The **Waimea Canyon** is a spectacular gorge that defies description. When Mark Twain was here, he called it "the Grand Canyon of the Pacific." Indeed, the layers evident on the sides of the canyon are reminiscent of the grander canyon in Arizona. Each layer represents a different eruption and subsequent lava flow. The canyon is 10 miles long, 1 mile wide and more than 3,600 feet deep.

To get to the canyon, take Waimea Canyon Road from Waimea. They *want* you to go up from Kokeʻe Road in Kekaha because they hope you'll buy

something there, but the views are better going up from Waimea. On your return from the canyon, you can take Kokeʻe Road (between the 6 and 7 mile markers) down for a different view of the coast.

Before you go up the road, check your gas gauge. There are no stations up there, and you've got a 40 mile round trip ahead of you with a 4,000 foot elevation rise. The temperature is 10–15 degrees cooler up there, and a sweater might be wise, depending on conditions. There are more good hiking trails in this area than anywhere in Hawaiʻi. For more hiking information and a detailed map of the trails in the Waimea/Kokeʻe area, see HIKING under ACTIVITIES on page 136.

To reach the canyon, turn *mauka* onto Waimea Canyon Road just past the 23 mile marker near a church. The road twists and turns its way up the canyon's side. On the way, keep an eye out for **Niʻihau**. There are some great views of

Splendid Waimea Canyon is yet another facet of Kaua'i's personality.

that private island from up here. (Even on cloudless days there's almost always a cloud over Ni'ihau. Its land mass causes them.) Past the 10 mile marker is the **Waimea Canyon Lookout**. This is one of several vantage points and definitely worth a stop. From here on you will probably see lots of wild chickens about. They thrive in this environment.

The canyon lookout is an awesome vista. At one time three rivers, fed from the island's center by the Alaka'i Swamp on Mt. Wai'ale'ale, all ran down the gently sloping shield volcano, emptying into the ocean at separate points like the spokes of a wheel. That's what created the now dry valleys you see on your way out to Polihale. When a fault caused the collapse of part of the volcano's flank, the three rivers were forced to combine and ran down into the fault. This new, opportunistic river carved a place for itself in the splintered and fractured lava flows. The results are extraordinary.

As you drive upward, there are numerous areas along the road from which to view the canyon. From the **Pu'u Ka Pele Lookout**, the **Waipo'o Falls** are visible after a heavy rain, especially in the winter. The hike there (see HIKING) is fabulous. The **Pu'u Hinahina Lookout**, located past the 13 mile marker, has a **Ni'ihau Viewpoint** in addition to its canyon lookout. If it's clear, the view of **Ni'ihau** is great.

Shortly after this lookout there is a paved road on your left leading to the **Makaha Ridge Tracking Station** run by the military in conjunction with the **Pacific Missile Range Facility**. The road drops 2,000 feet over a relatively short distance and can be a real brake burner. Shortly before the gate at the station you will see several dirt roads leading into a pleasant forested area with picnic tables.

Looking at the map you'll see that there are dirt hunter-roads all along this part of the coast. The views from the edge of the ridges are mind boggling, but they are only open on weekends and are *supposed* to be used by hunters.

Past the 15 mile marker is the **Koke'e Museum** (335–9975). This is a good place to stretch your legs. The museum itself has several interesting displays and their three-dimensional map of the canyon really gives you a sense of what you are seeing. We've found the personnel there to be extremely knowledgeable. The **Koke'e Lodge** (335–6061) next door is a good place to get lunch. (Actually, it's the *only* place to get lunch.)

As you ascend the road, note how different the vegetation is up here. Remember how it was down at the bottom near Waimea? Here it is always cool, and there is more rainfall than on the plain below.

Just past the lodge (on the opposite side of the road), Waineke Rd. to Mohihi Rd. makes a wonderful diversion if you happen to have a 4wd vehicle. You can drive 6 miles into the interior of Koke'e, visiting beau-

tiful sights along the way. The map of the area is on page 138.

At the 18 mile marker is the **Kalalau Lookout** where most people stop. We suggest that you drive right past it and go to the *far* superior, but less used, **Pu'u o Kila Lookout**. You are not about to see another canyon lookout. You are about to be treated to one of the greatest views in the Pacific. The **Kalalau Valley** is the largest valley on **Na Pali**. It was inhabited

The sometimes misty forests of Koke'e demonstrate the contrasts found on the Garden Island.

The Kalalau Valley is best viewed not from the Kalalau Lookout, but from the Pu'u o Kila Lookout.

until 1919, and its beach is only reachable by an 11-mile hike or by kayak (see ADVENTURES). For now, just revel in the view. Clouds are always moving in and out of the valley, so if it's cloudy, wait a while before you give up.

A REAL GEM

It's well worth it. The earlier you go, the fewer clouds there tend to be. You can usually see clouds coming from the interior of the island. When they encounter the valley, they sink. Sinking air warms, and warmer air can hold more moisture. So if conditions are right, during normal trade winds, the clouds disappear into humidity in less than a minute right before your eyes. If the winds are the opposite, coming from the ocean, clouds back up in the valley, and it won't clear up.

According to historians, there used to be a *steep* trail into the valley from here leading down across a ridge called *kapea*, a Hawaiian word for scrotum. It was so-named because it was so steep that it made your…well, *you* figure it out.

Hawaiian geese, called **nenes**, tend to hang out at the lookouts. These are endemic to Hawai'i (found nowhere else) and are what you get when you take wayward Canadian geese and isolate them in the tropics for a million years. They've adapted to higher altitudes, lost most of the webbing in their feet and have no fear of cars or people, so be careful driving around at the lookout. They also try to make their living begging food from visitors. Please try to resist.

This is the end of the road. As the crow flies, Ha'ena on the north shore is less than 7 miles away, but you ain't no crow. They tried to build a road from here to Ha'ena in the '50s. Anybody who has ever hiked the **Alaka'i Swamp Trail** before they installed a boardwalk could tell you that a road in these parts is next to impossible. The results of this boondoggle are monuments in the form of heavy earthmoving equipment still stuck in the swamp where the prison work crews left them. A stroll from here down part of the **Pihea Trail** can be a pleasant diversion. This is where the road to Ha'ena was supposed to start.

In 1870, Queen Emma made a famous trek through the **Alaka'i Swamp** to the Kilohana Lookout. (As an aside, Alaka'i means "to lead," because it's impossible to get around in there without a guide.) She had a hundred people accompany her and stopped at awkward times to insist on hula demonstrations. Her guide vowed never to go into Alaka'i again, and the trip became legendary throughout the islands.

By not having a road completely encircling the island, Kaua'i has been able to escape the fate that has befallen O'ahu. As long as the dots aren't connected, there will always be parts of Kaua'i that are remote.

WEST SHORE SHOPPING

Past Lawai you come to **Hanapepe**. It's tough to find the downtown shops open, so try to do your shopping here on Friday evenings (Art Night) when the galleries are open.

The open air **Sunshine Markets** are in Kalaheo (Tues. at 3:30 p.m.), Hanapepe (Thurs. at 3:30 p.m.) and Kekaha (Saturdays at 9 a.m.).

On your way out to Waimea Canyon for an early morning hike, stop in at the **Thrifty Mart Bakery** just past the 19 mile marker on the left side for a cup of coffee and some tasty and *very* reasonably priced baked goods. Donuts sell out early.

Pick up some sandwiches or picnic food at the deli in the **Big Save** in Waimea to put in your backpack. Check out **Collectibles & Fine Junque** for Hawaiian collectibles just

down the street.

An excellent stop to purchase a T-shirt is **Forever Kaua'i** in Kekaha at the Waimea Canyon Plaza at the intersection of Kokee Road and Old Mana Road. Also try the yummy locally made baked goods at the Menehune Food Mart.

WEST SHORE BEST BETS

Best Sunset View—Anywhere along the shore, or a couple miles up Waimea Canyon Road

Best Treat—Shave Ice at Jo-Jo's Clubhouse in Waimea

Best Hearty Food—Chili and cornbread at the Koke'e Lodge

Best Place for Quiet Contemplation— To the right of the viewing platform at Pu'u o Kila Lookout

Best Swimming—Salt Pond Beach Park or Queen's Pond at Polihale (if calm)

Best Place to Get Away From It All and Write the Great American Novel— Waimea Plantation Cottages

Best Place to View Ni'ihau—Along Waimea Canyon Road or from Pu'u Hinahina Lookout

Best Place to Have Good Brakes— Makaha Ridge Road

The nenes of Koke'e are accomplished beggars. This one flew off in a huff when we said no.

Ke'e Beach and its reef lagoon offer some of the best swimming on the North Shore. This is how it looks from the Kalalau Trail.

BEACHES

Because Kaua'i is older than the other major Hawaiian Islands, it is blessed with having more sand beaches per mile of shoreline than any other. No part of the island is without sandy beaches. Many are accessible by merely driving up and falling into the sand. Others are deliciously secluded, requiring walks of various lengths. Some are local secrets; others are unknown even to most locals. In this section we will describe virtually all of Kaua'i's beaches starting from the north shore and working our way around the island clockwise. All of these beaches are located on the maps of the various areas.

County **beach park facilities** are sometimes less than pristine, though they have improved significantly recently.

BEACH SAFETY

The beaches of Kaua'i, and Hawai'i in general, are beautiful, warm and unfortunately can be dangerous. The waves, currents and popularity of beachgoing have caused Hawai'i to become the drowning capital of the U.S. If you're going to swim in the ocean, you need to bear several things in mind. We are not trying to be killjoys here, but there are several reasons why Hawai'i's beaches can be particularly dangerous. The waves are stronger here in the open ocean than most other places. Rip currents can form, cease and form again with no warning. Large "rogue waves" can come ashore with no warning. These usually occur when two or more waves fuse at sea, becoming a larger wave. Even calm seas are no guarantee of safety. Many people have been caught unaware by large waves during ostensibly "calm seas." We have swum and snorkeled most of the beaches we describe in this book on at least two occasions (usually more than two). But beaches change. The underwater topography changes throughout the year. Storms can take a very safe beach and rearrange the sand, turning it into a dangerous beach. Just because we describe a beach as being in a certain condition does not mean it will be in that same condition when *you* visit it.

Consequently, you should consider the beach descriptions as a snapshot in calm

times. If seas aren't calm, you probably shouldn't go in the water. If you observe a rip current, you probably shouldn't go in the water. If you aren't a comfortable swimmer, you should probably never go in the water, except at those beaches that have lifeguards and protected pools, such as Lydgate State Park. But during abnormally high seas, even these are potentially hazardous. Kaua'i averages nine drownings per year—58% of these are visitors. We don't want you to become part of that statistic. There is no way we can tell you that a certain beach will be swimmable on a certain day, and we claim no such prescience. There is no substitution for your own observations and judgment.

In general, the north shore beaches are calmest during the summer months (meaning April–September). The south shore is calmest during the winter months (meaning October–May). North shore high surf is stronger than south shore high surf since our location in the northern hemisphere makes us closer to northern winter storms than southern hemisphere winter storms.

A few of the standard safety tips apply. Never turn your back on the ocean. Never swim alone. Never swim in the mouth of a river. Never swim in murky water. Never swim when the seas are not calm. Don't walk too close to the shore break; a large wave can come and knock you over and pull you in. Observe ocean conditions carefully. Don't let small children play in the water unsupervised. (In fact, it's best to keep them at the protected ponds such as Lydgate.) Fins give you far more power and speed and are a good safety device (besides being more fun). If you are comfortable in a mask and snorkel, they provide considerable peace of mind, in addition to opening up the underwater world.

Lastly, don't let Kaua'i's idyllic environment cloud your judgment. Recognize the ocean for what it is: a powerful force that needs to be respected.

When frolicking at a beach, especially a rocky one, **reef shoes** are invaluable for protecting your feet from cuts. They can turn a marginal beach into a fun beach.

People tend to get fatigued while walking in sand. The trick to making it easier is to walk with a very gentle, relaxed stride while lightly striking the sand almost flat footed.

Beach conditions are usually best in the first half of the day. And remember that weekends—like weekends everywhere—are more popular with local beachgoers, so it's best to plan your beach activities for weekdays, if possible.

One thing you should be aware of is that in Hawai'i, all beaches are public beaches. This means that you can park yourself on any stretch of sand you like. The trick, sometimes, can be access. To get to a public beach you might have to cross private land. The county and state have procured easements to many of the beaches. On our various maps, we have marked these public access routes in yellow. This, along with descriptions and directions, will assist you in finding the beach of your choice. But public access is an involved and often murky subject. We did our best to get it right, but there *may* be some that are marked where *somebody* may object. (E.g., "This *used* to be public access, but the county easement wasn't filed properly when the moon was full, and my attorney talked to their attorney, and together they drafted this 85-page document describing the protocols necessary when accessing every fourth Tuesday…") You get the idea. Use your best judgment.

The beaches that are *supposed* to have **lifeguards** are Hanalei Beach Park,

Wai'oli, Anahola, Wailua, Lydgate, Po'ipu Beach, Salt Pond and Kekaha. Ke'e's situation was in flux at press time.

When we mention that a beach has facilities, it usually includes restrooms, showers, picnic tables and drinking water.

A WORD ABOUT SHELLS

Hawai'i's creatures produce only a tiny fraction of the shells you'll find in other parts of the world, so it's illegal to take any from the beach. Once we were snorkeling at Larsen's when a visitor asked us, "How come I don't see any such and such type of shells anymore? We were here 5 years ago and saw lots of them. I have a whole bag of 'em back home in my garage." We told him, "Maybe we don't have much anymore because they're all in that bag of yours in the garage."

NORTH SHORE BEACHES

❖ **Ke'e Beach**—This is as far as you can go *by car* on the north shore. The

beach here is called Ke'e (also called Ha'ena *State* Park) and is a swimming, snorkeling and sunbathing favorite. The

A REAL GEM sand volume here varies tremendously. Some summers the sand fills the lagoon, creating a sand swimming pool knee-deep. During these times *on calm days* the snorkeling just *outside* the reef is unreal. Tons of fish, clear water and so many turtles you'll lose count as you cruise out the reef opening on the left side and head right. Maybe it's our imagination but the snorkeling seems even better here than a few years ago. But calm seas are the *only* time you should consider *leaving* the lagoon. During winter months and at other times, large waves may wash over the reef, creating an excess of lagoon water. Since Ke'e has the only reef opening, this water has only one place to go to equalize the volume—out the reef opening on the left side. That's why it's important to observe ocean conditions carefully. Big waves mean big currents in the reef openings and big problems for you unless you stay away from the reef opening.

The park is equipped with facilities. There may or may not be a lifeguard here. (Long story.) The stream you crossed ³⁄₁₀ mile back makes an ideal place to rinse off the saltwater, but be careful—the rocks can be slippery.

If the parking area seems full of cars, take the dirt road to the right for a couple hundred feet and stay to the left. There you may find a perfect place to park. One turnout even has a picnic table. Even when drivers are circling the regular parking area like vultures, we often find a good place to park here. Keep going farther back on the dirt road for even more spots.

The highway's end is also where the Kalalau Trail begins. It leads to **Hanakapi'ai Beach** and **Kalalau Beach**, which are described in the ADVENTURES section.

❖ **Ha'ena Beach Park**—This very pretty beach has complete facilities. It is located across from the Dry Cave. Plenty of parking near the beach. Sand is very coarse (and therefore comes off very easily). Although you might see people swimming here, the shore is totally exposed, lacking any reef protection. The smallest of waves has a surprising amount of force. A popular surf spot off to the left of the beach is called Cannons. Since the beach is very steep, a small wave could knock you over and the backwash could pull you in; therefore, swimming is hazardous except dur-

A beachgoer wonders if it's too late to return his snorkel gear.

ing very calm seas. Camping with county permit.

❖ **Tunnels (Makua) Beach**—One of Kaua'i's snorkeling nirvanas. This superb beach has a wide-fringing reef that is so large it can be seen from space. (Don't believe me? Locate it on the map, then look at the cover of this book. The reef is very prominent in this shot taken from the space shuttle.) There is often a lateral rip current, but it's *normally* quite weak, making Tunnels a good snorkeling spot most of the time. The beach is quite popular, and you will often see SCUBA divers here, as well as surfers and windsurfers. All this makes it sound crowded, but crowds are a relative thing. You will find fewer people here than on O'ahu's *least* crowded beach. Plus, a lack of street parking keeps the numbers relatively low. The kaleidoscope of underwater life is usually profuse and definitely worth your time to explore. See section on SNORKELING on page 172

A REAL GEM

for some useful tips. See also the SCUBA section; both are in the chapter called ACTIVITIES. Public access is by either of two short dirt roads past the 8 mile marker on 560. The first one is ⁴⁄₁₀ mile past the 8 mile marker. The second one is almost ⁶⁄₁₀ mile past the 8 mile marker. The second one has easier access. Get there early to assure a parking spot. If they're full, take Alealea Street before the 8 mile marker, park near the sand, and walk to the left along the beach. (It's a half-mile walk, but it's pretty.)

❖ **Kepuhi Beach**—The snorkeling is good here but not nearly as good as Tunnels. You'll rarely find many people on this beach, so if you're in the area and want easy access but no crowds, this is the beach for you. This long strip of sand is fronted by an even longer coral reef. The makeup of this reef causes a slightly stronger current. Check out conditions before you snorkel. Because most of it is not located directly off the main highway, it tends to be forgotten, even by locals. It is, however, still used on occasion by throw-net fishermen. Access is at the eastern end of Alamoo Road. See map on page 48.

❖ **Wainiha Beach Park**—Hazardous surf and its location at the mouth of the Wainiha River make it murky and unsuitable for anything other than shoreline fishing and beachcombing.

❖ **Lumaha'i Beach**—This is the long, wide, golden, glorious beach you see just after you've passed Hanalei Bay. Pictured on countless postcards and posters, this beach was made famous as a location for the movie *South Pacific*. This is where Mitzi Gaynor spent considerable time washing that man right out of her hair. (If you don't know the song, that last sentence must sound awfully stupid.) If you're looking for a huge, picture-perfect stretch of sand on the north shore, Lumaha'i shouldn't be missed. If you're looking for safe swimming, Lumaha'i shouldn't be touched. This beach, along with Hanakapi'ai on the Na Pali Coast, are the two most dangerous beaches on Kaua'i. Exposed to open ocean, the waves here, even small ones, are frighteningly powerful. We've come to this beach after seeing it absolutely flat at Ha'ena Beach Park, a few miles away, only to be utterly assaulted by Lumaha'i's waves. Put simply, most of Lumaha'i is almost never safe to swim. The waves, currents and backwash are not to be underestimated. Lumaha'i Stream on the left side is sometimes crossable during calm seas and low stream flow. It serves as an estuary for 'o'opu during the summer when the shifting sands tend to cut off the river from the ocean. During this time, the closed river mouth is sometimes safe to swim. But absent these conditions, swimming in Lumaha'i Stream has caused numerous individuals to be swept out to sea. Surfers

and boogie boarders often use the left side of the beach near the rocks, but unless you're an expert on Hawaiian surf, this should not be attempted.

Separated by lava rock to the right (east) of Lumaha'i is **Kahalahala Beach** (technically part of Lumaha'i, but who's quibbling). Swimming here is a different story. You access it from a marvelous 3–4 minute walk down through lush jungle to the beach 100 feet below. During calm, summer days the water here can be like a crystal-clear swimming pool. There's a tide-pool for keikis to splash about, a fair amount of shade and a tall rock that some people love jumping off. (Our general rule is never jump off anything you haven't checked out first.) When seas are calm here, this area is utter paradise. Big surf, however, which is not uncommon in the winter, makes this part of the beach nearly as dangerous as the rest of Lumaha'i.

Access to these beaches can be obtained either via a trail from the top of the lookout at the eastern edge of the beach (this gets you to the eastern part, which is the best part), or from the parking area just before you get to Lumaha'i River. See map on page 48.

❖ **Hanalei Bay**—The four beaches described below are all part of Hanalei Bay. With its single long crescent of sand, the bay is beautiful to look at but not great to swim in. Pounding shore break, backwash and rip currents, especially during the winter months, make Hanalei Bay less than ideal as a swimming beach. But that doesn't make it any less pretty. Large surfing waves make Hanalei Bay very popular with surfers, who come from other islands to experience the extremely long-lasting waves.

❖ **Waikoko Beach**—Easy access and good reef protection at this one portion

The Hawaiian Monk Seal

The endangered Hawaiian monk seal occasionally comes ashore after a heavy meal or to avoid a predator. Many people assume the seals are sick or injured and attempt to coax them back into the water. If you are lucky enough to encounter one, please leave it alone. Beaching is perfectly normal. The fines for disturbing one can range as high as $25,000. The seals dive as deep as 400 feet to feed and are considered the most primitive seals in the world with ancient social behavior. Unlike other seals, they don't come ashore in large numbers.

A monk seal snoozes at a Kapa'a beach, oblivious to the kite surfers just offshore. Then again, this photographer watched the same kite surfers for over 5 minutes, oblivious to the monk seal 10 feet away.

of Hanalei Bay make this a popular beach during moderate surf periods, but the water is shallow, which makes for marginal swimming conditions. The snorkeling is better than the swimming if stream flow isn't high. Located between the 4 and 5 mile markers as the road begins to ascend. There is a 20-foot-long path near the 15 MPH sign. See map on page 49.

❖ **Waiʻoli Beach Park**—Located at the end of either Heʻe or ʻAmaʻama Roads in Hanalei, the underwater topography focuses more of the ocean's force here, making the swimming hazardous except during very calm seas. Access is from Weke Road in Hanalei.

❖ **Hanalei Pavilion Beach Park**— Also located on Weke Road in Hanalei, it includes facilities and a lifeguard. Popular with boogie boarders and surfers, the shore break and backwash make for less-than-ideal swimming conditions most of the time.

❖ **Black Pot**—Located near the mouth of the Hanalei River, swimming conditions are marginal. During calm summer surf, boogie boarding is possible near the pier area. Black Pot refers to a large black cooking pot residents used to keep at the beach. This is the area where kayakers put in to paddle up the Hanalei River. The picturesque pier here makes a good sunset photo. Facilities available at beach. Camping with county permit.

❖ **Puʻu Poa Beach**—Located next to the Princeville Hotel in Princeville, the beach has a fringing reef and offers good snorkeling possibilities during calm seas. During the winter, the waters off the outer edge of the reef offer some of the best and most challenging surfing in the state (for experts only). Access is

through a cement path starting just to the left of the gate house at the Princeville Hotel. Getting to the beach necessitates negotiating 191 steps. (Yes, we counted...it was a slow day.) From here you can walk all the way to the mouth of the Hanalei River. The other access is to come from Black Pot Beach and wade across the usually shallow water at the mouth of the Hanalei River.

❖ **Pali Ke Kua (Hideaways)**—Fifty feet before the Princeville Hotel gate

A REAL GEM

house is a corridor off to the right (next to the Puʻu Poa tennis courts). This path leads *down* (120 feet below) to Pali Ke Kua Beach, also called Hideaways. The first half of the descent consists of stairs and a railing. The remainder is trail. All told, it takes 5–10 minutes to get there. There are actually two beaches here, with the second one off to the right separated by a rocky point. Both offer excellent snorkeling during calm seas. The salient underwater features are good relief and a diverse fish community punctuated by the occasional turtle. With marvelous coarse sand, large false kamani trees for shade and good snorkeling when calm, this beach is a wonderful place to spend the day. Though not as unknown as it was before we revealed it in our first edition, you will rarely find too many people here since it's still poorly marked.

While the beach can be a nice place to bring the kids, some may have trouble negotiating their way down the path. (In fact, *you* might have trouble, too, if it has been raining and the path below the steps is muddy.) When seas aren't calm, rip currents can form. Check ocean conditions carefully. Unusually high surf has been known to generate waves that can sweep

If you can negotiate the steps and path on the right side coming down to the sand, Hideaways delivers the right ingredients that make a great beach. And in the summer it's twice as long as this.

across the entire beach. The *other* part of Pali Ke Kua beach can be reached by swimming to the left from Hideaways or by walking a paved trail leading down from the Pali Ke Kua condominiums. That *other* path is a private trail available only to guests at Pali Ke Kua.

❖ **Queen's Bath**—When we revealed it in our first edition, Queen's Bath was an unknown gem accessible via a vague trail through the jungle and exclusive to our readers. I guess we're a victim of our own success. It's now so popular that they installed a parking lot and signs. Queen's Bath is actually a large pool the size of several swimming pools carved by nature into a lava shelf with an inlet from the ocean for fresh seawater to flow. (Shown on page 24.) If the surf is too high, you would never recognize this place as anything special. But at other times, Queen's Bath is a marvelous pool

A REAL GEM

to swim in. Fish get in through the inlet, making it all the more charming. (Bring your mask; no fins needed.) It's a great place to take your underwater camera. During the summer, if the ocean is *too* calm, the water is not refreshed as much as it should be. During high surf, it's dangerous as the water flows in and out of the pond. But the rest of the time, Queen's Bath is one of those places you will return to each time you visit Kaua'i. To get there, follow the trail off Kapiolani Rd near Punahele Rd in Princeville. Note the shape of the end of the trail on the map on page 49. A sign at the trailhead indicates that the "beach" is closed to swimming Oct. 1–May 1. That's a generality. It's presumably meant to convey that these are the winter months and that high surf, which is more common then, makes Queen's Bath unusable. The trail (slippery when wet) passes a marvelous seasonal waterfall on your right after a few minutes. (Good for rinsing off the salt when you're done.) After dropping 120

'Anini's 2-mile long fringing reef usually gives this beach the calmest water on the north shore.

feet, the trail encounters the ocean at the lava shoreline where a small waterfall drops directly into the ocean. Go to the *left* along the lava for 260 yards. (It'll seem like more.) Queen's Bath is recessed in the rock and is part of a horseshoe-shaped lava cut. Use the photo on page 44 or the inside cover to identify it. If you can't find it, the ocean probably isn't cooperating. During the winter, low tide is best.

❖ **SeaLodge Beach**—This wonderful pocket of sand is set in an indentation in

A REAL GEM

the cliff. With plenty of shade courtesy of false kamani trees and heavenly coarse sand (the kind that won't stick to you with the tenacity of a barnacle), SeaLodge Beach is a real find. This beach is sometimes empty of people because most don't know it's there. During the summer in particular, it's an ideal secluded beach. Access is via a trail at the end of the long cement drive-way located to the right at the end of Keoniana Road. The trail follows a stream part of the way then turns to the left just before you get to the top of a waterfall. (That sounds complicated, but it's not that bad.) Another trail from *Building A* at the SeaLodge resort intersects the trail after a few hundred yards. See map on page 49. Where the trail encounters the ocean, it veers to the left. Look for turtles in the water here. The snorkeling can be outstanding during very calm seas, but entry and currents need to be respected. Depending on the weather, the trail can be slippery and a bit tricky in areas. During periods of unusually high surf, waves have been known to travel all the way to the base of the cliff. Don't come here if this is the case. The entire picturesque hike should take between 10 and 15 minutes and is well worth it.

❖ **'Anini Beach Park**—Protected by a *long* fringing reef, 'Anini Beach has become a popular place for the rich and famous to build homes. The water can be very shallow, and the snorkeling is usually good in many areas. The swimming is among the safest you'll find on the north shore. The channel at the western end of the beach is where the water flows out, so stay away from this part. (See the left side of the map on page 46.) There are numerous areas along this stretch of sand to swim, snorkel or just frolic. There is a polo field across from the beach; check it out if you're there during summer. 'Anini Beach is a good place to learn windsurfing. Camping with county permit, facilities at the pavilion. The name used to be *Wanini Beach,* but the "W" was blasted away with a shotgun by an irate resident who felt it had been misspelled. Other residents assumed the gun-toting spellchecker must have corrected a mistake and the "new" name stuck. (*That's* typical Hawai'i.) Take the northern Kalihiwai Road (between the 25 and 26 mile markers) and stay to the left on 'Anini Road.

The far (west) end of the beach, on the other side of the channel, is known as **Wyllie Beach**. Residents of Princeville access it by taking a ¼ mile long trail from the end of Wyllie Road, which drops 20 stories. The easier way is to park near the channel on 'Anini Road and wade across the stream. Wyllie Beach is a thin ribbon of sand with lots of shade from false kamani trees (whose fallen leaves turn yellow, red, orange and brown). It makes a very nice stroll as the ocean gently laps at your feet (though the sand can disappear at high tide and surf). There is a touch more sand in nearshore waters (though still plenty of rocks) than at other parts of 'Anini.

❖ **Kalihiwai Beach**—Located at the mouth of Kalihiwai Stream, you drive down from either Kalihiwai Road. (It used to be a loop, but the bridge was knocked out by a tsunami in 1957, and they declined to rebuild it.) At the bottom of the road you encounter a picturesque bay with a wide sand beach lined with ironwood trees to park under. There are houses on the other side of the road. The beach is popular with boogie boarders in

Local children often play in the shallow stream at Kalihiwai Bay.

the summer and is a good place to see local keikis learning to ride waves. It's also a good place to just enjoy the water during the summer. During the winter surfers ride the large waves under the cliff area. The eastern (first) Kalihiwai Road is the best road to take to the beach. The only ding is that local dogs occasionally roam free, leaving—well, *you* know what they leave—behind.

❖ **Secret Beach**—Also known as Kauapea Beach and known to most

A REAL GEM

locals by the more enticing name of Secret Beach, this is a stunningly beautiful beach only accessible via a 10–15 minute hike. This fact, along with its former anonymity, caused it to become Kaua'i's premier nude beach. For the record, public nudity is illegal in Hawai'i, and police issue tickets there, so it's not as prevalent as before. This long, golden sand beach is not swimmable during the winter, but on calm summer days it can be a delight for swimming and offers good snorkeling. It's worth the trip year-round just to see its exceptional scenic beauty. There is usually a small waterfall to rinse off your gear and a few places where water squirts from the side of the cliff. The island off to your right is Moku'ae'ae Island, a bird sanctuary. To get to Secret Beach, turn right off the first (eastern) Kalihiwai road, then right on the first dirt road you encounter. (See map on page 46.) Take the trail to the bottom. (It's real slippery when it's raining.) Make a mental note of where it encounters the beach for your return.

❖ **Kahili Quarry Beach**—Where Kilauea Stream encounters the ocean is a beach sometimes called Rock Quarry Beach. There is good swimming on the left (western) side and good snorkeling on the right side during calm seas. Since this is a river mouth, the water can get murky at times. (Sharks, which like murky water, have been sighted here during periods of heavy stream flow.) This is a popular boogie boarding and surfing site. The river mouth can cause rip currents. Easiest access is from a dirt road off N. Wailapa Road. See map on page 46. A good hike near here is described under HIKING on page 147.

❖ **Waiakalua Beach**—A marvelous and undiscovered north shore beach. Although from your car it requires a steep, 5–10 minute walk to the beach 160 feet below, Waiakalua is an undisturbed, serene place to spend the afternoon. Medium coarse sand, a long, fringing reef, numerous pockets of shade and a fresh water spring at the far end add to the charm. Observe the reef from up on the bluff. Calm summer snorkeling can be interesting but shallow; watch out for rip currents. During other times, swimming can be hazardous. At the far end of the beach is a rocky point separating the two halves of the beach. The snorkeling around this point is exciting, featuring clear water teaming with big life. However, the rips, surges and surf make this area tricky—only advanced snorkelers need apply. Otherwise, just enjoy the beach. The cool spring at the far end offers sweet, fresh water. Bring an empty container and some water treatment pills—all fresh water obtained anywhere in nature should be treated to prevent bacterial disease. To get there, turn onto North Waiakalua Road and take the dirt road on the left side just before the end of the road. Park when you can't drive any more, and take the trail off to the left. The beach on your left at the bottom

Larsen's Beach has an excellent reef. But stay away from the channel near the top left of the photo.

is Waiakalua Beach. The beach boulders off to your right lead to **Pila'a Beach**. It can take 10–30 minutes to reach **Pila'a Beach**, depending on your boulder-hopping prowess. Otherwise, just stay at Waiakalua Beach. You'll probably have either one all to yourself. See map on page 47.

❖ **Larsen's Beach**—This has crystal-clear water, lots of beachcombing and seclusion. The beach is named after a former manager at Kilauea Plantation named L. David Larsen (the rascal who introduced the hated blackberries to Koke'e). This beach is splendidly isolated but can be accessed by walking down a gently sloping trail. Off to the right are a bunch of lava rocks that make for good snorkeling if conditions are right. To the left is a long crescent of sand broken by occasional outcroppings

A REAL GEM

of rock and reef. Underwater topography creates good conditions for beachcombing. Pakala Point is on the left side where the first beach ends and lava rock protrudes out into the ocean. Just before these rocks is **Pakala Channel**. (Shown near the top of the photo and on the inside back cover.) Most of the water you see breaking over the reef drains through this channel; therefore, *don't swim in or near the channel*. The water leading just up to the channel moves so swiftly at times that it seems more like rapids than a rip current. If the ocean is calm and you stay away from the channel, if the tide is right and you have some experience snorkeling, this place can be a snorkeler's paradise. Lots of coral and fish in shallow, crystal-clear water greet the eye. You may be the only one on the beach if you go during the week. This beach is *not* a swimming beach, just for snorkeling, due to the sharp reefs and shallow water.

One thing that can be *very cool*—if

The south side of Moloa'a Bay on a calm, sunny day is paradise found.

you're careful—is to get in the water at the southeast end (where the trailhead is) and let the current take you toward (but not into!) the Pakala Channel. Then get out and walk back.

The end of summer is when water at reef-fringed beaches like Larsen's has the poorest visibility because it has usually been many months since its had a good flushing by the high surf.

During periods of high surf, waves *tower* above the reef breaking on the edge, which can be quite a spectacle.

On the opposite side of Pakala Point are two pockets of sand that are even more secluded and offer good snorkeling. Larsen's is about 20 minutes north of Kapa'a; take the *north* end of Ko'olau Road (the second Ko'olau if you're coming from Kapa'a) just before the 20 mile marker. 1²/₁₀ miles from the north end of Ko'olau Road, take the left Beach Access road all the way until it ends. (See map on page 47.) Go through the cattle guard

and follow the trail to the bottom (which is 140 feet below you). The beach is a 5–10 minute walk down the hill. Note where the trail hits the beach for your return. If you pass through a herd of cows on the trail, try to discourage them from following you down to the beach. Cattle and beaches don't mix.

❖ **Moloa'a Beach**—A wonderful beach on calm days. The right (southeast) side is much nicer than the northwest side. Very pretty beach, but not a great swimming beach when seas aren't calm. **A REAL GEM** It's off the main highway and not as well known as other beaches. Take the first (southeastern) Ko'olau Road (before the 17 mile marker) to Moloa'a Road. The public access is near the end of Moloa'a Road. Parking can be limited. To get to the southwest side you'll have to walk 100 yards along the beach.

There you'll find the wading, swimming and boogie boarding the best and shade is plentiful. See map on page 47. Some residents lost access to their nearby houses when the tiny bridge to their neighborhood collapsed in the late '90s. Rather than make them wait years while county agencies squabbled over jurisdiction, the military base on the west side sent a dozen Navy Seabees to build them a new one *in one day* using donated materials.

❖ **Papa'a Bay**—Very picturesque, but access is a problem. You need to use the access to North 'Aliomanu Beach (see map) and boulder-hop along the shoreline for over 1,000 feet. In addition, it is one of the few beaches on Kaua'i where you may detect a fishy smell. See map on page 47. When the producer of the movie *6 Days/7 Nights* was here to film the plane crash scene, he apparently liked the location so much, he purchased all *240 acres* around the bay and has built quite a compound, which he calls **Tara**. Although Captain Hollywood owns the land around the bay, the *beach* is public.

❖ **'Aliomanu Beach**—This is really two beaches with different access points. The long, fringing reef offshore of the south beach is used heavily by locals for throw-net fishing, octopus hunting, pole fishing, torch fishing and limu harvesting. This beach, along with Pila'a and Larsen's, attracts families who have been limu (an edible seaweed) harvesting on the outer parts of the reef for generations. They pick the top part of the plant, leaving the roots to regenerate.

The northern (and better) beach is accessed from a parking lot 80 feet above the beach, requiring a 5 minute walk. (See map on page 47.) Although the nearshore waters are rocky, the beach is sandy and very pretty.

❖ **Anahola Beach Park**—The area around Anahola is designated Hawaiian Homelands, and most of the beach users are Hawaiian. Visitors aren't common but are certainly welcome. Swimming is safest where it is protected on the right (eastern) side of the bay to just before Kahala Point. Also nice is the northern end, which is lightly used and can be accessed from the first Aliomanu Road.

EAST SHORE BEACHES

❖ **Donkey Beach**—So named by drifters in the '60s who observed burros and mules being used by the sugar company to haul seed cane to the fields nearby. Donkey Beach has been a popular nudist beach on Kaua'i due to its location, but the land's new owners are doing much to end this practice. (Having purchased the land from the sugar company and selling house lots for $1 million plus, they're not too thrilled with the idea of naked beachgoers.) This long stretch of sand is also popular with surfers. Interestingly, surfing in ancient times was for chiefs only and was usually done nude. (I wonder if that's where the *term hang* loose came from...)

Access is ½ mile north of the 11 mile marker, north of Kapa'a. The uncrowded beach is very attractive, with a convenient tree in the middle for shade. The foreshore at the beach is steep, creating a pounding shore break and strong backwash. Swimming is sometimes hazardous. It's about a 10 minute (550 yard) walk to the beach. As you near the shoreline, veer to the right for the beach. To the left (north) past the stream and over the small hill is a secluded cove (cleverly labeled "secluded cove" on our map) where the snorkeling can be very good at times. You will probably have that cove all to yourself.

❖ **Kealia Beach**—Drive north of Kapa'a and you will often see lots of boogie boarders and surfers in the water here. (See map on page 59.) The powerful waves are fantastic but can be treacherous. The currents and backwash are sometimes ferocious. The northern end of the beach is more protected by a breakwater and can be good for wading and occasionally snorkeling on a calm day. If you have never ridden waves, be very careful or you might get drilled into the ground. If the surf is high, definitely leave it for the big boys.

❖ **Kapa'a Beach Park**—Located in the heart of Kapa'a, this is heavily used by locals. Like any beach located close to a population center, Kapa'a Beach Park is not as pristine as other beaches you will find. That said, the northern section (the part just before the lookout as you leave Kapa'a going north) offers interesting but shallow snorkeling. Check for currents. The rest of the park is not as memorable. It is, however, a good place for a beach stroll or to watch the sunrise. There are a few large sand pockets along the beach that are swimmable when the surf isn't high. Regular facilities here plus a swimming pool. The best thing about Kapa'a Beach Park is watching the kite surfers on a windy day.

❖ **Waipouli Beach**—Pretty but not a good swimming beach. There are a few small pockets along the southern portion of the beach that are relatively safe for swimming during calm periods, but be cautious. The area seaward of the beachrock fronting the beach is subject to strong currents year-round. This is normally considered a dangerous beach. There is a paved shoreline trail along much of this beach, which is perfect for jogging or a leisurely stroll.

Just north of Waipouli Beach is **Waipouli Beach Park**, also called **Fuji Beach** and sometimes **Baby Beach**. Conditions there are different. This can be a nice place to let keikis splash around in the ocean. Part of it (on Moanakai Street between Pahihi and Makana) is often protected by a long, natural sandstone breakwater. Only when the tide or surf are high does water flow over the sandstone and form a slight current to the left. Otherwise, it's usually flat calm. The sand is coarse, so you'll sink a bit more. Check to make sure the ocean isn't making a liar out of us and that it's clean enough. Since it's located in the middle of town, it sometimes gets a little dirty.

❖ **Wailua Beach**—Across from the Coco Palms Resort, from the mouth of the Wailua River to a rocky point to the north, this is an easily accessible beach. Just drive right up. It is popular with surfers and boogie boarders who appreciate the unprotected waves. Winter swells sometimes keep even these users out of the water. Swimmers should be aware of rip currents in several areas along the beach and pounding shore break during high seas. The river itself, which is crossable only during periods of *low flow*, can cause tricky water conditions, so caution is advised. The ocean and the river are constantly battling for supremacy, and the struggle can be dramatic. The ocean builds up a sand bar, and the river attempts to erode it. Sometimes the river is completely stopped up. When it finally breaks through the sand bar, it can be fascinating. The sand bar can erode in a matter of an hour or two, taking large amounts of sand with it. For a short time thereafter, ancient Hawaiian petroglyphs are exposed on rocks in the river mouth.

❖ **Lydgate State Park**—Located just south of the Wailua River, Lydgate (run by the county but still called a state park) is composed of a picnic area, a large patch of grass, restrooms, a nice, large playground, show-

A REAL GEM

ers, lifeguard and two marvelous boulder-enclosed ponds. These ponds are nearly always safe to swim, with the smaller one meant for the keikis (kids). These ponds were created to allow fresh sea water and fish into the pond, while protecting you from the ocean's force. And they work quite well. Lydgate is the most popular fish feeding place on the island. Mornings are the best times. Some chips, bread or rabbit food sparingly squeezed through a hole in a plastic baggie will usually win you lots of new underwater friends. If you are having trouble attracting a crowd, keep swimming slowly while staying reasonably close to the rocks. Fish like the rocks since they offer protection from predators. Once a few start eating, continue to swim slowly to attract the maximum crowd. For more tips on feeding the fish, see page 172. Please be careful to take the plastic baggie out with you. There are plenty of turtles in the area that can choke on the plastic. Access is just off Leho Road in Wailua. (See map on page 59.)

❖ **Nukoli'i Beach Park**—From Lydgate to the far end of the Radisson Hotel is a long sand beach called Nukoli'i Beach. This beach includes the area fronting the Wailua Golf Course. This entire stretch of sand, more than two miles in length, is never crowded, often deserted. This is surprising given its proximity to Kapa'a, but good for you. There is a road fronting the golf course, but it is eroding. In several spots it can be very narrow. If you just want to easily claim a large spot of beach for yourself, this is as good a place as any. The swimming conditions vary along the beach but are usually marginal. Currents and surf are the usual villains. The area in front of the golf course is the only part worth considering for swimming purposes. The snorkeling can be good when it's calm, and it's fun to hunt for golf balls in the water. You might even find a club hurled by someone having an off day. Access? Just drive right up from the dirt road between the golf course and the Radisson Hotel entrance (not far from the 4 mile marker). Or take the Radisson Resort entrance to access the southern portion of the beach. Facilities near the Radisson. One caveat: Natural currents sometimes bring to this beach flotsam, such as netting and ropes from passing ships.

❖ **Hanama'ulu Beach Park**—Water is usually murky due to the Hanama'ulu Stream. Sharks are often seen in the area. The waters around Ahukini Pier can offer interesting snorkeling when it's very calm. In general, a mediocre beach only good for beachcombing.

❖ **Ninini Beach/Running Waters**—Located below the Marriott, there's good snorkeling off to the left in front of the rocks on a calm day. However, even then it can be surgy and a bit tricky. Access via a walk through the 13th green and a steep trail to the bottom; see map on page 63. Take a drive over to the Ninini Lighthouse. If someone is working there at the time, ask if you can go to the top. The view from there is outstanding.

❖ **Kalapaki Beach**—With a gently sloping sand bottom and partial protection from the open ocean, Kalapaki

Beach is popular with visitors and locals alike. Swimming, bodysurfing, windsurfing, beginner surfing and boogie boarding conditions are usually good except during periods of high surf. Adjacent Nawiliwili Park behind the Anchor Cove Shopping Center is a popular picnic spot. Canoes and twin-hulled sailing camarans often come ashore here. Facilities near Anchor Cove Shopping Center. Access is by a road behind the shopping center or through the Marriott. See map on page 63. This is a good place to be when a cruise ship goes by. Because it's at Nawiliwili Bay (where the Hule'ia and Nawiliwili streams empty), the water won't be as clear as other water around the island. When calm (which is most of the time), it's a good place to teach your little one how to ride a boogie board.

❖ **Niumalu Beach Park**—Popular place to launch kayaks for trips up the Hule'ia Stream (where the opening scenes from *Raiders of the Lost Ark* were filmed). Camping by county permit. Other water activities are lousy due to its location so far up the river.

SOUTH SHORE BEACHES

❖ **Maha'ulepu Beaches**—This marvelous coastline is wild and undeveloped, actually consisting of three separate areas known as **Gillin's Beach**, **Kawailoa Bay** and **Ha'ula Beach**.

A REAL GEM

The whole of Maha'ulepu makes for fantastic exploring and beach walking, hence the gem. The swimming is often hazardous, and seas here are often choppy. Winter is best. Ocean entry is difficult in many places. There is a guard shack on the road to the beaches, and you may need to sign a release to drive on the land, which is open sunrise to sunset. Please take everything out that you bring in. The land company, can close this access down any time they wish, so locals are bending over backwards not to give 'em a reason.

Maha'ulepu is located past the Hyatt on Po'ipu Road after the road becomes dirt. Turn right at the dead end and follow the telephone poles. See map on page 73.

To get to **Gillin's Beach**, park on the right where the road starts to curve left. (See map.) This beach is named after the late Elbert Gillin whose rebuilt house is on the beach just off to your right. If you walk past it, you'll see a stream that may or may not reach the ocean. Take the trail that fronts the stream on its far (southern) side. After about two minutes you'll see a small triangle-shaped opening off to your left. This is an ancient open-roofed sandstone sinkhole with some cool features. The local community college has been doing some archeology studies there and sometimes has it gated off. This area is identified as a cave on the map rather than as an amphitheater because we didn't want the casual map reader to think that rock concerts were held there.

To get to **Kawailoa Bay**, continue on the dirt road until it is directly next to the beach. Windsurfing is popular from here to **Gillin's Beach**. They ride the waves faster than the wind, and it is a real treat to watch.

The trail to **Ha'ula Beach** (see map on page 73) requires a walk along an elevated field of lithified sand. (The trail starts at a fence opening where the fence encounters the ocean.) The constant assault from sea spray has caused the sandstone to erode into short but fantastically sharp and strangely shaped

pinnacles. This is a great place to observe the power of the ocean as it smashes into the cliff. Local fishermen drop their lines into the water from here since they can see their prey before they cast. When you reach **Haʻula Beach** (about a 10–15 minute walk), you will almost certainly have it all to yourself. The beach is backed by high sand dunes. Behind one you will find an old picnic table and BBQ. The beach is rarely visited except by occasional horseback tours from CJM Stables. The swimming isn't very good; in fact, it can be quite hazardous depending on conditions. But the beach is a beautiful place to enjoy your solitude. Over the ridge to the northeast is **Kipu Kai Beach**. Totally isolated, it's where the opening scenes of *The Lost World* were filmed. But the only way to get to it is by sea or over that ridge. And the horse trails over the ridge are generously sprinkled with evil, spiked stickers. Bring your kevlar pants.

You may or may not see an unattributed KEEP OUT sign on the shoreline trail leading to **Haʻula Beach.** Local fisherman fishing from the cliffs on weekends don't seem to pay any attention to it.

The area between **Haʻula Beach** and **Kawailoa Bay** contains other lithified sand dunes as well. Fishing from the top (labeled Cliff Cracks on the map) is incredible, but be careful—the dunes can be brittle, so don't fall in. The beach area just north of these lithified dunes often provides lots of goodies for the beachcomber.

Mahaʻulepu was the scene of a terrific slaughter in the spring of 1796. When King Kamehameha launched the first of two invasion attempts, he and his fleet of 1,200 canoes carrying 10,000 soldiers left Oʻahu at midnight, hoping to reach Wailua on Kauaʻi by daybreak. They were in the middle of the treacherous Kauaʻi Channel when the wind and seas picked up. Many of his canoes were swamped. Reluctantly, he ordered a retreat but too late to stop some of his advance canoes. When they landed at Mahaʻulepu, they were exhausted. They awoke to the sound of enemy troops who proceeded to kill all but a few escapees. The last thing these escapees wanted to do was go back to Oʻahu and tell their boss what happened. So they bolted all the way to the Big Island and kept their mouths shut.

❖ **Shipwreck Beach**—This beach was named for an old, unidentified wooden shipwreck now long gone. Also called **Keoniloa Beach**, it fronts the Hyatt. The public access road is between the Hyatt and the Poʻipu Bay Resort Golf Course. The beach is used mostly by surfers, boogie boarders, body surfers and windsurfers who stay toward the eastern end. High surf can create very unfavorable conditions. Even during calm seas, swimming is sometimes difficult. The Hyatt erects colored flags to signal ocean conditions—green meaning safe. (Though we've *never* seen a green flag. Their lawyer probably confiscated it.) The cliff off to your left is called Makawehi Point and is a popular place for pole fishermen. You will often see foolhardy young men jumping off the cliff into the waters below. (As did Harrison Ford and Anne Heche in *6 Days/7 Nights*.) The cliffs are a fascinating place to hike and are described in HIKING on page 153. The Hyatt has some outdoor showers near the beach area to rinse off, but they are technically only for the guests.

❖ **Brennecke Beach**—This beach was badly mauled by a hurricane back in 1992, but community volunteers brought

The water is nice, but entry can be a bit awkward from this spot. Shipwreck Beach can be a good place to sit and watch frustrated fishermen cast off (literally).

it back to life by hauling in sand and removing an ill-conceived seawall. Great boogie boarding and lots of turtles. Since it is so small, surfboards are not allowed near the shore. The waves are usually great and tend to break both far away and close to shore—perfect for both beginners and advanced. You can rent boogie boards across the street at Nukumoi Surf Co. Observe conditions carefully before you go in. Since this beach is more susceptible to change than most island beaches, you'll have to evaluate its boogie viability.

❖ **Po'ipu Beach Park**—This is the major center of beach activity on the

A REAL GEM

south shore. The swimming is nearly always safe just to the left of the tombolo. What's a tombolo? Glad you asked. It's a narrow strip

of sand joining two pieces of land. If you stand or lie on the middle of this one when the tide is right, the ocean waves will strike you from both sides of the strip; this is what builds up the sand bar. (Every few years, storms erase the sand bar for months at a time.) There are only three such examples in the state, all on Kaua'i (the other two are inaccessible except by kayak; they are Makapili Rock near Kilauea and Kipu Kai). Many people like to park their beach chairs at the end of the tombolo (also known as Nukumoi Point). Of course, their return trip isn't always dry if the tide is high. Snorkeling around the right side of the point can be fantastic. Park facilities are present. To the left is an area semi-protected by a breakwater. It's very popular with children. This park is a nice place to enjoy the ocean. The far right side isn't as protected but features excellent snorkeling and swimming if the surf isn't high.

❖ **Kiahuna Beach/Sheraton Beach/ Poʻipu Beach**—Take your pick with regard to the name. This beach fronts the Sheraton Hotel and Kiahuna Resort. It is postcard pretty and often safe to swim thanks to an offshore reef. Surfers ride waves outside the reef, but you should stay inside unless you really know your stuff. Boogie boarding and snorkeling help make this one of the most user-friendly beaches around. Access from the end of Hoonani Rd.

A REAL GEM

❖ **Koloa Landing**—An old boat launch used as a SCUBA spot. See SCUBA in the chapter on ACTIVITIES.

❖ **Baby Beach**—This stretch of sand is partially protected from surf by a natural breakwater of lava boulders forming a quasi-protected pool. The sand only extends a little way into the water, giving way to a lining of lava stones, so you'll be grateful for those cheap reef shoes you brought with you. These same shallow stones also capture some of the sun's heat, making the water a little warmer here. A REAL GEM for people terrified of the ocean, as well as little crumb crunchers, hence the name. Check conditions first. On Hoona (loop) Rd. off Lawaʻi Rd. See map on page 72.

❖ **PK's**—Named after the Prince Kuhio monument across the street on Lawaʻi Road. Almost no sand and entry can be awkward, but snorkeling is good at times. Also used for SNUBA and SCUBA.

❖ **Lawaʻi Beach/Beach House**—This tiny pocket of sand next to the Beach House Restaurant nearly disap-

If high surf is rockin' at other beaches, Baby Beach in Lawaʻi usually provides a calm respite.

Nowhere does shattered litter look more beautiful than at Glass Beach.

pears at high tide. The snorkeling in front of the restaurant is great, but the water is subject to currents during periods of high surf and needs to be respected. At other times it can be calm and a good place for the less-experienced snorkeler. SNUBA (not SCUBA) is also done here. Just stay near the shore around the restaurant.

❖ **Keiki Cove**—A minuscule pocket of sand just past Lawa'i Beach where the road almost clips the ocean. (A break in the wall hides stairs.) It's usually protected and an excellent place to let rug rats experience the ocean, but check it yourself first. See photo on page 35.

❖ **Lawa'i Bay**—Access is the problem here. There's no way to get here by land without crossing private property. But you can kayak here from Kukui'ula Harbor only a mile to the east. The beach is in a particularly lovely setting, backed by the National Tropical Botanical Garden. If you visit the beach, you're not allowed to venture into the private garden.

❖ **Palama Beach**—The only way to get to this beach is to take Kaua'i Coffee's dirt road past the 4 mile marker on Po'ipu Road. From there, take one of the feeder roads to the beach. (The feeder road is on the map, but the gate's probably locked.) All this requires permission from Kaua'i Coffee, which they probably won't give. If you're still with me, the beach is quiet and nearly always deserted.

WEST SHORE BEACHES

There aren't a lot of listings under West Shore Beaches. That's because it's almost *all beach*.

❖ **Glass Beach**—If someone told you that you gotta check out the beach near an old dump, would you believe them? Then if they said the reason to check it out was because stuff from the dump washes ashore, would you go? Well...you should. Glass Beach makes a rotten first impression. It's in the industrial part of 'Ele'ele backed by huge, ugly tanks full of gasoline. Add to that millions of pieces of broken glass, washed in from broken bottles and auto glass. The result? A colorful tapestry of sand and multicolored glass. (Come to think of it, doesn't glass *come* from sand?) This isn't a beach to frolic at or swim in. It's a good strolling beach, especially if you want to tie in a visit here with a hike along the Swiss cheese-type of lava farther east. That hike is described on page 154. The amounts of glass varies with tides and surf. Please don't take any of the glass litter. (Now *there's* a bizarre statement if taken out of context.) To get to Glass Beach, drive toward Hanapepe, turn left on Waialo Road going toward Port Allen. Before the ocean, go left on Aka Ula until it's dirt. Then take a right in the dirt and park at the beach. A 20 minute or so walk farther east leads to **Wahi-awa Beach**, a dark sand beach where tour boats sometimes moor for lunch. See map on page 83.

❖ **Salt Pond Beach Park**—This area is distinguished in that it has the only natural salt ponds in Hawai'i still used to make salt. Seawater is pumped into containers and allowed to evaporate. More water is added, and then it is transferred to shallower pans. The process is repeated until the water is loaded with salt. This is allowed to evaporate completely, leaving crystallized salt behind. (Excellent in kalua pig.) During the summer you'll likely see people practicing this process. The nearby park and its facilities are a popular place for locals to bring their families. The beach is separated by two rocky points. A natural ridge of rock runs between the two points, creating an area of relative calm inside. Swimming is usually safe, and children play in the semi-protected ocean water. The exception is during periods of high surf, which can make it unsafe. In Hanapepe past 17 mile marker off Lele Road.

❖ **Pakala Beach**—Those cars you might see parked on the side of the road shortly after the 21 mile marker belong to surfers carrying their boards to a very famous surfing site also known as **Infinities**, so named because the ride seems to last forever. The water is murky and only used for expert surfing.

❖ **Lucy Wright Beach Park**—Lucy Wright was a prominent member of the Waimea community when she died in 1931. It is a testament to how the townsfolk felt about her that the beach was named in her honor, especially in light of the more historic event that happened here. For it was at this spot that Captain James Cook first set foot in the Hawaiian Islands in January 1778. The beach itself is not a particularly good beach. The Waimea River mouth is nearby, and the silty water is less enticing than clear waters elsewhere. Some guidebooks label this a black sand beach, like the black sand beaches on the Big Island or Maui. That's not quite accurate. Though there *is* lots of black sand here—flecks of lava along with a green stone called olivine chipped from the river bed by the Waimea River—much of the "black sand" is simply fine sediment carried by the same river. Camping by county permit. Across the river are the remains of the Russian Fort called Fort Elizabeth State Historic Park. For more information on the fort, see page 83. The best part of the beach is watching the interplay of the ocean and river mouth, described on page 84.

❖ **Polihale**—This area consists of more than 15 *miles* of uninterrupted sand beach. There are three regions, called **Polihale State Park, Pacific Missile Range Facility** and **Kekaha Beach Park**. Except for a few small areas, the entire stretch is unprotected, which means it is exposed to the ocean's force. During periods of high surf, waves can travel up the beach and pull you in, so be wary. When the seas are calm, you might enjoy the water. The sand can get pretty hot out on this side—hot enough to fry your feet, so watch it. Take water with you. It's available only at Kekaha Beach Park and at the other end at Polihale State Park.

Kekaha Beach Park is the first region you encounter. High surf generates a particularly powerful rip current and waves can be unbelievably strong, so stay out unless the water is real calm.

Past Kekaha is one of the least appreciated (and used) stretches of beach on the island. **Kokole Point** marks the beginning of PMRF (below). The dirt road ⅔ past the 27 mile marker leads to the shoreline. 4WD drivers should read the part about driving on sand under the Polihale description below if you want to drive on the beach. At the beach here you can often walk for a mile (especially to the west) and not find a soul. Ni'ihau seems so close from here. There's no shade, and the same swimming warnings apply as Kekaha Beach Park. But it's a great place to enjoy a wide, sandy beach and an awesome place for a late afternoon BBQ.

Pacific Missile Range Facility (PMRF) is operated by the U.S. Navy. It is here that they train for ASW or Anti Submarine Warfare. They also conduct "Star Wars" missile tests here. Since the September 11th attacks the access situation has gotten more difficult, so call (335–4523) before you get here to make

arrangements. The beach on the northern part (adjacent to Polihale State Park) is **Barking Sands Beach**. If conditions are right, the sand dune (which has numerous kiawe trees) is supposed to make a barking sound with your every step. The likely cause is a combination of uniform grain size coupled with a thin coating of silica that sticks when dry. Don't feel bad if it doesn't happen. We've jumped up and down like idiots on that sand until we're blue in the face, and we haven't even gotten it to whine. The sand needs to be *real* dry. Local legend has it that the barking sound comes from nine dogs buried in the sand. They belonged to their master, a fisherman, in the days when dogs didn't bark. (Sometimes I wish those were *still* the days.) One day, they started acting antsy as the master tied them up before he went fishing. While he was out, a storm broke and forced him off course. A god gave the dogs the power to bark so they could guide their master home. Unfortunately, the dogs were so fearful waiting for their master that they ran around the stakes they were tied to. Around and around and around they ran until they buried themselves in the sand. The fisherman was depressed when he returned and couldn't find his dogs. He would go down to the shore every day looking for them, but he never found them. The dogs remain there to this day, barking for their master, hoping he will find them. (My neighbor's dog seems to bark for the same reason.)

Polihale State Park is the end of the line. You can't go any farther north on this part of the island without a boat. This is where the Na Pali Coast starts. Rain is rare in these parts. On the few occasions that it does rain hard, the road can get pretty sloppy. Other times potholes might slow you down but regular cars can almost always make it. The sand can get *real* hot in the summer. The four facility areas here tend to be poorly maintained but include showers, restrooms, picnic tables and drinking water (which you'll need).

The dunes of Polihale are famous throughout the islands. The beach averages 300 feet wide, and the dunes can get up to 100 feet high. Walking down a dune like that can be fun; walking up is a monster. Better to walk around unless you are training for the *Ironman Triathlon*. Locals drive their 4WD vehicles right onto the beach. If you try it, be aware that there is no AAA on the island, and you are a *long* way from Lihu'e. The first thing a tow truck driver will probably ask you is, "Do you own your own home?" It's probably cheaper to buy a new car. Remember the 4WD drive trick to driving on sand is to have low air pressure in your tires (15 psi is what we use), be gentle on the gas and *don't stop* in soft sand; let your momentum carry you. A cheap air pump from Wal-mart that plugs into the cigarette lighter can

refill the air. Even with all that, it's still possible to get stuck. Consider taking the carpet out of the trunk and driving on it if you're stuck.

To get there, you take Hwy 50 till it ends, veering right at the fork. (See map on page 82.) The first dirt road leads 3³⁄₁₀ miles to a large monkeypod tree. To the left is **Queen's Pond**. This is the one part of Polihale that often offers safe swimming. It is encircled by a small fringing reef, and the swimming inside the reef is good except during periods of high surf.

If you go to the right at the monkeypod tree, there's a soft sandy spot in the road 4½ miles from where you left the pavement. This is where many 2WD drivers stop and climb the dune to get to the beach. A smarter way is to backtrack till you see the loop road through the campsites. (It's 1 mile from the monkeypod tree.) It goes to the top and along the dune, getting you closer to the beach.

Beaches along **Na Pali** are not reachable unless you're up for an adventure. That's why they are described in the ADVENTURES section.

Semi-protected by reef, Polihale's Queen's Pond makes a fine wading pool much of the time.

Wet, warm and happy. Life is good...

If you want more from your Kaua'i vacation than a sun-tan, Kaua'i offers a multitude of activities that will keep you happy and busy. Among the more popular activities are helicopter tours, ocean tours of Na Pali, golfing, hiking, SCUBA diving and kayaking. You will find lots more to do here as well.

We've listed the activities here in alphabetical order. Beware of false claims on brochures. We've seen many fake scenes in some brochure racks. Computers have allowed photo manipulation to imply realities that don't exist (which *we* don't do).

Activities can be booked directly with the companies themselves. Ask them if they have any coupons floating around in the free publications or if there is a discount for booking direct. You can also book through **activity brokers** and **booths** which have become numerous and usually have signs such as FREE MAPS or ISLAND INFORMATION. Allow me to translate: The word FREE usually means I WANT TO SELL YOU SOMETHING.

What we're about to tell you will get this book pulled from some shops and badmouthed in some circles, but the truth's the truth. Their objective, as is the case with many concierges, is to sell you activities for a commission. *Occasionally* you can get better deals through activity booths or your concierge, but not often, because 25–30 percent of what you're paying is their commission (which they call a "deposit") for making the phone call. That's why calling direct can sometimes save money. Companies are so happy they don't have to give away ¼ to ⅓ of their fee to activity booths, they'll sometimes give you a discount.

Many of the activity booths strewn about the island are actually forums for selling timeshares. We are not taking a shot at timeshares. It's just that you need to know the real purpose of some of these booths. They can be very aggressive, especially now that so many timeshares are on the market. (To use a wilderness analogy—they are the hunters, you are the hunted. Don't let them see the fear in your eyes.)

Selling activities has become a *big*

business on Kaua'i, and it's important to know *why* they're pitching a certain company. If an activity booth or desk steers you to XYZ helicopter company and assures you that it's the best, that's fine, but consider the source. That's usually the company that the booth gets the *biggest commission* from. We check up on these booths frequently. Some are reputable and honest, and some are outrageous liars. Few activity sellers have ever done any of the activities unless they got it *free* and the company *knew* who they were. On the other hand, we *pay* for everything we do and review activities *anonymously*. We have no stake in *any* company we recommend, and we receive *no* commission. We just want to steer you in the best direction we can. If you know who you want to go with (because you read our reviews and decided for yourself), call them direct first.

A WARNING: Many of the companies listed have a 24-hour cancellation policy. Even if the weather causes you (not them) to cancel the morning of your activity, *you will be charged.* Some credit card companies will back you in a dispute if the 24-hour policy is posted, some won't. Fair? Maybe not. But that's the way it is.

Lastly, consider booking by e-mail before you come. Good companies can fill up in advance, and the Web can pave the way for your activities. Our site at **www.wizardpub.com** has links to *every* company listed here that has a site, even the ones we recommend *against*.

ATVs (also called quads) can be a fun way of seeing the back country, and how appropriate that we start this section with two companies that are *so* different.

Both are on the south shore. Our favorite is **Kipu Ranch Adventures** (246–9288). They have 3-hour rides of Kipu Ranch, the most beautiful ranch we know in Hawai'i. In addition to the lump-in-your-throat backdrop of Ha'upu Range along the pastures, they also descend into woodsier areas, along a stream and usually end up at a viewpoint almost no one on Kaua'i *ever* gets to see—the hidden valley and beach of Kipu Kai from the road that drapes across the mountain. (Because it's private and closed we *never* thought we'd get to see this sight.) They use big bikes and run their tours well. You won't be allowed to totally cut loose on your bike, if that's what you're aiming for. It's a tour. And, like the other company,

Think of an ATV as your own private tank.

you'll get dusty. But it's a fun way to see exceptional scenery. $95.

Kaua'i ATV (742–2734) uses a fun (and muddy) track that goes through an old truck tunnel and to a small waterfall. That said, we'd have a hard time thinking of *any* company on the island that had worse personnel than Kaua'i ATV. Their surliness and downright nastiness is breathtaking in its scope.

At the beginning, they announce to everyone that "these are *our* bikes, not yours. No hot dogging. If we catch anyone, you'll get two warnings." Then they tell everyone, *before they've even started the engines*, "Consider this your *first* warning." The attitude gets worse from here. And their guide's "facts" are often wrong. In general...they're *terrible*.

$130 for their 4-hour trip plus extra fees such as a collision damage waiver and photo fees.

Bike lanes or shoulders of some kind line the main highway from Princeville all the way around to Mana on the west side (though some are narrow in spots and some bridges force you into the traffic). Past Princeville, forget it.

There are many places to rent and ride mountain bikes. The dirt roads around **Po'ipu**, especially near **Maha'ulepu,** can be fun, though a bit dusty. Another good place is the cane road between **Kealia Beach** and **Anahola.** (Start at Kealia Beach and pedal north.) The **Kuilau** and **Moalepe Trails** can be exciting. (Described under HIKING on page 149.) The roads past the end of **Kuamo'o Rd.** in Kapa'a leading toward Wai'ale'ale and

the Jungle Hike described on page 150 are excellent for mountain bikes.

If you don't mind a long drive, the roads of Koke'e offer good choices. See the Koke'e map on page 138 and the west side map on page 82. Pay attention to Mohihi Camp 10 Road on the Koke'e map, and the roads on the west (ocean) side of Waimea Canyon Road starting from near the 11 and 13 mile markers on the west side map. The latter offer marvelous opportunities. The contour road is always fun. You can even travel down the spine of some of the ridges, such as Kauhao and Ka'awe-iki, if you have the stones to pedal back up. The ADVENTURES section has a bike/hike combo.

If you're interested in renting a mountain bike, call any of these companies: **Kaua'i Cycle & Tour** in Kapa'a at 821–2115 (the friendliest bike shop on the island), **Outfitters Kaua'i** in Po'ipu at 742–9667 and **Pedal 'n Paddle** in Hanalei at 826–9069. Expect to pay $20–$35 per day. Bikes with shocks are better but more expensive.

If you just want to go downhill, road trips down Waimea Canyon Rd. are available. They're fun but pretty short, and *not* comparable to Maui's more famous and longer downhill ride. With **Bicycle Downhill\Outfitters Kaua'i** (742–7421) you meet at 6 a.m. or 2:30 p.m. in Po'ipu, then drive up to the canyon in their van. Near the 12 mile marker you get out and coast downhill almost the entire way on 550 and 552, ending up in Kekaha before noon. $80. (Interestingly, one of their ads says "100% downhill" but shows a woman riding *uphill!*) **Kaua'i Coasters** (639–2412) has a similar ride, but they leave (and get back) earlier in order to see the sunrise from Koke'e. $65. Morning tours take around a dozen people and include muffins and coffee.

Keiki shreddin 'em.

Boogie Boarding

Boogie boarding (riders are derisively referred to as *spongers* by surfers) is where you ride a wave on what is essentially a sawed-off surfboard. It can be a real blast. You need short, stubby fins to catch bigger waves (which break in deeper water), but you can snare small waves by simply standing in shallow water and lurching forward as the wave is breaking. If you've never done it before, stay away from big waves; they can drill you. Smooth-bottom (hard shell) boards work best. If you're not going to boogie board with boogie fins (which some consider difficult to learn), you should boogie board with reef shoes or some other kind of water footwear. This allows you to scramble around in the water without fear of tearing your feet up on a rock or urchin. Shirts are *very* important, especially for men. (Women already have this aspect covered.) Sand and the board itself can rub you so raw your *da kines* will glow in the dark.

Your hotel activity desk may have boards. It should cost you $5–$7 per day, $15–$25 per week. Other places include:

North Shore—Hanalei **Surf Co.** at 826–9000, **Kayak Kaua'i** at 826–9844, **Pedal 'n Paddle** at 826–9069.

East Shore—Kayak Kaua'i at 822–9179, **Chris The Fun Lady** at 822–7759.

South Shore—Sea **Sport Divers** in Po'ipu at 742–9303, **Progressive Expressions** in Koloa at 742–6041, or **Nukumoi Beach & Surf Shop** at 742–8019 across from Po'ipu Beach.

Below are some beaches worth considering. Also check the BEACHES section.

◆ **Kealia Beach** in Kapa'a is excellent, but the waves are powerful.
◆ **Kalapaki Beach** in Lihu'e is a smart choice for beginners and the timid.
◆ **Brennecke Beach** has returned to its former glory. (For a decade it was poor after being chewed up by a hurricane.)

CAMPING

The ultimate in low-price lodging is offered by Mother Nature herself. Kaua'i is a great place to camp with 13 different areas—six state camping areas and seven county campsites. See map below. To camp at a state controlled site, you need to contact the **Division of State Parks** at 3060 Eiwa St., #306, Lihu'e, HI 96766, (808) 274–3444. (Our Web site has a link to a

Campsites Requiring Permits

State Parks Written in Yellow; County Parks are in Brown

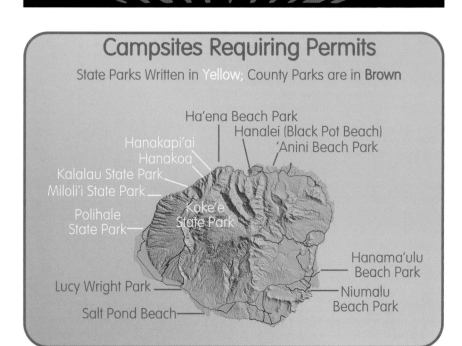

Ha'ena Beach Park
Hanalei (Black Pot Beach)
'Anini Beach Park

Hanakapi'ai
Hanakoa
Kalalau State Park
Miloli'i State Park

Polihale
State Park

Koke'e
State Park

Hanama'ulu
Beach Park

Lucy Wright Park

Niumalu
Beach Park

Salt Pond Beach

page where permit applications are downloadable.) You are *strongly* advised to get your permit before you arrive because the sites can fill up, especially during peak season (May–December). The state requires that you send a copy of the driver's license or passport of every adult who will be camping, as well as the names of any minors, along with your dates of travel. The permits are $5 per family per night (except Na Pali, which is $10 *per person*) and should be acquired as far in advance as you can. They recommend at least six months in advance during the busy months. *More for Na Pali.*

The state enforces permits with uncommon zeal, so when officers swoop in to check your permits, stand at attention and wipe that smile off your face.

For beach campsites see BEACHES.

County sites require a county permit. Write to: **Division of Parks and Recreation**, 4444 Rice St., #150, Lihu'e, HI 96766, (808) 241–6660. They will send you an application. The cost is $3 per person per night.

Car camping from 4WDs at Koke'e State Park is lovely—especially Sugi Grove—and is convenient if you plan to hike much there.

If you need to rent camping or hiking gear, your best sources will be **Pedal 'n Paddle** in Hanalei at 826–9069 or **Kayak Kaua'i** in Hanalei at 826–9844.

LPG can be found at **Kmart** or **Wal-mart** in Lihu'e. For white gas or butane call **Gaspro** in Lihu'e at 245–6766.

Good places to buy gear include the variety stores around the island: **Pedal 'n Paddle** (826–9069) in Hanalei, **Waipouli Variety** (822–1014) in Kapa'a and **Discount Variety** (742–9393) in Koloa. Others are **Wal-mart** and **Kmart** in Lihu'e and **Cost-U-Less** in Kapa'a for food.

Kaua'i's waters contain abundant fish. Of course, it's one thing to have 'em and another thing to catch 'em. Whether you want to go deep sea fishing, sit by a lake, or cast off a cliff, you will be pleased to know that all are available on Kaua'i.

DEEP SEA FISHING

If deep sea fishing's your game, there are several charter companies around. They all provide the necessary gear. Tuna, wahoo (ono) and marlin, among others, are all caught in these waters. The seas around the islands can be rough if you're not used to it, and it's fairly common for someone on board (maybe you) to spend the trip feeding the fish. We advise that you take Dramamine or Bonine *before you leave*. Scopolamine patches work well but have side effects that can temporarily affect vision (can make close-up vision poor for a week). Other alternatives may be available. See your doctor. (I've always wanted to say that.) Some people feel that greasy foods or citrus before or during your trip is a no-no; *many* swear by ginger tablets. Some seriously suggest putting a cherry seed in your bellybutton. (And hope the fish don't laugh at you.)

Most boats troll nonstop since the lure darting out of the water simulates a panicky bait fish—the favored meal for large game fish. On some boats, each person is assigned a certain reel. Experienced anglers usually vie for corner poles on the assumption that strikes coming from the sides are more likely to hit corners first.

You should know in advance that in Hawai'i, the fish belongs to the boat. What happens to the fish is entirely up to the captain, and they usually keep it. You may catch a 1,000-pound marlin and be told that you can't have as much as a steak from it. If this bothers you, you're out of luck. If the ono or another *relatively* small fish are striking a lot and there is a glut of them, you might be allowed to keep it—or half of it. You *may* be able to make arrangements in advance to the contrary.

Before deciding *who* to go with, decide if conditions warrant going at all. It might be calm on one side of the island and rough on another. Current ocean conditions can be obtained by calling 245–3564 for Hawaiian waters, 245–6001 for the weather forecast.

Reputable charter companies are:

Hawaiian Style Fishing at 635–7335 has a 25' boat. Unlike most boats there's no deck hand, so it'll be a bit more hands on (literally). If the trolling's not working they'll bottom feed. A good, flexible outfit. $95 for a half day.

'Anini Fishing Charters at 828–1285 fishes off the north shore. Light and medium tackle are their specialty, but they'll go heavy if you like. $95 for a half day, Bob will stay out longer if things are really jumping. 33' craft will take 6 people, minimum of 4.

Kai Bear at 639–4556 has a 38' and a 42' Bertram. Their motto is, "If you find a nicer boat, I'll pay for your trip." (Gotta love their confidence.) Half day is $99, their deluxe half day is $149. Half day private charters are $550. Out of Nawiliwili.

Sport Fishing Kaua'i at 742–7013 has 33' and 38' Bertrams. Medium to light stand-up tackle and 3 fighting stations. 4–6 people per boat. $95 for four hours, $135 for six hours. Out of Port Allen.

True Blue Charters and Ocean Sports at 246–6333 fishes off the east shore and specializes in the big stuff. Their 4-hour trip is $99, 6-hour trips are $129. They will go out with 4 people, to a maximum of 10 on their 55' craft. Based out of Nawiliwili.

Open Sea at 332–8213 has a 36' Hatteras. $95 per person, plus they'll do private charters to Ni'ihau.

FRESHWATER FISHING

There are dozens of lakes (actually manmade reservoirs) strewn throughout the island. Largemouth bass are plentiful. You'll also find smallmouth bass and a tough-fighting South American import called tucunare or peacock bass. Avoid fishing when the water is real muddy after a heavy rain; fish won't bite.

The **Pu'u Lua Reservoir** in Koke'e (on the west side, see map on page 82) used to be stocked with trout, until an endangered bug put a stop to that. They won't be restocking it until they figure out if the trout are eating the bugs. What's there is still fishable, and trout season in Koke'e is restricted to the first Saturday in August, then 16 consecutive days, then weekends and holidays until the end of September. (Subtract from this the square root of pi and the result is your birthday.)

Division of Aquatic Resources, Department of Land and Natural Resources at 274–3344 can fill in any additional blanks you may have.

Companies that do guided freshwater fishing trips: **Cast & Catch** (332–9707), **Fishing in Paradise** (245–7358) and **JJ's Big Bass** (332–9219).

Places to obtain licenses are:

Lihu'e Fishing Supply at 245–4930 in Lihu'e and **Waipouli Variety** at 822–1014 in Kapa'a. Squid and shrimp can be obtained from most supermarkets.

With its bountiful nightly rainfall and warm, sunny days, Kaua'i is a perfect environment for golf. Its nine golf courses are diverse, ranging from a wealthy sugar magnate's private course donated to the island, to a world class resort course rated #1 in the all the islands by *Golf Digest*. If golf is your game, Kaua'i is sure to please.

The prices described under Fees in the table (next page) reflect the highest category of fees. Check the specific course descriptions below for more information and possible discounts. Many have additional twilight specials.

PRINCEVILLE RESORT KAUA'I; THE MAKAI COURSE 826–3580

Designed by Robert Trent Jones, Jr. and first opened in 1972, the **Makai Course** consists of 3 sets of 9 holes called the **Ocean,** the **Lakes** and the **Woods.** For 18 holes you get your choice of two with **Ocean/Lakes** being the most popular. The **Woods** course has a windy reputation. The **Lakes** offers an impressive 9, with holes 3–7 commanding outstanding views. Hole 9 requires a buttery touch as it shoots over the water onto a small green located just behind it. The **Ocean** is the most challenging and interesting of the three, as well as the longest. The 6th and 7th holes offer dramatic views of the north shore coastline from the edge of a steep cliff. In fact, hole 7 shoots across a menacing gorge.

Located off Highway 56 inside Prince-

COURSE	PAR	YARDS	RATING	FEES
Princeville Resort Kaua'i;				
Makai Course	72	6306	69.7	$125*
Prince Course	72	6521	71.0	$175*
Wailua Municipal Course	72	6585	71.9	$25–$35
Kaua'i Lagoons Golf and Racket Club;				
Mokihana Course	72	6108	68.0	$120*
Kiele Course	72	6164	69.1	$170*
Po'ipu Bay Resort	72	6021	69.0	$185*
Kiahuna Golf Club	70	5631	66.5	$75*
Puakea Course (10 hole x 2)	80	7040	74.0	$65*
Kukuiolono (9 hole x 2)	72	6154	70.0	$7

* Indicates power cart included in fee.

ville; see map on page 49. Fees are $125 for standard, $110 if you're staying at Princeville resort. Kama'aina rate is $47–$57. Carts are included. Walking is allowed, but you pay for a cart anyway.

Note: The proper golf attire rule is more rigidly enforced at Princeville courses.

PRINCEVILLE RESORT KAUA'I;
THE PRINCE COURSE 826-5070

Now you've reached golfing nirvana. This course is often rated #1 in all the islands by *Golf Digest*, and for good reason. With 390 gorgeous acres to work with, Robert Trent Jones, Jr. took full advantage of the cliffs, gorges and natural rolling scenery. When it opened in 1990, the Prince Course was hailed by *Golf Digest* as the best new resort course in the country. Since then, it has become known throughout Hawai'i as one of the most challenging and rewarding courses one can play, usually rated as the best in the state. The design stresses unobstructed expansiveness, with the rolling topography and deep gorges serving as the main hazards and obstacles. There are nine miles of cart paths, and the layout allows for considerable room between holes. Hole 6 offers a delightful march toward the ocean cliffs. At hole 7, you must shoot over a gorge onto a narrow finger of land containing the green and little else. The 14th green is accompanied by a charming waterfall coming out of a hole in the mountain. You won't find a lot of flat areas on this course, but you will find tough, challenging, world-class golfing. In fact, if you're *really* into self-flagellation (*hey,* getting pretty personal, aren't we?), the black tees measure a whopping 7,309 yards with a rating of

ACTIVITIES

74.6. The Clubhouse is spectacular (except for the restaurant). If you've never played golf before, this probably isn't the course on which to learn. But if you have a little experience and don't mind being humbled a bit, this course can't be beat.

Located just before Princeville off Highway 56, see map on page 46. Fees are $175 for standard, $150 if you are staying in Princeville, $130 if you're staying at the Princeville Hotel and $60–$85 for kama'ainas.

WAILUA MUNICIPAL COURSE 241-6666

At one time this course had been rated as the best *municipal* course in Hawai'i and one of the best in the U.S. In the '90s it fell into disrepair due to an obvious lack of concern by groundskeepers and management. It has enjoyed a comeback of late—they're putting in the effort and money, and it shows. Today Wailua rates as a pretty good municipal course.

As it parallels the beach on Kaua'i's Coconut Coast, Wailua constantly reminds you that you are near the ocean. The smell of sea air, the constant crosswind and the roar of the surf are all comforting companions, making this course extremely popular with locals. (The $10–$15 kama'aina rates might also be a factor). Weekends are very busy, Tuesday and Thursday are slowest. While the course is long, there are relatively few hazards, making it a leisurely course. Wind is always a consideration here. Hole 17 requires restraint, lest you drive it into the sand. (The *real* sand and its accompanying surf.) The locker room and other facilities are no-frills. Singles are paired up. Rates are $32 on weekdays, $44 on weekends (plus $14 for the optional cart, $5 for a push cart). A five-round pass is $135. Club rental available for $15.

KAUA'I LAGOONS; MOKIHANA COURSE
241-6000, OR (800) 634-6400

Formerly the Lagoons Course, it's one of the two courses operated by Kaua'i Lagoons and is not part of the Kaua'i Marriott. Designed by Jack Nicklaus and opened in 1989, the **Mokihana** has become popular with locals due to its lower fees. Not as challenging as the **Kiele** course, the **Mokihana** also seems to receive less maintenance and has been relegated to the status of the less deserving cousin course. While the **Mokihana** offers a pleasant golfing experience, it is not as spectacular as some of the other courses and might disappoint those who have been told to "make sure you golf at the Marriott." The adjacent airport and its accompanying jets can be a bit annoying. If your golfing days are few and precious here, consider playing the **Kiele** or driving to the north shore. But if you have golfing days to burn, the **Mokihana** is a pleasant course.

Located at Kaua'i Lagoons, take the Rice Street entrance and proceed past the hotel. Fees are $120, with discounts if you are staying at one of several resorts. (For example, Marriott customers pay $75.) Price drops to $65 after 11 a.m. Carts are included in the price. Kama'ainas pay $45.

KAUA'I LAGOONS; KIELE COURSE
241-6000, OR (800) 634-6400

This is considered one of the tougher courses around and is replete with thick, lush, woodsy areas along the cart paths and luscious ocean views. Also designed by Jack Nicklaus and opened in 1988, the **Kiele** was the finest course on the island until the **Prince** opened up on the north shore. It's still outstanding. The greens at hole 16 command a fabulous view of the ocean chiseling its way

inland. Many of the holes are difficult and rewarding. It's usually rated in the top 100 courses by various magazines.

Located at Kaua'i Lagoons, take the Rice Street entrance and proceed past the hotel. Fees are $170 with discounts if you are staying at one of several resorts. (For example, Marriott customers pay $120.) Kama'aina rates available. Carts are included in the price and are mandatory. Price drops to $99 at noon.

KIAHUNA GOLF CLUB 742–9595

At one time Kiahuna Golf Club's owners boasted that their Robert Trent Jones, Jr.-designed course was the best on Kaua'i. Those days, if they ever existed, are *long* gone. Now it is somewhat run down, and its current owners seem to have lost interest. There is a slightly cramped feel to it. The course's main boast is not its play, but the *heiaus* and other ancient structures on the course. The greens are often extremely slow. With a par of 70 and fairly easy holes, **Kiahuna** is good for the ego but lacks

pizzazz. In general, the only reason to golf at **Kiahuna** is for the price. If you can swing it (so to speak), you're better off at one of the other courses.

Located on Kiahuna Plantation Drive off Po'ipu Road (520), see map on page 73. $75 for standard 18 holes, $45 for 9. Kama'aina rate for 18 holes is $40. Carts are included in the price and are mandatory. Only a $10 discount for playing after 11 a.m. It was for sale at press time, so we're hoping new owners will breath some life into her.

PO'IPU BAY RESORT (HYATT) 742–8711

With its location on the "sunny south shore," **Po'ipu Bay Resort** is a sprawling 210 acres of wide open golfing. In fact, if it has a flaw, it's that it is too wide open. Even course personnel privately mumble about a dearth of hazards. But this nit-picking aside, **Po'ipu Bay Resort** offers spectacular scenery, impeccable grooming and attention to detail. (They like to brag that they imported their bunker sand from Australia and Idaho.) Designed by

For those who venture off the fairway here at Po'ipu we have some advice: Take the stroke.

(here he is again) Robert Trent Jones, Jr., our only real complaint is that the grass in the rough is allowed to get too soft and shaggy. If you roll just slightly off the fairway, even when you see where it went, it's easy to lose your ball unless you step on it. (Go ahead…say it: *If I shot better I wouldn't be in the rough.* Ooo, that hurts.) The links style course is nicely designed with particularly smashing views from holes 15–17. Look for turtles in the water when you're near the *heiau* (an ancient Hawaiian structure) on hole 16. During winter months you might even see whales off the coast. The course is not as challenging as Princeville's Prince Course (but it can be windier), and players less comfortable in the game will enjoy it as much as the more advanced. Collared golf shirts are requested. They have GPS distance locators in the golf carts—which is cool—but we're uncertain as to their accuracy. Even after the government improved GPS signals, we found we could drive carts to within 15 yards of a hole, yet the locator would indicate 40 or 50 yards to go.

Located off Po'ipu Road (520); see map on page 73. Fees are $185 for the general public, $125 for Hyatt guests and a kama'aina rate of $75. Carts are included in the price and are mandatory. At noon price drops to $120. By the way, so you don't go blind looking for it, there *is* no such place as Po'ipu Bay.

KUKUIOLONO GOLF COURSE 332–9151

In 1919, sugar magnate Walter D. McBryde donated his personal 9-hole golf course and some surrounding land to the people of Kaua'i. This land, complete with a trust, has been cherished by Kaua'i residents ever since. To get into the park, you pass through a magnificent metal gate with lava stone pillars. Once inside,

the personal nature of the course is apparent. The links are not as lavish as others on the island; its location in Kalaheo does not afford it much rainfall, and the maintenance budget is not in the same league as the big boys. And it was not designed by Robert Trent Jones, Jr.; in fact, they don't know *who* designed it. But this course might leave you with a smile. They even sell bird seed to feed the ubiquitous tame chickens. The price can't be touched. $7 *per day* with power carts costing $6 and pull carts $2 per nine holes. Club rental for $6 available, but check in advance. Course personnel can be snotty and unprofessional, but don't let it get to you. It's the course that's the star here. If you're playing 18 holes, play from the blue tees for the back nine— 6,154 yards of pleasant, easy-going golf. Especially good for beginners since there aren't many hazards. If you want to personally thank Mr. McBryde, you'll find him buried near the 8th tee, in the middle of his lovely and cherished Japanese garden. This charming garden is worth a look, and local weddings occur here almost every weekend.

Open to everyone, this course is located $8/10$ of a mile from Highway 50 on Papalina Road (the only stoplight in Kalaheo). Look for a gate on your right. No advance tee times.

PUAKEA GOLF COURSE 245–8756

This is a surprisingly good course considering it's unfinished. There are only 10 holes. (An additional 8 were in the works at press time.) The designer, Robin Nelson, must have gotten a good price on sand because he used *a lot* and placed much of it rather sadistically. There's also very little flat ground, keeping the challenges alive. Fairways are spaced far apart. Shortly after it was opened,

Puakea (then called Grove Farm) was rated by *Sports Illustrated* as among the top ten *nine*-hole courses in the country. (Either they couldn't count or they didn't have a list for *ten*-hole courses.)

The views of Ha'upu Mountain are beautiful. The last three holes are memorable. At 8 it's a par 3, but precision is required as a pond edging right up to the green is in front of you. Number 9 summons a solid hit or the sizable gully you need to shoot over will snare a ball. And at 10 they used up all the extra sand they couldn't stuff around the other 9 holes.

In all, Puakea is a fun and rather difficult course. Play 10 for a short but sweet golf game, or go again for a long 20 holes. Located behind Kukui Grove Shopping Center, see map on page 63. Fees for 20 holes are $65 for the general public, $45 for 10 holes and a kama'aina rate of $40. Carts included in price and mandatory. Collared shirts requested. Club rental available for $15.

First, I need to get something out of the way. Flying a powered hang glider (known as a trike) is different than any other type of aircraft. When I was growing up, I used to have a recurring dream that I could flap my arms and fly like a bird. My father flew little Cessnas, which, though fun, felt more to me like a car in the air than flying like a bird. I had forgotten my flying dreams until **Birds in Paradise** (822–5309) began giving lessons in these odd-looking aircraft. I was skeptical at first. Is this for real? Is it safe? Are you *really* allowed to do this? After checking into it a bit I discovered that these newest generation crafts are *far* safer than they were two decades ago. As soon as my instructor

Flying along in a powered hang glider is as close as you'll ever get to feeling like a bird.

and I took off, I realized that a person *really could* fly like a bird. *This* was what the flying bug felt like! I was so smitten with the craft that I eventually paid the owner to teach me, and now I fly trikes myself. So, although I have *no* personal interest in any company teaching trikes in Hawai'i, my perspective isn't as remote as it is for most activities. After all, it's not possible to *anonymously* review Birds in Paradise because I now know the pilot. (We're both members of the small ultralight community.)

With that explanation, powered hang gliding is an activity I love and recommend. Don't confuse this with hang gliding. This craft has an engine, it's bigger and more stable, and it even has a powered parachute attached to the craft...just in case. (A safety feature they're just beginning to install on traditional airplanes.) Trikes take off and land on regular runways, and the ease and grace of the craft is glorious. (Rent the movie *Fly Away Home* if you want to see what they're like.)

Trikes have become quite a love of mine and are, in my opinion, the safest form of ultralight flight available. (I'm not a daredevil and wouldn't fly them myself if I felt unsafe in them, though any time you're in the air you're potentially at risk—even on the airlines.) I grin like a fool *every* time I fly and have never reviewed an activity that generates more enthusiastic responses from other participants. It seems that whenever I see people coming off a trike (I use the same airport that Birds in Paradise does), passengers are *frothing* at the mouth with excitement, proclaiming that it's the best thing they've ever done on vacation.

The pilot, Gerry Charlebois, is certified as an Ultralight Flight Instructor by the EAA and is an internationally known professional hang glider. Though I can't review him anonymously, I can tell you that he is widely considered one of the most skilled trike pilots in the nation with over *8,000* hours in trikes. And, although I have hundreds of hours in trikes myself, I'm still in awe at the deftness with which he handles his craft.

They have a camera mounted on the wing to take a roll of photos of you during the lesson (for $25 extra)—just in case no one back home believes you. There's a 270-pound weight limit. The cost of a half hour in-air lesson is $100. It's $175 for a hour with 2-hour flights available. Expensive? Perhaps. But it's so unspeakably cool that the memories will stay with you for a lifetime.

HELICOPTERS

If ever there was a place made for helicopter exploration, it's Kaua'i. Much of the island can be seen only by air, and helicopters, with their giant windows and their ability to hover, are by far the preferred method for most. Going to Kaua'i without taking a helicopter flight is like going to see the Sistine Chapel and not looking up. You will see the ruggedly beautiful Na Pali Coast and marvel at the sheerness of some of its cliffs. This is an area where razor-thin, almost two-dimensional mountains rise parallel to each other, leaving impossibly tall and narrow valleys between them. You will see vertical spires and shake your head in disbelief at the sight of a goat perched on top. The awe-inspiring Waimea Canyon—dubbed "the Grand Canyon of the Pacific" by Mark Twain—unfolds

Na Pali by air is like no other place in the world.

beneath you. A good pilot will come up over a ridge, suddenly exposing the glorious canyon, often timed to coincide with a crescendo in the music you hear in your headphones. You will see the incredible Olokele Valley with its jagged twists and turns and stair-step waterfalls. It is impossible to keep track of all the waterfalls you will see on your flight. You will get a different view of Kauaʻi's fabulous north shore beaches and reefs. You might see whales, depending on the time of year. And best of all, you will be treated to the almost spiritual splendor of Waiʻaleʻale Crater. You have never seen anything like the crater—a three-sided wall of waterfalls 3,000 feet high, greens of every imaginable shade and a lushness that is beyond comprehension. Many people find themselves weeping when they enter the crater. Others find that they stop breathing—it happened to one of us the first time. If it has been dry lately, it's simply great; if it's been "pumping," it is spectacular.

When you are finished with the flight, you will either be speechless or babble like a fool—it happens to everyone.

Bear in mind that we're not rabidly pro-helicopter. In our Maui book, *Maui Revealed*, we were lukewarm on flights there (fearing a bang-for-your-buck deficit). But on Kauaʻi it's absolutely worth it.

One concern you may have is safety, and that's a valid point. As far as the industry safety record is concerned, there have been crashes and "incidents," when a craft has had to make an unscheduled landing. You can ask the companies directly about safety, but you should be aware that over the years when we've tried it, we're often misled or directly lied to. Not every time, but many times.

When we checked with the FAA, we

discovered that, like many things, safety evaluation isn't that simple. A company might be cited for maintenance violations—*that* sounds ominous. Then you find out that the maintenance was carried out properly, but a log was dated incorrectly or the company didn't fill out a particular form. Should we steer you away from them for this reason?

In the end it comes down to a matter of judgment. Below is a list of companies that we feel are qualified. Others on the island have not been evaluated. Not all have spotless safety records. Things happen—a warning light comes on and you have to land immediately. Even if it was a false alarm, it is still considered an "incident." These companies struck us as honest and forthright in their concerns about safety.

As far as seating is concerned, the front seat is the best. To console you, some companies might tell you otherwise when they direct you to a back seat. From the front, the island rushes at you with incredible drama. The problem is that seating arrangements are made on the basis of weight. Lighter people are generally seated up front. If you are seated in the back, the **right seat** is the best since much of the action will be on the right side. (By common agreement companies fly clockwise around the island,

making Na Pali and other areas best from the right side.) Although companies won't guarantee you the *front* seat, ask them if they'll at least keep you on the *right side* of the craft and let them know you'll consider them weasels if they don't comply. Most will accommodate. If they don't, consider going elsewhere.

A-Stars have two passengers up front and four in the back, leaving two people in the middle. Helicopter companies like these crafts since they can fly six passengers at a time. There are usually no windows to open, so glare may be a factor with your pictures. **Bell Jet Rangers** have one passenger up front, three in back. They have a small window to open to get better pictures. The back middle seat on the Jet Ranger is a poor seat and some people complain about the open window making things windy. Between the A-Stars and the Bells, we like A-Stars for comfort and visibility and Bells *only* for photography (due to the sliding window). **Hughes 500** aircraft have two in the front and two in the back, a great arrangement. The Hughes has the pilot sit on the left side, out of the way. (*Some* new A-Stars like Air Kaua'i's and Jack Harter's do as well.) Hughes have large, removable windows. While the back is a bit cramped and doesn't allow the forward view that other back seats allow,

Company	Phone #	Status	Helicopter Type	2-Way *	Departs
Inter-Island	335–5009	Recommended	Hughes 500	Yes	Hanapepe
Air Kaua'i	246–4666	Recommended	A-Star	Yes	Lihu'e
Jack Harter	245–3774	Recommended	Jet and A-Star	Yes	Lihu'e
Will Squyres	245–8881	Qualified	A-Star	No	Lihu'e
Safari	246–0136	Qualified	A-Star	Yes	Lihu'e
Island	245–8588	Qualified	Jet and A-Star	Yes	Lihu'e
Ohana	245–3996	Qualified	A-Star	No	Lihu'e, Hanapepe
South Sea	245–2222	Qualified	Jet and A-Star	Yes	Lihu'e
Heli USA	826–6591	Qualified	A-Star	Yes	Princeville
Ni'ihau	335–3500	Specialized	Agusta	No	Hanapepe
* Indicates whether craft contains a microphone for you to talk to the pilot.					

their side views are better. Unfortunately, only one recommended company uses these, **Inter-Island**. It's because the Hughes cost more to operate than Bells and don't carry six people like A-Stars.

All helicopters on Kaua'i are allowed to fly 500 feet over most scenic areas. (Companies that claim only *they* can fly that low...are full of beans.)

This is a hard section to write. You're going to spend a lot of money, and we *really* want to point you in the right direction. Most of the companies do a pretty good job, but they're very different. (Of course, like another activity that comes to mind—*wink, wink*—even when a helicopter ride over Kaua'i is bad...it's still good.) The difference between helicopter companies is the difference between a very pleasant flight and really experiencing the island. It's the difference between coming off the craft with a pleasant smile and coming off with a stupid grin on your face that won't leave all day. Between having a tale to tell and experiencing something so moving that it will stay with you for a lifetime. All this said and done, our favorites are **Inter-island**, **Air Kaua'i** and **Jack Harter**.

RECOMMENDED COMPANIES

Inter-Island—The most unusual helicopter trip on the island. When you get into the Hughes from Hanapepe's Port Allen Airport (a good take-off point), the first thing you notice is that the doors are off. Now *that's* a view! During the flight they do something no one else was doing at press time—they *land* at an inaccessible waterfall. After 30 minutes or so of frolicking in the pool (did you bring your swim suit?) and deli lunch, it's back in the chopper to finish the trip. Front seat passengers usually go in back and vice versa—*cool!* Their route is a bit different

than other operators with some impressive locations. It gets pretty cold and sometimes wet in the back and the wind in your eyes and hair might be an annoyance (so pony-tail those long locks), but the 60+ minutes in the air and 30 on the ground provide a flight that you can't get elsewhere. While not as comfortable or cushy as the other flights, it's a fun, if pricey, adventure. $250. Waterfall landings only when weather permits.

Air Kaua'i is our favorite...*sometimes.* They fly A-Stars that have been enhanced, like a luxury car with all the extras. Some of these touches are now offered by other companies, but Air Kaua'i has them all. Like the *extra large* windows so visibility from the back seats is much better. Their A–Stars are air conditioned and have the pilot sitting on the left side, out of the way. They use the expensive noise-cancelling headphones. These don't filter out all external sounds, just selective sounds. (We men know all about filtering out selected sounds.) Also, the pilot's voice doesn't totally stomp on the music, and their sound system allows the pilot to randomly choose the music throughout the tour instead of a single tape. This is important since the music in one location may work better than at another. They even turn off the chopper during loading, a time luxury others at Lihu'e Airport don't attempt. Chuck, the owner and operator, is probably the best tour pilot on the island. He was born to do this. He doesn't fill the tour with mindless chatter the way some others do and abides by our personal helicopter tour mantra: DON'T SPEAK UNLESS IT IMPROVES THE SILENCE. There's a time to talk and a time to shut up. The island, after all, is the star. Some pilots seem to forget that. His narration seems the perfect mix.

You won't feel rushed on his tour. Notice how we personalized this description? It's because other pilots at Air Kaua'i aren't nearly as good, a problem that leads to consistency. The other pilots are still flying the best A-Stars on the island, but their narration is badly lacking by comparison and this can have a surprising impact on the whole experience. $230 for an hour but they usually discount to $172.

Jack Harter—The guy who started it all rarely flies these days, but his company's tours are still in demand, so book in advance. They use a Bell Jet and an A-Star (the later keeps the pilot on the left side). Jack has 60–65 minute flights for $179 and an excellent comprehensive 90–95 minute flight for $239. He's the only one with such a flight. It's a good flight for those wishing to take lots of photos since it's not at all rushed, the Bell's windows slide open (ergo, no glare but some wind), and the pilot will have more time to accommodate your photographic wishes. Harter and Inter-Island are the only companies with no on-board music, but their narration is the

most detailed *and accurate* of any company we've ever flown with on any island. The lack of music might take away some of the emotional tone of a Kaua'i air tour, but their knowledge of the island and concern for accuracy is to be applauded.

OTHER QUALIFIED COMPANIES

Safari—We're not a big fan of their tours. At least they use the noise-canceling headphones. One interesting difference, however, is that they videotape

If you ever saw Jurassic Park, *you'll remember this waterfall (real name Manawaiopuna Falls). The only other way to see it is by helicopter (unless your last name happens to be Robinson).*

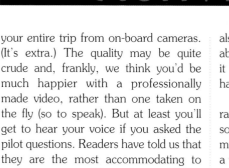
your entire trip from on-board cameras. (It's extra.) The quality may be quite crude and, frankly, we think you'd be much happier with a professionally made video, rather than one taken on the fly (so to speak). But at least you'll get to hear your voice if you asked the pilot questions. Readers have told us that they are the most accommodating to larger passengers. They advertise "Safari coined the phrase: 'Cadillac of helicopters' and other helicopter tour operators have used derivatives through purported third party mediators." Uh...what in the world does *that* mean? $199 an hour.

Will Squyres—Uses air-conditioned A-Stars with pilot on the left and noise-canceling headsets. $159 for an hour. Perhaps because they're big and have the bookings, we've noticed that they do tours on days when we personally wouldn't want to fly due to marginal weather—not from a safety point of view, but a quality-of-product standpoint. If it's too cloudy to see much and dumping rain around much of the island, how much bang for your buck are you getting?

Heli USA—Leaves from Princeville, so their tours are slightly more concentrated over scenic areas. They are a *huge* company, and their pilots seem a bit more like bored tour bus drivers. *(On your left is such-and-such falls, on your right is such-and-such bay.)* Flights from 30–60 minutes. Overall, an unimpressive effort and our least favorite tour but prices start about about $100.

South Sea—Large company. Not the best but not the worst (any more) in our opinion.

Island Helicopters—Cheap if you go to a timeshare presentation that they push when you call up.

Ohana—This is a company with a safety record that concerns us. We're also disappointed that when we've asked about their safety record, we've been told it was "excellent" and that they'd never had a crash. That is profoundly untrue.

Prices from the various companies range between $100 and $230 per person for a flight of between 45 and 75 minutes. These prices sometimes include a video. Many companies have coupons available in ads or give discounts for booking direct or online. (Just ask them.) Charter rates are between $675 and $1,100 per hour.

Be wary of some of the information imparted during some of these flights, especially from bigger companies that may have pilots from the mainland with little knowledge of Kaua'i. They mean well, but often their "facts" are way off.

HELICOPTER TIPS

- Never take a flight less than an hour; you will only get your appetite whetted. It's too rushed.
- With a still camera, zoom lenses work best since the size of the field changes rapidly.
- Use fast film—ASA/ISO 200 or 400.
- Beware of the glare from the inside of the windows, and don't let your camera touch a vibrating window while shooting. Circular polarizers reduce glare as does dark clothing.
- Don't get so caught up taking pictures that you lose the moment. It's hard to soak up the magic of your flight through a camera viewfinder.
- If you're in a craft that has two-way communication, don't be afraid to ask the pilot to turn so you can take a shot of something. Most will.
- If you're prone to motion sickness, take something *before* you fly.
- Remove any earrings before putting on the headphones.

ACTIVITIES

- If you can't hear the pilot over the music, ask him to adjust the sound.
- If there are four or more of you, consider chartering a helicopter. It might actually be cheaper and will allow you to call many of the shots during the flight. "Pilot, please hover here for a few minutes, and turn a little more to the right." If only your group is on the flight, you are effectively chartering the flight whether you realize it or not, so take advantage of it.
- Morning is usually the best time for flights (though Na Pali looks best in the afternoon). Rainy weather brings more waterfalls.
- If you do a helicopter trip, make it early in your stay. It'll help orient you to the island.
- When you see people getting off a helicopter after their tour, try not to be downwind from them. They are often foaming at the mouth from their experience and might drool on you.

For an off-island helicopter experience, **Ni'ihau Helicopters** at 335–3500, owned by the powerful Robinson family, flies groups to their privately owned island of Ni'ihau. For $280 you get a 3-hour flight, circumnavigating Ni'ihau and landing at one of its beaches for snorkeling and a picnic. The problem you encounter with them is that they require at least 4 people on a flight and don't usually have enough customers to ensure a flight for you. Even if they do, their twin-engine Agusta is almost always being chartered for commercial work (such as the military, which uses it for electronic warfare exercises). If you are determined to take the flight, contact them as much in advance as possible to maximize the chance that they can organize a flight, but don't be surprised if it doesn't work out.

AIRPLANE TOURS

If you don't like helicopters and still want to see Kaua'i by air, **Fly Kaua'i** at 246–9123 provides tours by airplane. It's nowhere *near* as thrilling as a helicopter tour, but a bi-plane is snazzy. At $150 per person for an hour-long flight ($89 for 30 minutes), it's not any cheaper than a helicopter, but they only take 2 passengers at a time, so tours are more personalized. Kevin, the owner/operator, is the most skilled fixed-wing airplane pilot we've ever flown with and makes the absolute best of his airplane.

Of all the Hawaiian Islands, none offers more trails or better hiking than Kaua'i. You could spend an entire month on Kaua'i, hiking every day and not see half the trails that the island has to offer. And those are just the official *maintained* trails.

We have added *lots* of new hikes to this edition. We've also made some close-up maps to assist on specific hikes. Additionally, there are several *excellent* hikes listed under ADVENTURES since they're a bit...different.

If you plan to do a lot of hiking, contact the agencies below for information packets on their trails:

Division of State Parks
3060 Eiwa St., Room 306
Lihu'e, HI 96766
(808) 274-3444

Division of Parks and Recreation
4444 Rice St., Room 150
Lihu'e, HI 96766
(808) 241-6660

We defy you to find a finer setting for lunch than this one along the Po'omau Canyon Ditch Trail.

If you need to **rent** camping or hiking gear, your best sources will be **Kayak Kaua'i** in Hanalei at 826–9844 and in Kapa'a at 822–9179 or **Pedal 'n Paddle** in Hanalei at 826–9069. For walking in streams or anything slippery, nothing beats **tabis**. Like felt-covered mittens for your feet, they provide impressive traction on mossy rocks. (No ankle support, though.) **Waipouli Variety** (822–1014) and **Kmart** in Kapa'a are your best bets.

Good places to buy other gear include the variety stores around the island: **Village Variety** (826–6077) in Hanalei, **Waipouli Variety** (822–1014) in Kapa'a and **Discount Variety** (742–9393) in Koloa. Don't forget **Wal-mart** and **Kmart** in Lihu'e.

NOTE ABOUT GPS USE: We don't put latitude and longitude on our maps because some GPS receivers will read incorrectly, relative to the standard benchmark government topographic maps. This is because Hawai'i topos use what's called OLD HAWAIIAN DATUM, which can make you think you're ⁴⁄₁₀ mile south/southeast of where you *really* are. (We pulled out *lots* of hair before we figured out *that* one.)

Lastly, a hiking stick can be helpful on some trails. We sometimes even use two on long hikes and find that they greatly ease climbing and descending and give better balance, in addition to their usefulness in probing mud puddles. It's also useful during the months when tiny **crab spiders** are active. Their minor bites aren't dangerous, just annoying, especially if you get one in the face. Just wave a stick in front of you if you notice any on the trail. In a flash of brilliance, they were brought to the islands on purpose to attack a farming pest. Didn't work—smooth move, guys! (Next, they'll probably want to bring in *tarantulas* to get rid of the mosquitoes.)

ACTIVITIES

KOKE'E/WAIMEA CANYON AREA

In Koke'e State Park you'll find exceptional hiking, with the additional benefit of higher altitude and its accompanying cooler temperatures. The map on page 138 shows the layout of the trails and dirt roads. The dirt roads, even when graded well, become *very* slick when wet. As a result, you may have to walk to some of the trailheads, lest you find yourself stranded. It's a good idea to check in at the Koke'e Museum (335–9975, open 10–4) before you hike to get up-to-date information.

By the way, some of the trails in Koke'e require a 4WD vehicle (or a *long* walk) to get to them. As an alternative to a 4WD, consider renting a mountain bike and bringing it up to the canyon in your car. Then ride it out and hide it in the forest near the trailhead, and you will find that your hiking options greatly increase. One such hike is listed under ADVENTURES on page 188.

The Po'omau Canyon Ditch Trail

Formerly called The Ditch Trail, this is an outstanding hike and one of our favorites in the park. This trail was closed for over a decade after 1982's Hurricane 'Iwa and a series of landslides scuffed it up, but it was reopened in the 1990s. It sports incredible views, lush and exotic surroundings and a dizzying finger of land that sticks out into the canyon and overlooks two glorious waterfalls at one shot. It also has a smashing grassy overlook with a canyon view custom made for a picnic lunch. This is a truly beautiful trail. Originally cut in 1926 to assist Koke'e Ditch workers, it's unofficially kept up by volunteers. There are two segments. The first is moderately strenuous at most, and the second is fairly strenuous. Long pants can be useful if the blackberry bushes (and

their evil thorns) are sticking out into the trail. The footing is occasionally obnoxious, especially on the second half, and there are opportunities for the genetically clumsy or the vertiginous to take a long roll.

To get there take, Waineke Road (across from the Koke'e Museum) to Mohihi (Camp 10) Road and drive on the main dirt road. Either park at the intersection of Mohihi and Kumuwela Road and walk a mile on Mohihi Road to the trailhead, or drive farther, until you're 1%10 miles from Hwy 550. From here, it's a ¾ mile walk to the trailhead. (4WDs won't have a problem with the last ¾ mile, but cars may unless it's *real* dry and you're *real* confident it will stay that way.) The unmarked trailhead is *on your right* angling back toward the road exactly 2¼ miles from Hwy 550. (If you come to a bridge with metal slats, you've gone 600 feet too far. The trailhead is *just before* a road turnout and was only marked with a HIGH FIRE DANGER sign at press time. Look for it on your right when the 30-foot high wall of rock and dirt on your left is about to end. See map. If you have to cross a concrete walkway at the beginning of the trail, *you're on the wrong trail.*)

Almost as soon as you start the trail, you will come to a wild ginger grove. This is your canary in a cage. If the gin-

ger grove is too thick to walk through, it means you are unlucky enough to be here toward the end of this trail's volunteer-run maintenance cycle and that the rest of the trail is overgrown, as well. Might want to do a different hike.

The trail winds its way through primordial-looking jungle with ferns, birds and often the sound of running water to keep you company. Toward the end of the first half, there is a narrow ridge of land on your left; look for it. This is only for the intrepid, as the drop on either side is rather conclusive. At the end is a vista from a poet's dream. On the far wall is a thunderous cascade pounding its way down. Next to it is a multi-step waterfall plunging into a deep pool with the awesome canyon all around you. You will probably interrupt other visitors—bleating goats are almost always perched up here.

After the ridge, continue on the trail until it encounters a spur to Kumuwela Road. Either circle around on the road, or continue on the second half of the trail. It's a tad hairier in spots but worth it. Half a mile from the end, you cross a stream. If you take the short trail to the left first, you will be rewarded with a perfect place to have your lunch. It's the grassy bank of an old waterfall (before the ditch cut it off), which overlooks the valley in a setting that is right out of a movie. Sit under the sugi tree for a while, and you won't *ever* want to leave.

At the end of the trail, you can walk two miles on Kumuwela Road (or take Kumuwela and Waininiua Trails) back to Mohihi Camp 10 Road and your awaiting car. Now *there's* a hike to savor!

Pihea Trail to Alaka'i Swamp

This trail starts at the end of Waimea Canyon Road at the Pu'u o Kila Lookout. It combines awesome views of Kalalau Valley and takes you through the

The Alaka'i Swamp Trail's boardwalk meanders to a spectacular end at a sheer cliff overlooking the island's north shore 4,000 feet below the lookout.

ACTIVITIES

Koke'e Trails Map

The nature of the terrain at Koke'e makes it difficult to convey the type of hiking each trail provides. This accurate computer-generated shaded relief map is drawn from an angled perspective to give you a feel for the lay of the land. Since this is a perspective map, the mileage scale should be a little smaller at the top of the map (since it's "farther away" from your eyes) and a little bigger at the bottom of the map.

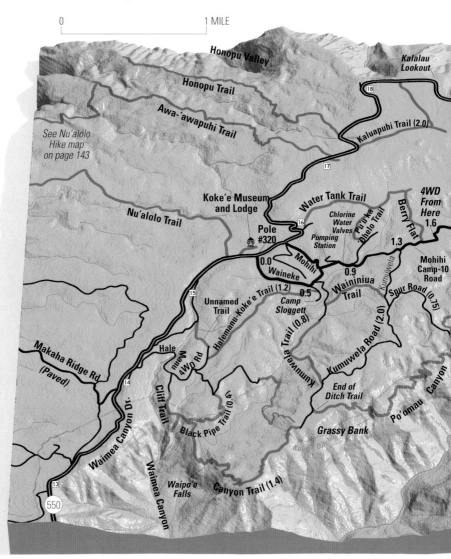

0   1 MILE

Note: Distances given for trails are one way. Distances listed along Mohihi-Camp 10 Road are from the intersection of Waineke Road and Waimea Canyon Road near telephone pole 320. Don't be fooled by a sign at that intersection saying Kumuwela Road.

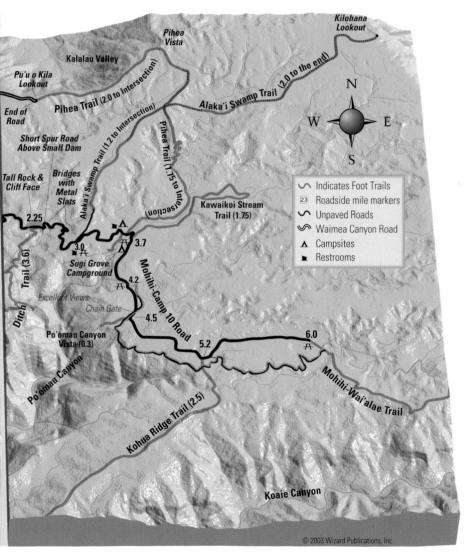

Kilohana Lookout

Pihea Vista

Kalalau Valley

Pu'u o Kila Lookout

Alaka'i Swamp Trail (2.0 to the end)

Pihea Trail (2.0 to Intersection)

End of Road

Short Spur Road Above Small Dam

Alaka'i Swamp Trail (1.2 to intersection)

Pihea Trail (1.75 to Intersection)

Tall Rock & Cliff Face

Bridges with Metal Slats

2.25

3.0

3.7

Kawaikoi Stream Trail (1.75)

Ditch Trail (3.6)

Sugi Grove Campground

4.2

Excellent Views

Chain Gate

4.5

Mohihi-Camp 10 Road

Po'omau Canyon Vista (0.3)

5.2

6.0

Po'omau Canyon

Kohua Ridge Trail (2.5)

Mohihi-Wai'alae Trail

Koaie Canyon

⌒ Indicates Foot Trails
23 Roadside mile markers
⌒ Unpaved Roads
〰 Waimea Canyon Road
Λ Campsites
■ Restrooms

highest swamp in the world. The terrain in the swamp is like nothing you've ever seen, and we've been told many times that it was the highlight of many people's hiking experience on Kaua'i. You're insulated from the mud *most* of the time by a wooden boardwalk.

The Pihea Trail skirts the edge of Kalalau Valley, passing through native 'ohi'a and fern forest. (See map on previous page.) About a mile into it, a very short but *steep* spur trail leads to the Pihea Vista. Nice, but tricky to walk up to—it's optional. (Long legs help.) Just past this junction, the trail is covered in most spots by a boardwalk to keep you from wallowing in the mud. (The part of the trail before the boardwalk is sometimes muddy, so be forewarned.) When the trail intersects the Alaka'i Swamp Trail, go left (east); it's about 2 miles to the end. The Alaka'i Swamp Trail leads to the edge of a cliff where the Kilohana Lookout affords a majestic view of Ha'ena on the north shore, clouds permitting. Imagine hiking to this point before the boardwalk was installed. Then imagine that the hard part was *still to come*. That's because the ancient Hawaiians used this trail to get to the north shore when the surf precluded going by sea. Once at Kilohana, they went over and down the 3,400-foot cliff to the valley floor and along the sloping valley to the ocean. All this for west siders to visit family on the north shore in the winter. (Remember this the next time you think you're too busy to drive across town to see Mom.) Along the trail you'll see old telephone poles. They were erected by the military after the attack on Pearl Harbor and stretched across the swamp, down the cliffs of Kilohana and into Hanalei. They served as a backup communications line in case

the Japanese captured Lihu'e.

Even without the view at the end it's probably the most unusual hike on the island. Full grown trees on the flats rarely exceed 5 feet tall. Submerged grasses, vines and moss-covered trees sheltering endemic birds (found nowhere else) make this a memorable hike. Fog rolls in and out constantly, adding to the mystery of the scenery. You've *never* seen wilderness like this. While you're on this boardwalk, you'll have the same thought as everyone else—"My *God*, this must have been a wretched hike before they installed this." Darned straight! It's about 8 miles round trip from your car, but you can just go as far as your desire takes you. The boardwalk system was created in the late '90s and was quite a task. Even with it, expect to get a little muddy from patches where the boardwalk was left out. If you want to avoid the sometimes sloppy stretch of the Pihea Trail, you can just do the Alaka'i Swamp Trail from its beginning off Mohihi Camp 10 Road. (See Map.) You'll probably need a 4WD or mountain bike to get to the Alaka'i Trailhead off Mohihi. Pihea's car access from the end of Waimea Canyon Road makes it the better route.

Canyon Trail to Waipo'o Falls

Another favorite, this one is also moderately strenuous and will probably take you 2–3 hours (including the dirt road to the trailhead), depending on how long you linger. Along the way you will get unparalleled views of the canyon from the other side, visit two waterfalls and find a cold pool to swim in, if you like.

You park your car at the top of Hale Manu Valley Road between the 14 and 15 mile markers on Waimea Canyon Rd. and walk $^8/_{10}$ mile down the road (with a 240-foot loss in elevation) to the trail-

head, unless you have a 4WD. *See* map.) As soon as the trail starts, you have the option of going to the lookout off to your right. You might want to save that for the end, since other views will be better.

After you are exposed to the great canyon views, you will come to the top of a ridge. Keep an eye out for goats on the opposite walls. Look south for a provocative-looking rock arch, out where it's impossible for man to have created it. (You will see it closer from waterfall #2.) The light in this part of the canyon is usually best in the late afternoon (around 3 p.m.).

Just past and below the ridge, you will come to an intersection, indicating Fall #1 and Fall #2. Number one is tiny, but the pool is cool and refreshing. Fall #2 takes a two-step plunge down 800 feet. You're at the top. These falls sometimes flow a bit low, especially in the summer, so don't be disappointed. Just enjoy the delicious scenery, complete with wild ginger everywhere, before making your way back.

Nuʻalolo Trail / Nuʻalolo Cliffs / Awa-ʻawapuhi Grand Loop

This is a great hike! It takes most of a day and is strenuous, but you're treated to views that will stay frozen in your mind for a lifetime. If you're up for a long day hike on Kauaʻi, this is the one. And you may be surprised at how few people you see along the way.

First, the gory details. It's either $9^8/_{10}$ or $11^3/_{10}$ miles (the latter if you have to walk Waimea Canyon Road back down to your car) and involves about 2,000 feet of altitude change, 1,500 of which is climbing the last leg. But *oh,* the sights you will see. The vertiginous may object to a place or two, but they won't want to miss it.

There are three trails. Nuʻalolo Trail starts near the Kokeʻe Lodge and heads toward the ocean, Awa-ʻawapuhi brings you back up, and Nuʻalolo Cliffs links the

Nuʻalolo Valley looks radically different from every angle.

two. When you finish at the Awa-'awa-puhi trailhead, you're 1½ miles up the road from your car. So either leave a car there, or you'll have to walk back down the narrow road to your car.

This hike is downhill for the first third, mostly flat for the second and a gentle but constant incline for the last third.

Start at the Nu'alolo Trailhead just south of Koke'e Lodge. (This is better than doing it from Awa-'awapuhi first.) *Coming from the lodge*, the 3⁸⁄₁₀ mile-long trail is on your right. After a short climb you'll descend a forest that will change from bird-filled koa forest to patches of wild flowers to dryland forest to exposed ridge. All are a tribute to the rain's infatuation with increasingly higher altitudes. The trail will split in a few

Take a break along the Nu'alolo Cliffs Trail.

places but quickly rejoins. By the way, part of this trail is open to hunting during some parts of the year. It's highly unlikely that you'll encounter a hunter, but it's probably best to avoid practicing those new pig calls you just learned.

About 3 miles into the hike is the turnoff for a hunter trail. Bypass it. At 3⁴⁄₁₀ mile is the intersection of Cliff Trail. Don't take Cliff Trail just yet; instead continue another ⅓ mile to Lolo Vista Point. Swallow hard. You're on the upper edge of an Eden-like valley. The view will take your breath away—and then some. Nu'alolo Valley is unimaginably beautiful, and the Na Pali coast looks endless beneath you. This is the bluff where Harrison Ford had his tree-choking tantrum in *6 Days/7 Nights.* (Though *he* got here by helicopter.) Surely it can't get better than this. Think again. As you go back and start the 2¹⁄₁₀ mile long Nu'alolo Cliffs Trail, you are almost immediately presented with an even more dramatic view—if that's possible. This trail was rerouted when Hurricane 'Iwa rubbed out the old inland trail in 1982. So here *you* are, at the back of the valley looking toward the ocean, half a mile below and a mile in front of you. *This* has got to be the best view on Kaua'i, right? So you'd think.

After a rest at the picnic shelter a little farther, the trail turns into deeper forest. This stretch is one of the loveliest in the park, where birds abound and the scenery is delicious. There are a few false trails that lead to nowhere. Stay on the main trail. After playing in your own personal waterfall (yep, it's got one of those, too, though it's occasionally dry) you hit the Awa-'awapuhi Trail. The highway is to your right, but you head left ⅓ mile.

Nothing can prepare you for what you are about to see. Just when you thought it couldn't get any better the

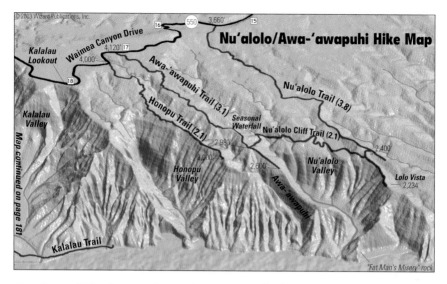

© 2003 Wizard Publications, Inc.

Nu'alolo/Awa-'awapuhi Hike Map

Kalalau Lookout
Waimea Canyon Drive 4,120' 17
4,000'
16 550 3,660' 15

Awa-'awapuhi Trail (3.1)

Honopu Trail (2.1)

Kalalau Valley
18

Kalalau Trail

Nu'alolo Trail (3.8)

Seasonal Waterfall
Nu'alolo Cliff Trail (2.1)

2,980

3,000
Honopu Valley

2,600

Nu'alolo Valley

2,400

Lolo Vista
2,234

Awa-'awapuhi

Map continued on page 181

"Fat Man's Misery" rock

Awa-'awapuhi Lookout steals your heart with cliffs so sheer and green they can't possibly be real. Can *this* be the same Nu'alolo Valley you saw before? High altitude-flying white-tailed tropic birds laugh and soar *beneath* you. Knife-edge ridges you didn't even know were there stand against the cliff. This is a side of God's handiwork that you never knew existed. Revel, savor, remember.

The view from past the guard-rail is even better, but you're unprotected. If you fall, the first step is a fairly jarring 2,000 feet. To the right is the almost vertical Awa-'awapuhi Valley. Check out the spires at the valley mouth.

Rested? Good. It's time to pay the piper. You're at 2,600, feet and the road is 3¹⁄₁₀ miles away at 4,120 feet. Fortunately, it's fairly gentle most of way.

SOME WARNINGS: You should start this hike no later than 10 a.m. (earlier if possible). Hiking boots are a good idea. This is not a good trail if it's been raining a lot in Koke'e. Avoid when muddy, or bring your bobsled. Hiking *up* Nu'alolo when muddy is awful—another reason we

come back up via Awa-'awapuhi. As for water, bring at least twice as much as you think you'll need. After all, the first ²⁄₃ is downhill or fairly flat, so lugging the water that far is relatively painless. Drink up before you start your ascent, and dump any water you don't want to carry. That's infinitely better than walking up Awa-'awapuhi dry (as *we* did the first time). There's a brochure at the museum that identifies marked plants on the Awa-'awapuhi Trail. It's great if you took the trail *down* (which we advise *against* since you're better off taking Nu'alolo down), but you're probably too pooped to care coming up. Besides, many of the markers have been removed.

Kuku'i Trail

While gazing into Waimea Canyon, you may wonder if there's a trail down into it. Yup. And lucky for you it's down the road at a lower elevation near the 9 mile marker, so you *only* have to descend (and, of course, ascend) 2,300 feet. Ah, but what views you'll see on your way down as the canyon changes

ACTIVITIES

in appearance. It's 2½ miles to the river below. (Not much distance to lose almost half a mile in elevation, so the grade is steep.) At the bottom is Wiliwili Camp. Make *sure* you bring enough water for the trek back up. Too many people underestimate the climb, and they're fantasizing about water on the way up.

If you don't want to go all the way down, there's a good viewpoint ⅓ mile into the trail and a *spectacular* viewpoint at the bench 1 mile into (and 750 feet below) the trailhead. Past this, the trail goes through forest.

Mohihi–Wai-ʻalae Trail

First things first. If you don't have a 4WD vehicle, you probably won't be doing this trail unless it's *real* dry and you have *lots* of confidence it won't rain. That's because it starts at the end of Mohihi Camp 10 Road, 6 miles from Waimea Canyon Dr. (Hwy 550). See map on page 139 and the description of the road in the Poʻomau Canyon Ditch Trail hike.

If you are blessed with a 4WD vehicle, you'll be treated to one of our favorite trails on the island. Not for any sweeping views—you only get one or two of those. This trail shines because it passes through one of the finest forests you'll ever see.

After parking at the end of Mohihi Road near picnic tables, you'll take the trail down a few minutes, across a foot bridge, and walk toward and to the right of more picnic tables. A sign there saying FOREST RESERVE marks the continuing faint trail to the right of the sign.

Down through a forest of sugi trees, you'll have to cross a stream that you can usually boulder-hop. A few dozen feet after the stream there's a shack. Don't pass it! The trail angles back to the right.

From here it's not so confusing. The trail gains 250 feet, levels out and climbs a bit more until you come to a shaky bench. From here there's a grand view of Koaiʻe Canyon, part of Waimea Canyon.

In all Kauaʻi it's unlikely you'll ever find a more pristine forest than along the Mohihi-Wai-ʻalae trail.

Ti plants grace the end of the 'Okolehao Trail. Turn around and you'll see more of the island from up here than perhaps any other trail on the island.

Soon a flatter area ushers in a world of moss. It's as if someone had a bucket of life and splashed it all over the ground. Be careful not to walk on the mosses themselves.

Around 2 miles from the car brings a plateau with a rain gauge. Until now the trail has been fairly wide. From here it's narrower, with passages through ferns, and there are a few areas that require care as they're on the side of a hill.

If you're game, the next mile is well worth it. It will drop to a luxuriant fern forest, then keeps getting better and better. When you're about 2½ miles from your car, the trail completely levels out. The forest has gotten more and more exotic looking. Gone are the introduced plants of Koke'e. This is an old growth, native forest that looks utterly primeval. The ground is soft and gentle, like walking on thickly padded carpet, and the area feels ancient and undisturbed. The

87 inches of rain this area gets per year are absorbed by the forest floor. Walk slowly and observe how life bursts from every nook and cranny. Native birds, though not numerous, show little or no fear of humans. We've been lucky enough to be here on a sunny day, but even rain won't obscure the healthiest, happiest and most prosperous forest you may ever walk through.

Although the trail keeps going for many, many miles, 3–3½ miles is a good turning-around point. (There are mile markers.) Though this last portion is *reasonably* marked, keep track of where you've been for your return. Try to start early—by 9 a.m., if possible, so you can take your time on this trail. Camping at Sugi Grove can be handy for this.

NORTH SHORE HIKES
Hanalei 'Okolehao Trail

So, you've been especially gluttonous

ACTIVITIES

since you've been here, and the guilt is keeping you awake at night. Here's your chance to work off that lu'au you attended. This trail is a puffer. It gains 1,250 feet in less than 2 miles. That means the grade is steep, tiring and unrelenting. It will seem much longer than it is.

The first ⅔ mile is on the dull remains of an old road. You've left your car and immediately started climbing. By the time the road ends and the *real* trail starts (at a huge power pole whose lines swoop into the valley below), you'll probably hate the trail and hate us for mentioning it. Look to the left, and the trail continues through forest. It's prettier, as it quickly starts climbing the ridge, but just as strenuous. Climb, climb, climb, climb. Then climb some more. There are breaks in the vegetation affording grand views, but you couldn't care less because you're puffing so hard. After about 30 miles (really 1⁹⁄₁₀, but you'll swear we're lying) you are richly rewarded. A lovely plateau dotted with ti plants offers impossibly sweeping views. You can see ⅕ of the entire island, weather cooperating, from Anahola all the way around to the end of the road at Ke'e. Behind you, you'll see Wai'ale'ale and the Hanalei River chiseling its way out of the mysterious center of the island. The Kilauea Lighthouse, Hanalei Bay...no-where is there a more expansive view.

Was it worth it? Only you can say, but we think so. Is the hard part done? 'Fraid not. Coming down is also hard because the constant downhill is hard on the knees...and 'okole if it's wet and you slip.

To get to the trailhead, cross the Hanalei Bridge past the 1 mile marker on Hwy 560 on the north shore. A little more than ½ mile into the road take a

right. At the Chinese cemetery (isn't that an unusual grave in front of you?) hang a left, then a right past the gate. Climb till the end or until you run out of sweat.

Incidentally, the word 'okolehao refers to liquor made from ti roots. In the old days, bootleggers planted ti up here to supply them with raw materials.

The Pools of Mokolea

For those looking for a beautiful, wild shoreline hike but don't want something too long and strenuous, this may be the ticket. It only travels ¼ mile each way from your 4WD car (or ½ mile from a regular car) but has some tasty rewards.

From the 4WD trailhead (directions below) you either go up and down next to a wire fence, or around—either way ending on the lava bench. You'll soon see tide-pools. Fish and crabs scatter at your approach. Lots of ancient metal equipment and parts are scattered along the shore. For 100 years the sugar company dumped worn-out gear here. What was once junk has been transformed by a century of melting rust into an intriguing part of the landscape.

More tide-pools and more lava. It's slow going because you're mostly boulder-hopping on lava rocks, so take your time. Only 800 feet from the end of the road is a large, Jacuzzi-sized hole in the lava where the ocean surges in and out. It's great to watch, but beware of large sets of waves that can surprise you. (This goes for much of the walk along here. Monster surf needs to be evaluated.)

At ¼ mile is Mokolea Point. What a spectacular place! Waves often pummel the area, creating rivulets of water flowing across the lava bench. During low surf a wonderful lava pool graces the area. Several small pools behind the large rock make nice soaking pools if the

The Pools of Mokolea top off a short but sweet shoreline hike.

surf isn't too high. Moderate waves sometimes wash over the bench, replenishing the pools. Overhead, white-tailed tropic birds and shearwaters often soar on the thermals. Kilauea Lighthouse and Crater Hill are 1⅓ mile across the water.

Just past the pools is the end of your hike. The ocean has cut a trench in the lava all the way to the cliff. When there's surf, the ocean comes roaring into the trench, which gets narrower and narrower, eventually undercutting the cliff in a small pocket. The result is a violent ricochet as the water and compressed air explode out of the trap that the lava has set for it. It's like a dragon, breathing water instead of fire. Some waves even hiss as they are expelled. Sometimes rogue waves pound with such ferocity you think the ground will split beneath your feet. Some explosions of water may shower you, so be careful there.

You can get to the marginally defined trailhead from one of two ways. A dirt road off Kilauea Road in Kilauea is ¼ mile from Keneke and the Kong Lung Center. (See map on page 46.) This 1⁷⁄₁₀ mile road (most suitable for 4WD vehicles) terminates on the Mokolea peninsula. Though a sign at the dirt road implies it's private or closed, county documents show it as a *public* access. An alternative way is to take Wailapa Road between the 21 & 22 mile markers off Hwy 56 near Kilauea. Then take the smooth dirt road to Kilauea Bay. Park and find the best place to wade across the stream (unless it's raging) and head toward the right.

The Kalalau Trail

The ultimate hike is also the most famous hike in all Hawai'i. Eleven miles of switchbacks, hills and beautiful scenery. This hike can be a real adven-

ACTIVITIES

Surprises, such as this freshwater cave at the shoreline, await those who hike to Kalalau Beach.

ture. Because of this, we discuss it in detail under ADVENTURES on page 180.

EAST SHORE HIKES
Sleeping Giant (Nounou Mountain)

This is a moderately difficult trail. Actually it's three different trails. The vertical elevation you will gain from the East Trail is 1,000 feet. A thousand feet sounds like a big rise (OK, it *is* a big rise), but this is a hike worth experiencing. Nearly the entire hike is through forests with pretty views. This is a real trail, not an abandoned road like some hiking trails. Of the three trails, the East is the prettiest, longest (at around 2 miles each way) and the least steep, though it involves the most elevation gain. If you take the eastern route, at the third switchback after the ½ mile stake the trail seems to split into 2 paths. *Do not take the left fork, which is on the side of the mountain!* This is probably a pig trail and not

part of the main trail. You won't like it. In fact, other trails that deviate from the main trail are usually bad. Take the time to savor some of the luscious views of the entire east shore from spots. When you get to the main fork in the trail (diligently guarded by hala trees with their A-frame, cage-like roots), take the fork to the left for 3 or 4 minutes to the picnic tables. From here you can see the entire Wailua Valley from Anahola to Lihu'e. The view is not to be missed and well worth the climbing effort expended. Anyone who becomes dizzy from heights should be aware that there are areas along the east side trail where the beautiful sweeping view off to one side is quite steep.

Up at the picnic tables, there is a short trail dipping south across the giant's neck up to his forehead and nose. Or is it his chin? Hard to say. The view from up there is, literally, a once-in-a-lifetime experience. The vista is

without rival. Think *real hard* before you take this part. It is steep, and the spine is almost vertical on both sides. A wrong step, or a slip anywhere near the nose, would almost certainly cost you your life. Just before the summit there is a short trail to your left leading to the hole in the giant's chin, seen from the bottom of Kuamo'o Road. This part of the Nounou Trail is what they call a real 'okole squeezer. Stop at the picnic table unless you are very brave, very foolish and very well insured.

If you take the West Trail or the Kuamo'o-Nounou Trail, you'll find the climbing steeper. A good workout; we like to climb it daily if we've enjoyed a few too many restaurant reviews lately. Kuamo'o-Nounou Trail and West Trail combine at a magnificent strand of Cook Island pines (a very tall and straight pine tree thought, during the Age of Discovery, to make good ships' masts).

Of the three trails to the top, we recommend either the East Trail or the Kuamo'o-Nounou Trail. (The latter has a stretch where mosquitoes might mug you. Use a repellent.) The map on page 59 makes it easy to find the three trailheads.

Kuilau Ridge Trail

This trail begins 1¾ miles past the University of Hawai'i at Manoa, Kaua'i Research Station. The trailhead marker is on the right side as you are coming west on Kuamo'o Road. Park at the Keahua Arboretum.

This is a very nice hike. The first part is a gentle but constant incline that takes you past a myriad of birds. Watch and listen for them. At the end of the incline (about 30 minutes), you will come to a small picnic area overlooking a lovely valley. If it's clear, you will get a stunning view of Mount Wai'ale'ale. This is a nice place to have lunch or just enjoy a long sip of water. *Make sure you go past the picnic tables.* The payoff is 5 minutes later. You will be rewarded with a wonderful razorback, winding, rolling, trek into paradise. *Gorgeous!* There are lush hillsides filled with ferns of every size and shape. Off in the distance you can see the ocean at Kapa'a and all the way to Lihu'e at another point. Very nice. Turn around where the Kuilau Trail ends and the Moalepe Trail begins (see map on page 58) ½ mile past a quaint wooden bridge. (Or continue onto Moalepe Trail, if you like, though Moalepe isn't in as good of condition.) The entire hike should take you 2½ to 3 hours if you hike at a semi-steady pace. Bring water. Hiking boots recommended but tennis shoes OK.

The Powerline Trail

The Powerline Trail is a dirt road cut through mostly untouched wilderness. It was carved by the electric company to facilitate the installation of (surprise!) powerlines in the early 1900s and goes from northeastern Kapa'a to southern Princeville. The road was left to the elements until it was improved in 1996 to put in newer and uglier poles. Only time will tell how long the road stays nice. (I heard many estimates as to the road length, so I took a motorcycle right after they spiffied it up—10¼ miles from gate to gate, according to the odometer.)

This trail is best taken as a shuttle, starting from Kapa'a side (the prettier part of the trail) past the end of Kuamo'o Road, just past the Keahua Arboretum. (See maps on pages 58 and 46 for the two trailheads.) You could leave your car there and take The Kaua'i Bus back from the north shore, but you'd have to take a cab up Kuamo'o Road to your

Otherwise, just take the trail until you get tired, then come back.

There aren't any long climbs, just lots of small ones on the hilly first half of the hike. The second half is mostly a gentle descent into the north shore. The area is lush and undisturbed for most of the way—except for the road and those pesky poles. (I guess we shouldn't whine too much about the poles. If they weren't there, the trail wouldn't be either.) The area is so lush that the absence of plants on the trail is easily visible from space. Look at the front cover—the Powerline Trail is unmistakable. Watch for waterfalls along the way, though none are close enough to visit. At about halfway you will be able to see the ocean on the north shore. What a lovely sight! You can see great distances at many places along the trail. This hike, though tiring, is a fine way to see Kaua'i's wild side. Surprisingly, the trail is usually drier on the northern end than the southern end.

Along the trail there are numerous short spur roads leading to individual poles. Some offer great views. Since the road stays fairly near the poles all the time, and since the main road is easy to stay on, you shouldn't get lost. (Before they improved it, people got lost on it all the time.) It ends at a gate on Kapa ka Road. (Kapa ka Road is between the 27 and 28 mile markers on Highway 56.)

Jungle Hike

If you want a *taste* of the steamy jungle and forest (but without the need for a machete and a gallon of insect repellent), this might be what you're looking for. It leads to a government stream gauging station and passes through some magnificent scenery. Your reward at the end is a small, picturesque stair-step little falls where two streams come together adjacent to a water diversion ditch. (The word ditch has ugly connotations, but often these small dams can make a nice place for a picnic.)

To get there, take Kuamo'o Road (580) all the way until it becomes dirt. (A sign at the Keahua Arboretum says 4WD ONLY, but the road's not *that* bad…probably.) The pavement stops, but you won't. You'll cross a couple streams and stay on the dirt road. When it eventually dead ends, go right and look at your odometer. At ½ mile is a Y. Take the left fork. At 1¼ miles is a left branch. Don't take it; go straight. Then at almost 1½ miles is another Y, then a gate; take the left fork. (If the gate's locked, you have to walk an extra ³⁄₁₀ mile.) At 1⁸⁄₁₀ miles is the second gate. The map on page 191 shows all of this. (This road can get a bit junky between scheduled maintenance. Without a 4WD you *may* have to stop sooner.) Park here and walk down the dirt road. The gate is on state land and was erected to prevent vehicles from going any farther, but it's perfectly legal to go through the gate and continue on foot. Near this gate is where they filmed the ENTRANCE GATE scenes in *Jurassic Park*. It probably won't stop a T-Rex, but it'll keep your car out. The views into Wai'ale'ale Crater from this dirt road can be exceptional, especially in the morning. After walking 10–15 minutes from the gate (½ mile), you'll come upon an ascent. There will be an old turnout on the left side. Keep a sharp eye open for it; it's easy to miss. The trail leading off to the left from this turnout immediately parallels for a short time a water ditch and passes through extremely lush territory. The ferns, birds and trees are abundant along this easy-to-follow but sometimes slippery trail. A pleasant 10–20

This jungle hike is fairly easy and rewards you with a nice place for a picnic.

minute trek up and over a 150-foot high ridge will bring you to a nice, freshwater pool, formed by the small dam. The area around the dam is covered with plant life and can be slippery. A wonderful, secluded spot to eat lunch.

The falls are actually formed by two streams. If you swim across the pool and climb the rocks, then take the right fork for only a few (slippery) minutes you'll come to a small, hidden falls. At the base is something we call the **Jacuzzi**. During low to moderate stream flow the falling water creates bubbles and jets of air that feels remarkably similar to a spa (albeit a cold one). It's *wonderful* to soak in. Just stay out if the flow is too heavy and read page 34 for precautions on swimming in streams. Use your own good judgment.

If you don't want to walk *over* the hill, you can walk *through* it. Where the ditch becomes a tunnel (at a circular cement opening), you can access the tunnel that

goes under the mountain. Most people will have to duck the entire 800 foot length and, of course, if the water flow rate should change while you're in there, you'd have a big problem to deal with. Hmm, maybe that over-the-hill trail isn't so bad after all. Anyway, it's an adventurous option that we've done (when the flow wasn't too high and we had a flashlight), and it's a hoot.

Hoʻopiʻi Falls Hike

Waterfalls have an amazing ability to bring piece of mind. Although Kauaʻi is studded with many waterfalls, most of them are inaccessible for one reason or another—but not this one. There are two falls on the Kapaʻa Stream—and one of them is named Hoʻopiʻi. Some locals call the first one Hoʻopiʻi—government maps give that name to the second falls.

Look at the map below. There are additional trails in this area, but the one

Some call this Ho'opi'i Falls. Others use that name for the next falls down the river. These keikis couldn't care less. They're just enjoying the sound.

to a trail. Go downstream and eventually there's a side path leading down to the first falls. Wow, what a place! A flat lava bench offers a magnificent place to sit and breathe in the falls. The only way to get under those falls is to go downstream and wade back upstream.

Back on the trail, the path eventually parallels the stream. Once there, you need to stay within 10 feet of the stream to stay on state land. A nearby landowner's rep told us he intended to ensure you don't need to stray more than 10 feet, by work-

shown is on state land. The top of the map on page 59 shows you where Kapahi Road is. An old *public* dirt road (now used as a trail) is on your left as you come down Kapahi Road. Please be respectful of the neighborhood here. One resident even posted an irate review of our book on amazon.com because he was upset that we told you how to get to these falls.

Walk down the dirt road and it leads

ing with the state to clarify the trail at the one point it deviated from the stream.

This area is lush and the sound of the stream hypnotic. Just before the second falls the trail crosses the stream, terminating at the top of the falls. (There's no easy way to the bottom.)

If you don't bring mosquito repellent, bring an extra pint of blood for the walk through the woods. Tennis shoes are OK

Ho'opi'i Falls Map

Kapa'a Stream

Kealia Stream

Falls

Old Dirt Road

Falls

Kapahi Road

Trails approximate

Kawaihau Road

© 2003 Wizard Publications Inc.

See top of page 59 to get here

unless you cross the stream for the second falls. Bring water and your camera!

Hiking to Wai'ale'ale

A question we're often asked is *How can I hike to the summit of Wai'ale'ale?* The answer is…you can't. In ancient times Hawaiians used to hike up a ridge on the northeast side of the crater (the ridge that's over the Tunnel Hike on page 188). Near the summit they had rope ladders for the final portion. A landslide and lack of use in the 1800s shut off that route. In the 1970s a person tried, with a helicopter overhead to give radio guidance, and he failed.

The other route used to be through the Alaka'i Swamp, and some government maps still show that trail. It's been gone for years, and even people born and raised here aren't able to make it through the swamp anymore. The rain gauge at the top is now read by helicopter.

SOUTH SHORE HIKES
Po'ipu Shoreline Sandstone Hikes

The lithified cliffs of **Makawehi** next to Shipwreck Beach, as well as the **Maha'ulepu** area, offer excellent shoreline hiking. The Makawehi cliffs are eas-

ily accessed by taking the trail from the parking lot between the Hyatt and the Po'ipu Bay Resort golf course (or simply walking to the east end of the beach). It's over half a mile long, formed from sand dunes deposited here during the last ice age. The wind and salt have clawed and thrashed at these cliffs with impressive results. Take your time and wander about. Look for (but don't remove) fossils in the sand, and enjoy the views.

Maha'ulepu is described in detail under BEACHES on page 108. Another good hike is to start from the end of the dirt road at the low cliffs west of Gillin's Beach House (on map). It's wonderful to walk along here when the surf is raging. At one place there's a hole in the floor of the cliff, allowing you to see the ocean exploding beneath your feet on the lithified bench below. This area looks like an alien landscape. Weekends bring fishermen who tend to leave reminders of their hobby here.

You could walk all the way to the Hyatt, if you wanted. The wind, pounding surf and beautiful cliffs create an amazingly relaxing walk, even if the ground is a bit lumpy. About ⅔ of the way to the Hyatt, the cliff gives way to a sandy pocket affording a luscious view of the cliffs.

Melted Metal and Keyhole Cave at the Swiss Cheese Shoreline

Here's an area that's alluring despite numerous reminders of the sometimes untidy nature of man. It starts near the industrial part of Hanapepe (technically 'Ele'ele) and leads to an isolated beach. Along the way the Swiss cheese-type of lava shoreline provides ample opportunity to explore how the ocean carves up the land, while an old dump site makes for some surprisingly interesting discoveries.

ACTIVITIES

Keyhole Cave is just one cool reason to check out the Hanapepe shoreline.

Start by driving to Glass Beach (see directions on page 112). After the beach the road continues, terminating at an old cemetery. Here you may see trash or junk cars. That's because this area used to be (and to an extent still is) a place locals use to dump equipment. Go to the lava bench below and head to the right. You'll see that the sides of the cliff are embedded with old junk, mostly metal and glass. (That's where Glass Beach got its glass.) On the lava is an amazing assortment of ancient engine blocks and car frames. I know it sounds ugly, but you have to see what the ocean has done with them. Many of the hulks have completely melted from the rust, often interwoven with the lava itself. Nature has had almost a hundred years to reclaim the metal, and the results of this long-time environmental abuse are oddly fascinating. Even old porcelain and ceramics have been rounded so that

you'd swear they're stones.

After exploring the junk area, backtrack by heading left along the shoreline. You'll see areas where the ocean has chiseled its way inland. Continue along the shore (east), and you soon come to a lava arch. Water floods under the arch, filling and draining the swimming pool-sized opening in seconds, creating a chaotic, washing machine effect. (Look, but don't swim.)

Tides and surf can alter the shoreline here. There are several blowholes that blow when the wave direction is just right. Always be alert to the potential of large waves.

Past the arch is a 20-plus-foot-long cave we call **Keyhole Cave**. It's got a small opening on the bottom where the ocean surges in and out. At the back is a keyhole-shaped opening. It's fascinating to watch the interplay of the cave and the ocean here.

There are other holes, then a tall column of lava looking down toward the frothing ocean. Although you've left the old dump site behind, local fishermen use this coastal area on weekends and don't always clean up their mess. Try not to let it bother you.

You can either continue along the shoreline or occasionally use the old road paralleling the coast. (Most likely you'll use both.) The land owner doesn't want you driving on the road but has traditionally let people walk along here. The coffee trees behind the shoreline, however, are off limits.

After 20–40 minutes (depending on how often you stop and explore—hopefully a lot) you come to Wahi-awa Beach. It's a lovely looking bay, though the water visibility is usually poor due to river runoff. During the week, if the tour boats aren't there for lunch, it's often empty.

Horseback Riding

If you want to let someone else do the walking while you tour the island, horseback riding is available from several outlets.

CJM Country Stables at 742–6096 has three rides available. An 8:30 a.m. Breakfast Ride—2 hours of riding, 1 hour for a continental breakfast. The ride is mostly along or near the coast to a "secret" beach (it's Ha'ula). $80 per person. Then there's a 9:30 a.m. and 2 p.m. Hidden Beach Ride—2 hours of riding on mountains and along the coast. Beverages included. $75 per person. Lastly, a beach/swim ride for $90. No riding experience necessary. 250-pound weight limit. CJM is a mixed bag. The positive side is their location. It's great to

walk so close to the shoreline and to see Ha'upu Mountain. On the negative they are a single-file, nose-to-tail outfit, no passing, no running, read-the-rules kind of company where the leader may spend the entire trip on his cell phone (which has happened to us). They take lots of riders and feel a bit like a rider processing machine, but the rigid structure will make beginners feel pretty comfortable. Experienced riders may be chomping at the bit (wow, I *finally* got to use that horse phrase in the proper context!) for some more spark.

Esprit de Corps (822–4688) is mostly for experienced riders. They have numerous rides. (The 5-hour is the best.) This includes up to an hour of training/refreshing. Unlike most companies, they'll let you trot and canter—a lot if you like. They ride a dirt road (Moalepe) with pleasant views of the mountains. They *strongly* stress proper riding habits—drilling you on posting (rising trot)—and it's more of a riding adventure instead of an animal tram ride like CJM. Their depth of knowledge is admirable and freely shared. Ask about the tasty rose myrtles along the way. Prices are $112 for the 2-hour intro, $216 for the 5-hour (which includes lunch and swimming) and $346 for the all-day trip.

Princeville Ranch Stables at 826–6777 has a marvelous 4-hour ride to a "secret" waterfall (Kalihiwai Falls—it's the falls seen from the bridge right after the 25 mile marker on the north shore.) $120 per person; includes 1 hour for swimming and a snack. There's a 220-pound weight limit. Bring your camera and something to swim in. There's also a 90-minute country ride for $65, and a $110 3-hour bluff ride above 'Anini Beach. Kayakers often paddle to Kalihiwai Falls, but expect to see your guide run them off if the kayakers

didn't pay Princeville Ranch for the privilege of seeing "their" waterfall. Personally, we find it a bit annoying that these recent leaseholders would cut off a waterfall that's been visited for centuries, citing the weak, overused villain "liability" (conveniently ignoring a state law that protects them from liability if you get hurt). Feel free to punish them by withholding your business if you agree. (OK, end of rant.)

Garden Island Ranch at 338–0052 has lots of rides, but good luck trying to get your call returned.

Silver Falls Ranch inland (mauka) of Kilauea at 828–6718 takes you around their working ranch. $78 for the 2-hour ride. For $105 it includes another hour and a trip to their small waterfall and large pool. Swim and lunch there.

JET SKIING

Jet ski rentals are outlawed on Kaua'i, so if this is what you came to the island to do, you're out of luck.

A kayak can be a marvelous way to see Kaua'i. The quiet, peaceful nature of kayak travel appeals to many. There are four rivers on Kaua'i you can kayak and, of course, there is the open ocean.

RIVER KAYAK TRIPS

We've kayaked all the rivers in several kinds of craft. We prefer the rigid two-person, self-bailing kayaks for beginners, single person self-bailers for those that have kayaked before. Some use canoes, but we're not as fond of them since they can fill with water if tipped. (Inflatables are terrible since they are easily deflect-

ed by wind—called weathercocking, in case you're taking notes.)

Of the four rivers, the **Wailua** is by far the most popular. In fact, it's getting a bit *too* crowded, if the truth be told. It's very scenic, and there's a **waterfall** on the north fork you can hike to if you like. (Some brochures call it the most spectacular waterfall on the island. That's bunk, but it's a nice one just the same.) It's 5 miles round trip and takes most people about 2½ hours plus stopping or hiking time. Since large boats take passengers to the Fern Grotto, kayakers should always stay on the north side of the river. If you want to visit the Fern Grotto, consider pulling ashore *before* the docks. To be honest, the grotto is not the same as it used to be and is barely worth the effort to get there. The best part about kayaking this river is the scenery and hiking to the waterfall. Just enjoy the Wailua for its lushness, and watch out for the large boat tours. (Ignore advertisements mentioning a rope swing. The state kept cutting it down—finally cutting the *tree* down—because of liability fears.) The African Village scene from *Outbreak* was filmed on a secluded plain here on your right; look for it. The wind will probably be in your face coming back, so hug the north bank tightly to minimize the wind. The earlier you leave (we start at 7 a.m. and strongly suggest you do, too) the less wind coming back and you'll avoid crowds on the river and at the waterfall. That means renting the night before and getting to the river around 6:45. **Paradise Outdoor Adventures** may let you keep kayaks overnight, as might **Kaua'i Water Ski**.

The **Hanalei River** is the longest and goes mostly through plains. (Beautiful plains, but plains.) There are no powerboats past the mouth where you put in,

so it'll be quieter. It takes about 3 to 3½ hours (7½ miles) round trip for most people to kayak this peaceful river. After a heavy rain, waterfalls etched in the distant valley walls can enhance the trip. The wind usually helps you a little coming back.

The **Hule'ia River** in Lihu'e is 5 miles round trip (2 hours or more). It starts from Nawiliwili Harbor and the water flow is not great, so expect ickier water here. There are majestic mountains on your left as you go out, and you will pass the Menehune Fishpond and an area where they filmed the swing-on-a-vine-to-the-waiting-airplane scene from *Raiders of the Lost Ark*. (Keep an eye out for the opening to the fishpond.) The last navigable part is our favorite part of this river. This river goes through a wildlife refuge, but you'll see and hear more birds on the Hanalei River. The wind will probably be in your face coming back.

The **Kalihiwai** is short but *very* sweet. You can kayak it in an hour if you decide not to do the additional hike to Kalihiwai Falls. Put in at Kalihiwai Beach. You might see the waterfall from where you stop kayaking. The scenery is the best of the four, and you might want to do it if you have any juice left after a Hanalei River trip. Expect to be hassled if you visit the falls in any way that doesn't bring money to the horse-back company that leases the land where the falls are.

Although we recommend unguided trips, there are many companies that do guided river kayak trips. (Kayak companies make more money on guided trips, so expect to be steered toward them.) If you're apprehensive and want a guided river trip, consider **Paradise Outdoor Adventures, Chris the Fun Lady, Kayak Kaua'i** or **Outfitters Kaua'i**. Most charge around $85 per person.

There will usually be two people per kayak on these trips. **Paradise Outdoor Adventures** has single kayaks available (for an extra fee) in addition to doubles for their tours.

If the ocean surf's up, how about a day on the river instead?

On the Wailua, first you kayak, then you hike...then you frolic!

outrigger canoe awaits to bring you back to your car. We recommend the morning trip. The hiking and paddling are not overly tough, though you'll get wet and muddy. The guides do an excellent job, they handle the food well, they're great with kids (who *love* the part where they feed some pigs and peacocks) and they don't rush you during the trip. It's not cheap at $119 per person, 20 people max. They have a less desirable trip that omits Kipu Falls and lunch for $80.

OCEAN KAYAK TRIPS

Ocean kayaking can be an experience of a lifetime. The crown jewel is a summer Na Pali Coast trip. *National Geographic* named it the second best adventure in the United States. (Rafting the Colorado was #1 and dog sledding in Alaska was #3.) Na Pali can be an *incredible* trip for those who can do it, either guided or unguided. We try to do it every summer and camp along the way. For more information on the Na Pali trip and for precautions on ocean kayaking in general, see ADVENTURES on page 176.

The best river trip we've seen is **Outfitters Kaua'i's** 7-hour Hule'ia River kayak/hike trip called the Kipu Ranch Tour. About two miles of kayaking then half a mile of hiking to a small falls. Then it's on a tractor-pulled wagon to lunch at a second waterfall. After eating, you head to Kipu Falls (see page 67) and its rope swing. You'll finally hike back to the river where an

Kipu Kai in winter is also delightful. Put in at Maha'ulepu and head into the trade winds, which help coming back. (We've dragged SCUBA tanks there during calm seas, and the diving is excellent.) Guided trips have started at Nawiliwili and picked up paddlers down the coast. Another nice, fairly short trip is to put in at Kukui'ula Small Boat Harbor in Lawa'i on the south shore and paddle 1 mile west (passing Spouting Horn) to Lawa'i Bay, a very pretty beach.

What if I want to rent a kayak and paddle the ocean on my own? Well, unlike all the other Hawaiian islands, Kaua'i is a very difficult place to rent a kayak *for the ocean*. Whether it's because companies want to make more money guiding you or because Kaua'i's ocean waters are not as calm (probably a little of both), most will turn you down cold. If you have some experience, try **Paradise Outdoor Adventures**. They have double kayaks with rudders (important for the ocean) and, if they think you're up to it, they may rent to you.

RENTING A KAYAK FOR THE RIVER

Prices change a lot in this competitive business. Most companies offer single-person kayaks for $25–$30 per day, with two-person kayaks for $45–$60 per day. Sometimes they are cheaper if you are willing to arm wrestle timeshare salesmen. Most cars will hold 2 or 3 kayaks on the roof.

THE KAYAK COMPANIES

The companies described below provide a variety of services.

Paradise Outdoor Adventures at 822–1112 is a good place to rent kayaks. Located on ocean side of the highway in north Kapa'a. They're the best at showing you proper paddling techniques and their knowledge is refreshing.

Chris The Fun Lady at 822–7759 is a good place to rent kayaks. Located on the ocean side of the highway in Kapa'a, they have excellent gear and extras.

Pedal 'n Paddle in Hanalei at 826–9069 specializes in one-stop shopping. They rent kayaks, camping supplies, mountain bikes and snorkel gear.

Kayak Kaua'i in Hanalei at (800) 437–3507 or 826–9844 and in Kapa'a it's 822–9179. From May through September they have one-day guided Na Pali tours for $160 per person. Lunch included at either Miloli'i or Nu'alolo Kai. They also have trips to Lawa'i Bay on the south shore. The more involved the trip, the better it is to call them in advance, *especially* for Na Pali.

Outfitters Kaua'i in Po'ipu at 742–9667 sometimes has guided one-way, 7-mile ocean tours, past Lawa'i Bay to Glass Beach for $119. They also have Na Pali trips for $165. Wailua River kayak tours are available as well as the awesome trip described under RIVER KAYAK TRIPS.

Aloha Canoes & Kayaks at 246–6804 also does trips at this river.

Activity Warehouse in Kapa'a rents kayaks at pretty good prices. But the service isn't as good. Beware that they also push timeshare presentations here.

Kaua'i Water Ski & Surf Company at 822–3574 has river kayaks available— $20 for single kayaks, $40 for doubles.

Wailua Kayak & Canoe at 821–1188 operates near the Wailua River and you'll probably be able to walk your kayak down to the boat launch on a kayak dollie. Their gear (seats and such) are not as good as others, and customer service is scant.

In addition to standard bus tours, there are two other land tours worth considering.

Hawai'i Movie Tours at 822–1192 takes people in vans to various locations around the island where movies were filmed. (See page 23 for more on movies that have been filmed on the island.) You see clips of the pertinent movie scenes on monitors in the van while they show you where and how they were filmed. The quality of the tour very much depends on the quality of the guide, and overall the company does a pretty good job. Best seats are right side, middle of the van. The half-day trip is a pricey $113 and includes lunch. They also have a 4WD van tour of more remote areas for $95. Hawai'i Movie Tours is not the only movie tour, but it's the best one out there.

Kaua'i Tours at 245–8809 provides 4WD tours. Trips include the Kilohana area (which is private and gated), the mountains behind Wailua town (which are open to the public) or a non-4WD road tour of Waimea Canyon area. Prices are $60–$100. The Wailua trip includes a 4-mile hike.

Ocean Tours

When Hollywood needs a beautiful, remote coastline studded with majestic cliffs and glorious valleys to film movies, they often choose Kaua'i's Na Pali Coast. *The Lost World, 6 Days/7 Nights, King Kong* and others have all used a Na Pali backdrop to convey an idyllic paradise. From the sea, this area of the island takes on a magical quality. Many people dream of seeing the Hawaiian Islands by sea. The Na Pali region is surely the most popular area to cruise, but there are others, as well. This can be a fantasy trip. Rough seas are rarely part of the fantasy, but they can be part of reality depending on conditions.

Kaua'i boat tours of Na Pali gained a worldwide reputation because the boats left from the north shore and spent virtually all of their time touring what is arguably the most spectacular coastline in the world. They zipped in and out of sea caves in rubber rafts and catamarans and snorkeled at an isolated beach. It was an unrivaled experience and became legendary among travelers. But this reputation is now dated and somewhat misleading, because in the late '90s *everything* changed. The government forced the boating companies to relocate to the west side, which is a *much* different experience. Don't get us wrong. Seeing Na Pali by boat from the west side is still an incredible thrill that we highly recommend. Soaking up this coastline and being on a boat are exquisitely relaxing. But from the west side you'll only see half of Na Pali (and not the best half), and ¾ of the trip isn't even along Na Pali.

Nothing stays static in this section. Awhile ago the situation changed *again* when a judge spanked the state for kicking all the boaters out of the North Shore. Today, *some* of the boaters are allowed to operate out of Hanalei—at least that was the case when we went to press.

The boats that leave *from Port Allen* travel 23 miles along the relatively uninteresting (by sea) Mana Plain, then head up the dry side of Na Pali before turning

around at Kalalau. (Boats that leave from Kikiaola Harbor shave 9 miles off the duller part—see map on page 82.) If boats would cruise past Kalalau to Hanakapi'ai, we'd be much happier, because that short stretch has some beautiful sights. But most turn back at Kalalau.

Boats that leave *from Hanalei* have a much better and more exciting route though the return trip is usually into head seas (meaning into the swells) and headwinds.

Some west shore companies switch to south shore tours in October and return to Na Pali in April, others can do Na Pali year-round. If you do Na Pali in winter, expect bigger seas.

TIPS

Many companies offer morning and afternoon trips. Morning trips usually have snorkeling and better food on board. Morning is also when you're more likely to encounter smoother seas and better weather.

Be wary of the information given during narrations. Many boat companies, like their helicopter brethren, are particularly prone to repeating inaccurate nonsense in their attempt to "educate" you and we've known some who literally made it up as they went along.

Seasickness can strike anyone. If you're concerned that it will be a problem, strongly consider taking Dramamine or something similar at least an hour *before* you leave. (The night before and morning of are best. It's useless to take it once you're on the boat.) Also, avoid any alcohol the night before. (A *big* no-no.) No greasy foods before or during the trip. And some think that citrus juices are a cause of seasickness. Ginger is a very good preventative/treatment. Below deck is a bad place to be if you're worried about getting seasick. Without a reference point, you're much more likely to let 'er rip down there. Scopolamine patches work but have side effects including (occasionally) blurred vision that can last a week. (Been there, done that, on a 10-day boat trip.)

From the west shore, the best views are off the right (starboard) side going out to Na Pali and off the left (port) side coming back. It's the opposite when you leave from the north shore. Also remember that most boats are a lot smoother in the back than the front, but you may get diesel fumes back there. Just slightly ahead of the back seats is our preferred position.

People come off these trips *toasted*, especially in the summer. Make sure you slather on the sunscreen, or you'll be sorry for the rest of your trip.

Since most trips involve driving to the west side early in the morning, consider doing the trip early in your vacation— when your body clock is still on mainland time and it's easier to rise early.

WHAT AND WHO

You have several options. There are sailing yachts that cover short distances up and down the coasts. Most power catamarans leave from Hanapepe (at Port Allen) and ply up and down Na Pali, except during the winter when many do south shore trips. Rigid hull inflatables, the modern and more comfortable version of the old rubber zodiacs, are a fun alternative to catamarans. Most of the companies have restrooms on some of their boats. Since some can change the boat they'll be using, check with them if this is a major concern, and to verify that the boat they will be using has a place that offers protection from the sun.

Over all, our favorites are **Na Pali Catamaran** on the north shore, **Holoholo** and **Liko Kaua'i** on the west shore.

POWER CATAMARANS

Power catamarans are the most popular way to see the Na Pali Coast. Catamarans slice through the waves rather than bouncing over them but they rock more. Most include an hour of snorkeling at Nu'alolo Kai or a site close to Polihale. (Nu'alolo's better; the site near Polihale is actually pretty mediocre. If you're at the latter site, the best snorkeling is away from shore, not toward it.)

Our favorite is **Na Pali Catamaran** (826–6853). Their 34-foot power cat takes up to 15 people and we like it better than any of the Port Allen operators simply because they leave from Hanalei. (They also do a good job.) $125 for the 4-hour tour includes snorkeling and a deli lunch. (They, and the two companies listed below mostly operate from March–October.) Morning is much better than afternoon here.

Hanalei Sport Fishing and Tours (826–6114) is also out of Hanalei but their 28-foot boat and $125 3½ hour tours aren't as good as Na Pali Cat.

The third north shore catamaran, **Captain Sundown** (826–5585), is a company we can't recommend.

Holoholo Charters (335–0815) has a large, 61-foot power catamaran. Their trips are distinguished in that they go to the "forbidden" island of Ni'ihau. For $156 (less in winter) the 7-hour trip leaves in the morning from Port Allen and makes a beeline to Kalalau Beach on Na Pali. In light seas they're close to shore; heavier swells call for greater distance. Then they tour part of Na Pali before heading to Ni'ihau where they snorkel. (Clean, clear water and lots of fish, but currents can sometimes make snorkeling there more work.) Continental breakfast and a good deli lunch included. After the snorkeling, the open bar serves drinks, but they refuse to serve cookies until they're 5 minutes from port. (Maybe they're afraid you'll toss them otherwise.)

There are two large trampolines at the bow for sunning, but they and the entire bow section are off limits most of the time while motoring. Easy steps into and out of the water from the boat. They also have afternoon charters that just go to Na Pali for $109 and some other trips. Holoholo is a good outfit and is easy to recommend. The boat is good, pretty stable, there's plenty of shade available, and the crew is very professional. They have a freshwater shower hose, adequate snorkel gear but no wet suits available. Our only complaint is that the boat design makes it feel crowded on nice days. Most of the seating is inside, but when it's reasonably calm and sunny most people want to be outside, which is somewhat spartan and lacking in seating, so people tend to crowd around the railings.

They also have another cat called the Leila, but we don't recommend it as much.

Liko Kaua'i Cruises at 338–0333 offers a relaxing 4-hour tour of Na Pali on a 49-foot power catamaran with 34 people. Leave from Kikiaola Small Boat Harbor near Kekaha and cruise north up the coast, often going as far as Ke'e Beach if the weather's good. (That's farther than any other west shore power cat goes and pleases us greatly.) On the way back you stop and snorkel at Nu'alolo Kai if conditions permit. Liko, a native Hawaiian, narrates with legends and stories. $110 for adults, $75 for keikis (kids), it includes snacks and sandwiches.

These passengers know what Hollywood knows…Na Pali is mesmerizing.

Captain Andy's Sailing Adventures at 335–6833 has 5½ hour Na Pali trips from Port Allen to Kalalau for $109. Snorkeling when conditions permit and deli lunch with an open bar of beer and wine. It would be a better product if they didn't pack *49* people on their nice 55-foot catamarans (and it feels crowded). They also keep snorkelers on a short leash and go to a poor snorkeling spot. It's a sailing cat, but they only sail a short time.

Kauaʻi Sea Tours at 826–7254 leaves from Port Allen for Na Pali trips for $119. They have a 60-foot power/sailing cat called the Lucky Lady, which rides well. We put them and Blue Dolphin (below) under POWER CATS because at best they'll probably only raise the sails while motoring downwind. (The sails are more for decoration since this type of vessel sails like a pig.) They also use 23-foot rigid hull inflatables, which aren't in the same league as Na Pali Explorer's nicer inflatable.

Ocean Odyssey at 742–6731 has a catamaran called Blue Dolphin similar to the Lucky Lady above, as well as a 56-foot trimaran. (The cat is better than the awkwardly designed 3-hull trimaran called Tropic Bird.) Up to 49 people, continental breakfast and deli lunch. They have a slide into the water. $119 for Na Pali trips. For an extra $25 you can try SCUBA (which is quite reasonable). Some days they also offer a Niʻihau trip similar to Holoholo's for $159.

Na Pali Eco-Adventures (826–6804) leaves from Port Allen in either their 34-foot or 40-foot power cat for trips up Na Pali year-round. The latter has a crowd-ed feel, like a block of floating benches. They'll go as far as Hanakapiʻai. 5-hour trips include snorkeling and lunch and are $115. (Ask them about the time in 2001 when a 20-foot juvenile hump-

back whale leaped onto their boat while they were eating, breaking the knee of an unfortunate passenger. Guess they shouldn't have been serving tuna fish.)

RIGID HULL INFLATABLES

Na Pali Explorer at 338-9999 leaves from the west side and heads north. Their 48-foot boat is amazingly smooth and fast for a zodiac—very impressive. There is some shade on board. They also have a less impressive 26-foot boat with no shade. $118 for the morning 5-hour Na Pali/snorkel trip. These include continental breakfast and a light lunch. $79 for the 3-hour Na Pali dash, no snorkeling.

RUBBER RAFTS (ZODIACS)

These used to dominate, but in today's world only a few still operate. **Na Pali Riders** (742-6331) uses them on 4½-hour trips but it's a decidedly mixed bag. Think of them as a low budget trip—without the low budget price. On the positive side they leave from Kikiaola Harbor and, during the summer season they go all the way to Ke'e on the north shore, so you'll see all of Na Pali. (Winter is whale watching heading south.) When they encounter dolphins, they get amazingly close. Also, zodiacs can be fun on calm seas. But if seas aren't reasonably smooth, it's a rough ride, because you'll feel every bump. On the negative side there's no shade or restroom, lunch is cheap sandwiches. Price is very steep at $120.

See also **Na Pali Explorer's** zodiac.

Captain Zodiac (826-9371) was a well-known company that's appeared and disappeared so many times lately, we've had a hard time keeping up. At press time they were linked up with Na Pali Eco-Adventures and their number was 826-9371. They were leaving from Port Allen, going only as far as Kalalau. Since that's the same route the larger (and smoother boats) take, we'd recommend against this trip at $115. If such a large percentage of your boat trip is going to be along the Mana Plain, take a cushier boat. Or if you want a rubber raft, go with Na Pali Rider since they leave Kikiaola Harbor, shaving nine of the most uninteresting miles off the trip.

PARASAILING

Parasailing is outlawed on Kaua'i. Hey, *that* was easy.

Kaua'i is the only Hawaiian island to offer river trips, and there are two ways to do it. You can take a riverboat ride up the Wailua River (often referred to as the only navigable river in all Hawai'i, but this is a relative term) or paddle your own kayak. **Smith's Motorboat Service** at 821-6892 and **Wai'ale'ale Boat Tours** at 822-4908 go 3 miles up the Wailua River and stop at the Fern Grotto, a large natural amphitheater with ferns all about. This is a popular place to get married. It's 30 minutes each way with entertainment and interesting information provided along the way. They spend 30–45 minutes at the site. $15 per person and they leave many times each day in their 100+ passenger boats. If you've heard of the Fern Grotto before, be forewarned that it really hasn't been the same since 1982 when Hurricane 'Iwa cleaned it out. It's nice, but not the wonder that it was before, and photos used in ads may be *very old* photos.

River trips up and down the Wailua River take you to the Fern Grotto, a fern-lined amphitheater.

You can also rent a kayak at any of several places and paddle the Wailua, the Hanalei River, the Kalihiwai River or the Hule'ia Stream. The best thing about kayaking the Wailua River instead of the riverboat tour is that you won't be restricted to the Fern Grotto. You'll be able to make a detour and hike to a pretty waterfall, often called Secret Falls. There are also guided river kayak tours. See KAYAKS.

Kaua'i is justly famous for many things: its incomparable lushness, gorgeous beaches and balmy nights. But Kaua'i is not famous for its diving. This is a shame because Kaua'i has some very good dive spots. Turtles are common, and many of them are downright gregarious. Lava tubes, ledges and walls are sprinkled around the island. Fish are abundant and varied. Coral growth is not as good as around the Big Island—at 22° latitude, Kaua'i is on the fringe of the coral belt. Kaua'i's many rivers and streams cut visibility in some areas, but you can still see more than 100 feet on good days.

Granted, you might find better conditions on the Kona coast of the Big Island or around Lana'i. It is dryer there and the lava's porous, so the ocean receives virtually no runoff. But this should not dissuade you from enjoying the wondrous underwater sights the Garden Island has to offer.

Kaua'i's ocean pattern is small summer surf on the north shore, larger summer surf on the south shore, and the opposite during winter months, so you should plan your diving activities accord-

ACTIVITIES

Dive Operator	Services Available	Price of Dive	Rent Gear For a Day	Boat Size / Passengers	Dive Computer	Ni'ihau 3-Tank Dive	Dive Certification	Rx Masks
Bubbles Below 332–7333	Boat Dives	$105 – $130 (2 tank)	No	35' / 8	Included	$245 – $270	$450	Yes
Dive Kaua'i 822–0452	Dive Shop & Boat Dives	$95 – $115 (2 tank)	$45	30' / 6-9	Included	$240 – $260	$355 – $395	Yes
Fathom Five 742–6991	Dive Shop & Boat Dives	$100 – $120 (2 tank)	$35	26' / 6	Included	None	$395 – $495	Yes
Hanalei Water Sports 826–7509	Shore Dives	$110 – $125 (2 tank)	No	N/A	No	None	$525	Yes
Mana Divers 335–0881	Boat Dives & Shore Dives	$95 – $115 (2 tank)	No	32' / 6	Included	None	$375	Yes
Ocean Quest 822–3589	Shore Dives	$80 – $95 (2 tank)	$35	N/A	Included	None	$395 – $495	Yes
Sea Sport Divers 742–9303	Dive Shop & Boat Dives	$100 – $120 (2 tank)	$40	32' / 6-10	Included	$255 – $275	$365	Yes
Wet-n-Wonderful 822–0211	Shore Dives	$65 – $95 (1 tank)	No	N/A	No	None	$375 – $425	Yes

ingly. Summer is very popular and the best companies book up early, so call them as soon as you know when you want to dive. The dive boat operators conduct their tours on the south shore year-round since the local government doesn't allow the boats to moor on the north shore. Some also have dives on the west side at Mana Crack and at Lehua Rock, off the coast of Ni'ihau. Those dives are generally considered advanced due to the depths involved. The Ni'ihau dive in particular involves at least 1½ hour travel time each way, so those who get seasick (and those who aren't sure) should take Dramamine or Bonine *before* they depart.

Off Ni'ihau, however, you're treated to ridiculously clear water, lots of big life (sharks, rays, dolphins and your best chance at a Hawaiian monk seal) and a close view of the "Forbidden Island." (The Robinsons, who own Ni'ihau, *hate* it when you call it that.) See ADVENTURES

for more on this dive. Book in advance to ensure space.

So you'll know our perspective when we review companies, we should tell you what we do and don't like when we go on a dive. On a bad dive, the dive master takes the group on a non-stop excursion that keeps you kicking the whole time. No time to stop and explore the nooks and crannies. Good outfits will give you a briefing, tell you about some of the endemic species here, what to look for and will point out various things on the dives, keeping it moving but not too fast. Bad outfits kick a lot. Good outfits explain the unique qualities of Hawai'i's environment. Bad dive masters may tell you what *they* saw (but *you* missed). Good companies work around your needs, wishes and desires. Bad companies keep everyone on a short leash. Good dive masters know their stuff and share it with you. Bad dive masters don't know squat but imply they know it all in order to

impress you. As divers, we tend to like companies that wander toward the boat for the latter part of the dive and allow you to go up when you are near the end of your tank, as opposed to everyone going up when the heaviest breather has burned up his/her bottle.

During times when we feel the diving conditions are bad (poor vis or big swells), we like to call around and ask about conditions. We appreciate the companies who admit it's bad, and we hold it against those who tell us how wonderful conditions are. (The company that fails this test the most is **Mana Divers**.)

IF YOU'VE NEVER DIVED BEFORE

Ocean Quest is your best choice. They will take you out for an introductory shore dive for $95 (one tank) or $135 (two-tank). They are *very* good with novices. (We took visiting family members to them for their first dive, and they were blown away by these guys.) **Mana Divers** is would probably be our second choice. (Just don't ask them how conditions are.) **Mana** has a one-tank shore intro for $95.

If you're interested in getting **certified** or did your book work on the mainland and want an open water referral, **Ocean Quest** is your best bet. The open water referral method allows you to do your class work at home, saving your Kaua'i vacation for the *fun stuff.*

RECOMMENDED FOR CERTIFIED DIVERS

As anonymous certified divers (who sometimes pretend to be novices), we are able to experiment with the different operators. The outfits we recommend are **Bubbles Below** and **Fathom Five** for boat dives and **Ocean Quest** for shore dives. They are all well-qualified, professional and knowledgeable. **Bubbles Below** has been the discoverer of many

great dive spots, and they are good with customers. The owners have been in business here for almost 20 years, and their love of the sport and knowledge of the seas are always evident. We've been a bit concerned with their consistency lately, but their reputation and track record should be solid enough to withstand a few bumps. They take a maximum of 8 on their 35-foot Radon. They prefer experienced divers. Discounts for multiple dive days available. **Ocean Quest** is also run by a local couple, George (aka Captain Nemo) and Jeannette. They are great folks who have a passion for what they do, and the personalized service really shows. We've never seen a better shore dive outfit. Experienced divers will love their shore dives, and beginners will find them perfect for their introduction to the world of SCUBA. **Fathom Five** is now the boat arm of Ocean Quest (see below).

A reasonable alternative if the above companies are full is **Mana Divers**.

Sometimes it's tempting to go with the cheapest dive operators. Remember that if you're herded in and out with a cheap company that doesn't know the underwater terrain, you may find that your "better deal" was no bargain at all.

DIVE SHOPS

There are three dive *shops* (as opposed to dive operators) on the island. In the past none made us feel warm and fuzzy (some are downright snotty). The wild card of the bunch is **Fathom Five**. Shortly before press time they were purchased by **Ocean Quest,** the shore dive outfit we like so much. They hadn't been operating Fathom Five long enough for us to generate an opinion as to their consistency, but we liked the changes we saw. Although their shop and boats are on the small side, they have *two* boats

(one is the certified boat, the other is the "rusty boat" for rusty divers and intros) so they don't mix intros with certifieds unless you want them to. (Certifieds will *love* that.) They feed you better than anyone else, get you on the boat quicker and have a good ascent policy. We also like how they'll keep and rinse your personal gear, if you dive on multiple days. If they maintain the quality of their boat dives at the same level they've kept their shore dive operation, they'll be the one to beat. They're on Po'ipu Road in Koloa.

Sea Sport Divers in Po'ipu (with a proposed satellite office in Kapa'a) is the largest shop with the best selection if you're looking to buy gear, but we don't recommend their boat dives. **Dive Kaua'i** is…in Kapa'a. Pretty average.

Even if **Hanalei Water Sports** weren't confiscatorily priced, they'd *still* be our last choice on the island.

For **renting gear**, any of the three shops will do fine.

For the heavy breathers among you, **Bubbles Below**, **Fathom Five** and **Dive Kaua'i** have 100s available.

Dive computers are available for your own *independent* dives and can be rented from **Fathom Five**. *Disposable* underwater cameras in a watertight box for SCUBA are available at most grocery stores and sundry shops. **Sea Sport Divers**, **Dive Kaua'i** and **Fathom Five** rent better cameras.

Some of the dive boats on Kaua'i feed you little or nothing between dives. I don't know about you, but I'm tempted to gnaw on the side of the boat after a dive. Bring a package of cookies with you. You'll probably be able to sell them to other hungry divers at prices confiscatory enough to pay for your dive. *(I have a bid of $8 for a chocolate chip cookie…Do I hear $9?)*

Shorties are usually sufficient for most

Tunnels Beach sports a fabulous reef, perfect for snorkeling, swimming and SCUBA.

people *in the summer only*. Surface water temperatures range from a low of 73.4° in February to a high of 80° in October. Any company that will *only* provide you with shorties doesn't seem to care much about your comfort.

Between morning and afternoon dives, morning is almost always best.

Nitrox (or enriched air) is available at **Bubbles Below**, **Dive Kaua'i** and **Sea Sport Divers**.

Kaua'i has many boat dive spots. Since the more resourceful operators are always finding new spots, and since you basically go where the boat operators go, we'll forgo a detailed description of all boat dive destinations. Suffice it to say that Sheraton Caves, General Store, Brennecke's Ledge, Turtle Bluffs, Amber's Arches and Fishbowl are all popular. Some sites, such as Sheraton Caves, are getting a bit over-dived.

Remember not to drive up to Waimea Canyon or the Kalalau Lookout after diving. As far as your nitrogen level is concerned, you're flying.

Below is a list of the best shore dives on the island:

◆ Ke'e Beach, north shore—If the seas are flat on a calm summer day, this area offers interesting shallow relief. The area near the reef drop-off is good, again on calm days.

◆ Tunnels, north shore—Easy access, lots of turtles, reef sharks, lava tubes, caves and nice underwater relief. Tunnels' allure is not its visibility, but the dramatic underwater topography. *If* you dive with someone who really knows the reef, this is unquestionably the best shore dive on the island and is often better than a boat dive. Low tide is best.

◆ Cannons, north shore—Similar to and almost as good as Tunnels. Easy access (from the roadside) a decided plus.

◆ The Hole, north shore—Located just off the Princeville Hotel. Like the name says, a hole in the reef. Acceptable underwater relief, easy access especially if you rent your gear from the dive facility just a few feet away, Hanalei Watersports. They will give you precise directions if you call them.

◆ Kahala Point, east shore—Entry and exit is a bugger on the lava rocks with crashing surf. Underwater relief is good and there are lots of fish. Near Anahola Beach Park.

◆ Koloa Landing, south shore—Easy entry, usually calm conditions year-round and decent coral near the shore. After slightly murky water on entry, the sea is usually quite clear. High tide is best.

◆ Nohili Point, west shore—If you're willing to walk with your gear for about 20 minutes on the sand (have I lost you yet?), you'll find good diving just past the big machine gun bunker. Lots of lobster and fairly pristine conditions are the highlight of this dive. Locals drive on the beach with their 4WD vehicles (after letting much of the air out of the tires), but you better be real sure of yourself before you try it in a rental 4WD. The fee for a tow this far out is just short of your first born male child. Only dive here during calm conditions, and be careful of the sharp rock ledge during entry and exit.

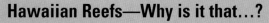

Hawaiian Reefs—Why is it that...?

What is that crackling sound, like bacon frying, I always hear while snorkeling or diving?
For years this baffled people. In the early days of submarines, the sound interfered with sonar operations. Finally we know the answer. It's hidden snapping shrimp defining their territory. One variety is even responsible for all the dark cracks and channels you see in smooth lobe coral. A pair creates the channels then "farm" algae inside.

Why are there so few shellfish in Hawai'i?
It's too warm for some of the more familiar shellfish (which tend to be filter-feeders and Hawai'i waters don't have as much stuff to filter). But Hawai'i has more shellfish than most people are aware of. They hide well under rocks and in sand. Also, people tend to collect shells (which is illegal), and that depletes the numbers.

Why do coral cuts take so long to heal?
Coral contains a live animal. When you scrape coral, it leaves proteinaceous matter in your body, which takes much longer for your body to dispatch.

Why do some of the reefs appear dead?
Much of the "coral" you see around Kaua'i isn't the kind of coral you're used to. It's called coralline algae, which secretes calcium carbonate. It's not dead, it's *supposed* to look like that.

What is the state fish?
Well, it used to be the humuhumunukunukuapua'a, but today we don't have a state fish. When the law expired it was not renewed because they "didn't want to revisit this partisan issue." (How can a state fish be *partisan?*)

What do turtles eat?
Dolphins. (Just teasing.) They primarily eat plants growing on rocks, as well as jellyfish when they are lucky enough to encounter them. Unfortunately for turtles and lucky for us, jellyfish aren't numerous here.

Is it harmful when people play with an octopus?
Yes, if the octopus gets harmed while trying to get it out of its hole. Best to leave them alone.

Why does the ocean rarely smell fishy here in Hawai'i?
Two reasons. We have relatively small tide changes, so the ocean doesn't strand large amounts of smelly seaweed at low tide. Also, the water is fairly sterile compared to mainland water, which owes much of its smell to algae and seaweed that thrives in the bacteria-rich runoff from industrial sources.

Why is the water so clear here?
Because relatively little junk is poured into our water compared to the mainland. Also, natural currents tend to flush the water with a continuous supply of fresh, clean ocean water.

Why do my ears hurt when I dive deep, and how are SCUBA divers able to get over it?
Because the increasing weight of the ocean is pressing on your ears the farther down you go. Divers alleviate this by equalizing their ears. Sounds high tech, but that simply means holding your nose while trying to blow out of it. This forces air into their eustachian tubes, creating equal pressures with the outside ocean. (It doesn't work if your sinuses are clogged.) Anything with air between it gets compressed. So if you know someone who gets a headache whenever they go under water...well, they must be an airhead.

If you have ever looked into a saltwater aquarium and marveled at the diversity of the fish life, snorkeling is an experience you might want to try. Anyone who has ever hovered over hundreds of colorful fish can attest to the thrill you feel from being in their environment.

Where to snorkel depends on how good you are and what kind of experience you want. The best place for beginners is **Lydgate State Park** in Wailua. There you will find an area protected by a ring of boulders that shields you from the strong ocean. Mornings are best. The intermediate snorkeler will find **Ke'e** or **Tunnels** on the north shore to be fabulous during the calm, warmer months. **Hideaways** is also great during calm seas. **Po'ipu Beach Park** on the south shore usually offers good snorkeling and calm seas in cooler months on either side of the tombolo. The BEACHES section has a description of all the beaches and the different characteristics they possess.

As far as gear goes, there are numerous places to rent gear on the island. We always snorkel wearing reef shoes and divers' fins (which fit over reef shoes). This way we can enter and exit the water without worrying about stepping on anything. Cheap reef shoes can be found at many places, including Kmart. Bootie socks or women's thin ankle-length socks will keep you from rubbing the top of your tootsies raw. Divers' fins can be rented at most dive shops. If enough people ask snorkel companies about them, they will start to carry them as well.

If you're looking to buy snorkel gear, you can pick it up pretty cheap at Wal-mart in Lihu'e on the highway or Kmart in Kukui Grove Shopping Center, also in Lihu'e.

Many people prefer to rent gear when they get here and leave it in the trunk, so they may snorkel when the opportunity arises. Your hotel or condo may have gear available. If they don't, try any of the following:

NORTH SHORE RENTALS:

Hanalei Surf Company at 826–9000 has pretty good equipment for only $5 per day, $20 per week. *Rx* available for nothing extra.

Pedal 'n Paddle at 826–9069 in Hanalei rents gear for $5 per day, $20 per week.

EAST SHORE RENTALS:

Chris The Fun Lady at 822–7759 on the highway in Kapa'a has pretty good gear for $5 per day, $15 for the week. *Rx* masks available, as well as fins that go over reef shoes (divers' fins).

Snorkel Bob has two locations: one on the highway in Kapa'a at 823–9433 and the other located on Po'ipu road past Koloa at 742–2206. You're likely to be drawn by the $2.50 per day gear but be tempted by the $6.50 or even *$11* gear. Although the equipment is pretty good, it's not *that* good. $4.50 gear is your best bet. *Rx* masks available. You can also rent on Kaua'i and return equipment to any other island.

SOUTH SHORE RENTALS:

Nukumoi Beach & Surf Shop at 742–8019 rents beach equipment including snorkel gear, boogie boards and the like. A good selection. Convenient, since they are right near Po'ipu Beach

Even when the ocean looks angry, Lydgate's protected ocean pool offers relatively safe snorkeling on all but the highest surf days. Morning is best.

Park. $5 per day.

Fathom Five at 742–6991 in Po'ipu has gear for $5 per day. Divers' fins available.

See also **Snorkel Bob** listed above.

SNORKEL TOURS

If you've never snorkeled before and desire lessons and assistance, **SeaFun Kaua'i** at 245–6400 offers guided snorkel tours for $75 per person (children under 12 cost $63). We once tried to teach a friend to snorkel and were unsuccessful even getting her to put her face in the water (she was terrified). We were very impressed that in only a few minutes they had her snorkeling like an expert. Even *non-swimmers* go out with them. For this price, they'll pick you up at your hotel, take you to a place like Tunnels or Lawa'i Beach and provide you with gear, wet suit (which makes you float), snacks and assistance. Prescription masks and video of your trip are available.

Hanalei Water Sports at 826–7509 has snorkel tours off the Princeville Hotel for $35.

SNORKEL TIPS:

• Tropical gloves make snorkeling much more enjoyable. You can grab rocks to maneuver in shallow or surgy areas. (Please don't grab coral, however.)

• Use *Sea Drops* or another brand of anti-fog goop. Spread it *thinly* on the inside of a dry mask, then do a quick rinse. The old-fashioned method of spitting in the mask is not very effective. (It's particularly frightening to see tobacco chewers do this. Yuck!)

• Don't use your arms much, or you will spook the fish. Gentle fin motion. Any rapid motion can cause the little critters to scatter.

• Fish are hungriest and most appreciative in the morning (before their coffee).

- If you have a mustache and have trouble with a leaking mask, try a little Vaseline. Don't get any on the glass—it can get *really* ugly.

- In general, it's not a good idea to feed the fish. It upsets the balance by giving some fish an unnatural advantage over others and has the perverse effect of reducing both fish counts and variety. That said, the fish at **Lydgate** are such longtime people-food junkies that you won't do any harm feeding them there. You can find rabbit or fish food at most grocery stores, Kmart or Walmart. Fill a Ziplock bag and, at the proper time, make a small slit in a corner to let the water fill the bag. You can dispense the food by squeezing the bag and using a slight wiggle motion to attract the fish. Be careful that the zip part doesn't unzip—a common occurrence. If you can get a few fish interested and they start darting around, others will come. Dispense the food *sparingly*; too much and they will grab a bite and run. If they have to compete, they will increase in numbers. Too much food also makes the water murky—fish don't like murky water and will depart. If you don't want to use rabbit food, a tightly compressed ball of bread works well. Again, dispense *sparingly*. Don't use frozen peas. Although many think that this food is benign, in fact, it can be harmful due to the fish's inability to digest it properly. We cannot stress enough the importance of not losing your plastic bag in the water. If a turtle encounters it, he will surely think it is a jellyfish and choke to death. If you encounter a bag discarded by a thoughtless jerk, please pick it up and wedge it in your suit until you get out of the water.

- Reef shoes or booties and fins that will fit over them can be rented at **Fathom Five** (742–6991) and **Sea Sport Divers** (742–9303).

- Several manufacturers, including Kodak and Fuji, sell disposable waterproof cameras. They are cheap and can provide wonderful souvenirs.

If you've always wanted to see what it's like to SCUBA dive but are a bit worried or don't want to go through the hassle, try SNUBA. That's where you take an air tank and place it on a raft that floats above you. Anyone 8 or older can SNUBA. From the raft there's a 20-foot hose attached to a regulator. There you are, underwater up to 20 feet deep, no tank on your back, no hassle. You'll have some instructions before you go under and the dive master stays with you the whole time. It can be an exciting way to see the underwater world for the first time. **Snuba Tours of Kaua'i** is at 823–8912. They do their thing off Lawa'i Beach on the south shore. $59. It should take a little over an hour.

Though not on par with the Grand Wailea on Maui, there are three spas on the island that are worth recommending. **Anara Spa** at The Hyatt (742–1234) in Po'ipu is the best with a fabulous full-service spa—guaranteed to turn you to jelly. **Ala Lani Spa and Tennis**

(245–3323) next to the Marriott also has full-service spa treatments. **The Princeville Health Club and Spa** (826–5030) in Princeville is also highly recommended. All offer the works and will relax you enough to breeze through the toughest IRS audit.

Ho, da shreddin's da kine, brah. (Just trying to get you in the mood.) Surfing is synonymous with Hawai'i. And why not? Hawaiians invented *da bugga*. Learning isn't as hard as you may think. Depending on conditions they may put you on a large soft board the size of a garage door (well…almost), so it's fairly easy to master, at least at this level.

Hanalei Bay is justly famous islandwide as one of the best and *most challenging* in Hawai'i. The section on BEACHES can assist you in picking beaches with surfing possibilities. **Cannons**, **Hanalei Bay**, **Kalihiwai**, **Kealia**, **Kalapaki**, **Infinities (Pakala Beach)**, are all well-known surf spots. If you want lessons, the best teacher we've seen is **Learn to Surf** at 826–7612. For $35 they'll spend 90 minutes with you at whichever beach has the right conditions. Good attitude and good place to rent a board.

Nukumoi Surf Co. across from Po'ipu Beach Park at 742–8019 books **Margo Oberg Surfing School**. Margo's a former surfing champion. You get 90 minutes of lessons for $48, but you may get one of her other instructors. **Windsurf Kaua'i** at 828–6838 gives 90-minute lessons for $60 in Hanalei Bay. Plus you keep the board the rest of the day. If you just want to rent a board, con-

tact your hotel activity desk or any of the following: **Progressive Expressions** at 742–6041 and **Nukumoi** at 742–8019, both in Po'ipu, **Hanalei Surf Company** in Hanalei at 826–9000, or **Kaua'i Water Ski & Surf Company** in Kapa'a at 822–3574.

By the way, a collection of surfboards is known in surfing lingo here as a *quiver*. And a little kid surfer who doesn't have a job or car yet is called a *grommet*. Just thought you'd like to know.

If you are into tennis, Kaua'i has no shortage of courts. Many hotels offer free courts for their guests. (Check our resort reviews.) If your hotel doesn't have one, you may contact the courts listed below to arrange court time. Kaua'i County has nine separate municipal courts scattered around the island, some lighted. They won't be as pristine as the private courts, but they are free to the public. You can call the county at 241–6670 to get the location of the court nearest you. **Ala Lani Spa and Tennis** (245–3323) has a stadium court if you brought your own crowd.

Other places to rent a court include **Princeville Resort Tennis Complex** (826–3620), **Kaua'i Coconut Beach** (822–6670), **Hyatt** (742–1234 and **Kiahuna** (742–9533).

At **Kaua'i Water Ski & Surf Company** (822–3574), you can waters-

ki the Wailua River. They rent a ski boat for $100 per hour, $55 for half hour. This includes the boat, driver, ski equipment and lessons, if you wish. Since you pay for the boat and not for skiing, non-skiers come along for free, up to 6 customers in the boat. If you've never skied before, it's *much* more tiring than it looks but gobs of fun.

Although Maui sees more whales than Kaua'i, they are still very common here. Whales work in Alaska in the summer, building up fat, then vacation here from December or January to March or April, when the females give birth and the males sing the blues. Only the males sing and they all sing the same song, usually with their heads pointed down. Humpbacks don't eat while they're here and may lose ⅓ of their body weight during their Hawaiian vacation. (I doubt that many *human* visitors can make that same claim.) These gentle giants are very social and have been known to come right up to the boats to check out the sightseers. Regulations prohibit the boat companies from initiating this kind of intimacy, but they get close enough to enjoy the whales. If you want to go on a whale watching boat tour, see OCEAN TOURS for a list of the tour boat operators.

If you want to try windsurfing (formerly known as sailboarding), you'll find that your options are limited on Kaua'i. Higher winds and more reefs mostly favor the more experienced. A notable exception is 'Anini Beach. Celeste at **Windsurf Kaua'i** (828–6838) specializes in lessons for beginners on the north shore. Rates are $75 per person for 3 hours of lessons and practice. '**Anini Beach Windsurfing** (826–9463) also offers lessons and board rentals. They charge $75 for a 3-hour lesson. $25 for an hour for rental, $75 for the day. Since county laws prohibit renting boards at the beach, you will probably have to pick up a board at another location if you don't want any lessons. Take it to Maha'ulepu or Salt Pond on the south shore, if you like. The west side just south of Pacific Missile Range Facility can also be very exciting for the experienced. There the winds that wrap around Na Pali can create ideal conditions. The folks at **Hanalei Surf Company** (826–9000) can be a good source for windsurfing information.

KITESURFING

One sport that's all the rage here in Hawai'i is **kitesurfing** or **kiteboarding**. Imagine a modified surfboard, shorter and boxier than a normal board, with fins at both ends and straps for your feet. Then let a special, controllable, two-line kite drag you along. Like windsurfing, you don't have to go the direction the wind takes you, you have control (though not as much as a windsurf board). It's harder to learn than windsurfing, but *oh,* what fun it is! More fun than windsurfing, if you can get over the steeper learning curve. At press time there wasn't anybody giving lessons on a regular basis that we could find. We expect that will change. If you want to see it check out Kapa'a Beach Park, the most popular local spot. Moanakai Road is a good place to hang out and watch them and it's where we took the photo on page 97.

OK, so 16 miles is a long way to paddle, whether over one day or several. But the wind, current and luscious scenery help propel you along.

The activities described below are for the serious adventurer. They can be experiences of a lifetime. We are assuming that if you consider any of them that you are a person of sound judgment, capable of assessing risks. All adventures carry risks of one kind or another. Our descriptions below do not attempt to convey all risks associated with an activity. These activities are not for everyone. Good preparation is essential. In the end, it comes down to your own good judgment.

NA PALI KAYAK TRIP

If you really want adventure, consider a kayak trip down the Na Pali Coast. June through August are normally considered the only months where ocean conditions permit kayak transit. Kayakers often put in at Ke'e Beach on the north shore, exiting at Polihale Beach on the west shore, a total of 16 miles. Along the way you will encounter incomparable beauty, innumerable waterfalls and sea caves, pristine aquamarine seas, turtles, flying fish and possibly dolphins. At night you can camp on beautiful beaches, sleeping to the sound of the surf. The experience will stay with you for a lifetime.

There are two ways to do this trip—either on a guided tour or on your own. Guided tours usually (but not always) do the entire trip in one day, offering a more structured—though less leisurely—way to see the coast. These trips, usually led by experienced guides, offer the *relative* safety of an expert. The drawbacks to this method are a lack of independent movement, a more brisk paddling pace (it's *tough* to do in one day) and usually the lack of an opportunity to camp.

Doing it on your own allows *you* to set the pace and the schedule. You go when you like, how you like, where you like and at the speed you like. You can rent a two-person kayak, if you desire. The drawback to going it alone is the lack of accompanying expertise. Consideration of this method necessitates a dispassionate evaluation of your skills, abilities, strengths and weaknesses. Although you don't need to be an

expert kayaker, it doesn't hurt to have experience. When we first did it on our own, our only kayaking experience had been a 3-hour trip up the Wailua River. After experiencing some trouble negotiating the kayak on the ocean, we came ashore and were fortunate enough to encounter someone who was able to instruct us in the proper paddling and loading techniques. On that first trip we experienced ideal conditions, which don't always occur, even during the summer. Please bear in mind that this trip is not for everyone. The Na Pali Coast is wild and unpredictable, and you are exposing yourself to the ocean's caprice. The usually calm June through August seas can become difficult with surprising suddenness. Most of the Na Pali boat companies can tell you stories about kayakers who had to be rescued when they got in over their heads (so to speak).

An excellent compromise is with **Kayak Kaua'i Outbound's** (826–9844) private guided trips. They'll send a guide with you for the first leg (to Kalalau Beach). Once you've demonstrated you're competent on the water, they'll leave. Camp there (with permits) and return at your own pace to Polihale where you can get pick-up service.

If you decide to do it on your own, here are a few things to keep in mind:

- Learn as much as you can about kayaking. (*Paddling Hawai'i* by Audrey Sutherland was our main reference when we made the trip.) Proper paddling and loading techniques are *essential*.

- In addition to other essentials, make sure you bring some waterproof sunblock, a hat, sunglasses, Chapstick and possibly Dramamine.

Sunset from the caves of Kalalau is your rich reward for a morning's paddle.

- Apply for camping permits *well in advance* (as much as 6–12 months in advance might be needed for some Na Pali campsites), and *make sure* you get a kayak landing stamp.

- Tell someone locally about your itinerary, leaving instructions on what to do if you don't arrive on time.

- Think through your food requirements. (You *won't* be living off the land.)

- Any water source you utilize along the way will require water treatment pills to avoid possible contraction of leptospirosis. Water filters that don't use chemicals are not considered reliable due to the corkscrew shape of the leptospirosis bacterium. Fresh water is present at the following beaches along the route: Keʻe, Hanakapiʻai, Kalalau, Honopu, Miloliʻi and Polihale, as well as some waterfalls that fall right into the ocean.

- Normal June through August conditions mean that the wind and currents are both pushing you in the direction you want to go, but *normal* doesn't mean *always*. Monitor ocean conditions by calling 245–6001 for National Weather Service weather, 245–3564 for Hawaiian Waters.

- Paddling in the early morning usually offers the calmest seas (sometimes like glass if you're lucky) and easier launchings.

- At press time only **Paradise Outdoor Adventures** (see KAYAKS in ACTIVITIES) would consider renting kayaks for completely unguided Na Pali trips. You'll have to convince them you're qualified.

- Unless you spring for pick-up service, you'll have to rent an extra car for a couple days and leave one at Keʻe Beach and one the at Polihale.

Here's some of what you can expect...

From Keʻe, Hanakapiʻai Beach is slightly over a mile. With campgrounds and a freshwater stream, Hanakapiʻai is a favorite place for hikers to camp (but a little too soon for you). Past Hanakapiʻai, you will start to see caves and waterfalls to your heart's content. Some of the caves are horseshoe-shaped, with separate entrances and exits. Explore 'em all.

Keep an eye out for dolphins and turtles, which become more plentiful as you get farther down the coast. At Kalalau, you have paddled 6 miles. If you're on your own, this is a good place to camp with half a mile of sand, fresh water and portable toilets. We like to pitch our tents in the caves near the beach. Kalalau is as far as hikers can go, so from here on you are in exclusive company.

Less than a mile past Kalalau is Honopu Beach. Landing crafts of all types, including *surfboards,* are prohibited. The only legal way to visit Honopu Beach is to swim there from Kalalau Beach (which can be hazardous if there's surf), or you can anchor your craft offshore and swim in (which can also be hazardous).

In all the Hawaiian Islands, and perhaps in all the world, you'll never find a more glorious, moving and mystical beach than Honopu. Unspoiled Honopu is only accessible by sea. It is actually two beaches, separated by a gigantic arch carved into Na Pali by Mother Nature's furious waves. During the summertime when the pounding Na Pali surf weakens, Honopu is reclaimed from the sea.

As you approach by kayak, you're left speechless by the sheer majesty of what unfolds before you. *Vertical* walls 1,200 feet high are the first characteristics you see from the sea. If you're lucky enough to visit here, the giant arch draws you toward it like a magnet. As you approach it, you can just make out the cascading waterfall around the bend. This is no mere trickle. This immense cataract can knock you down from its force. The stream continues through the arch and out to sea, providing a superb way to rinse off the saltwater. The southern beach of Honopu actually makes a better kayak landing than its northern counterpart, but the northern beach is the most dramatic, and its unfolding vista will surely stay with you forever.

Past Honopu, listen for goats. Although considered pests by island officials, it's charming to hear them from your position on the water. At 9 miles you come to a pair of reefs fringing a beach called Nu'alolo Kai. The waters inside the reef offer good snorkeling during calm seas (and you wouldn't be here if the seas weren't calm, right?). From your kayak, when the two signs onshore are aligned, you're heading toward the deeper channel and to shore.

In times past the Hawaiians mostly lived in the hanging valley above the beach. Access required scaling the vertical wall (actually, it's worse than vertical; it leans outward!) up a ladder and along a "trail" in the cliff, which was often nothing more

than cubbyholes for your feet. Worse yet was a large rock in the "trail" that was very difficult to get around. The Hawaiians even had a name for this dangerously placed immovable rock. They called it "fat man's misery."

Next, Miloli'i is 11 miles into your journey. Camping and fresh water make Miloli'i an inviting respite. There is a reef all along the beach and the same system to mark the channel as at Nu'alolo.

After Miloli'i, you will see a radio transmitter on top of a mountain belonging to Pacific Missile Range Facility. From the radar transmitter (helicopter pilots avoid getting too close to it, claiming they can feel their *da kines* cook), it's only 3 miles to Polihale. After your surf landing there, you can look forward to dragging your kayak through 500 feet of sand in searing heat, a task that would make a Himalayan Sherpa weep. (That pick-up service from Kayak Kaua'i sure sounds good, huh?)

Congratulations—you have now joined an elite club of adventurers who have braved the Na Pali. A not-so-quick shower at Polihale Beach, and you are ready to dance all night. Or maybe not.

An open-ceiling Na Pali sea cave called Queen's Bath is one of the many places to poke your kayak into during your voyage.

TRAIL

like paddling or the surf
~~~g. You can still see Na Pali.
Because the ultimate hike is also the
most famous hike in all Hawai'i—11
miles of switchbacks, hills and beautiful
scenery. See map below. Much of the
trail is narrow and not without hazards.
The trail calls for several stream cross-
ings. Don't cross if the water is too high.
Don't go if overnight hikes are a problem. To get the proper permits contact:
Division of State Parks, 3060 Eiwa
Street, Room 306, Lihu'e, HI 96766-
1875, (808) 274–3444.

Our map of the trail includes trailside
mile markers to give you an idea of distances. It is an accurate, computer-generated, shaded relief map drawn at a 45°
angle to give you a perspective of when
and how much climbing is involved—
altogether about 5,000 feet.

The first 2 miles of the trail leads to
Hanakapi'ai Beach. The second mile is
steep downhill (and tough coming back
up) and tricky in spots if you're a beginner hiker, but it's worth it. The views
along the coast are exceptional.

Hanakapi'ai is a beautiful but treacherous beach to swim. From here there
is a fairly tough 2-mile side trip to
Hanakapi'ai Falls, one of the more spectacular falls and pools on the north
shore. Many people like to reward themselves by swimming in the pool under
the falls. Watch out for falling rocks.

This is as far as you can go without a
permit. The authorities assume anyone
going past Hanakapi'ai will be camping.
If this is your plan, and you have your
state camping permit, keep on going.
Only 9 miles to go from here. At
Hanakoa, you have the choice of either
camping (if it's open), continuing to
Kalalau or taking the side trip to
Hanakoa Falls, which is even lovelier
than Hanakapi'ai. Less broken rock
around here means less *falling* rock, so
you stand a better chance of not getting
beaned by a falling rock if you decide to
linger under the falls. If you've come as
far as Hanakoa, go see the falls; it's less
than half a mile and worth the walk.

Back on the trail, your toughest
stretch is the last. From here to Kalalau
Beach you'll find lots of switchbacks and

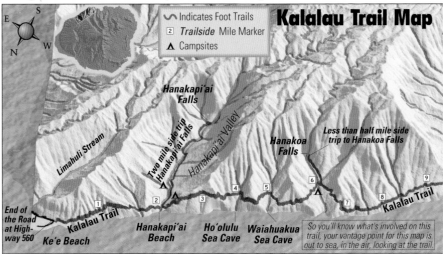

Kalalau Trail Map

⌃ Indicates Foot Trails
2 *Trailside* Mile Marker
⋀ Campsites

Hanakapi'ai Falls
Limahuli Stream
Two mile side trip Hanakapi'ai Falls
Hanakapi'ai Valley
Hanakoa Falls
Less than half mile side trip to Hanakoa Falls

End of the Road at Highway 560
Ke'e Beach
Kalalau Trail
Hanakapi'ai Beach
Ho'olulu Sea Cave
Waiahuakua Sea Cave
Kalalau Trail

So you'll know what's involved on this trail, your vantage point for this map is out to sea, in the air, looking at the trail.

Wild, raw and unforgettable—the Kalalau Trail.

a narrow trail at times. The views are stunning. Persevere and you will be richly rewarded. Wow! This is the glorious valley you see from the top of Waimea Canyon Drive at the Kalalau Lookout.

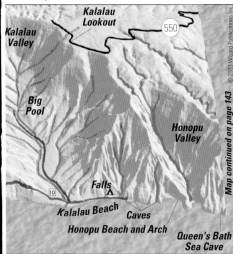

Kalalau
Lookout

550

Kalalau
Valley

Big
Pool

Honopu
Valley

10

Falls

Kalalau Beach   Caves

Honopu Beach and Arch

Queen's Bath
Sea Cave

Map continued on page 143

© 2003 Wizard Publications Inc.

The beach, the valley and the isolation all make Kalalau a magic place. There is a 2-mile trail inland, which takes you to "Big Pool," a large natural pool in the stream.

Have you ever read *Koolau the Leper* by Jack London? It's based on the true story of Koolau, who fled to Kalalau in the 1880s after authorities refused to let his wife accompany him to the Kalaupapa leper settlement on Moloka'i. On July 2, 1893, a ship carrying 12 police, 14 soldiers, the sheriff, many rifles and a howitzer came ashore to capture Koolau and the other lepers who had joined him. After Koolau shot two of the soldiers dead and a third accidentally shot himself in the head (oops), the authorities decided to leave Koolau alone. He died in Kalalau in 1896 from his affliction.

As you stand on the beach at Kalalau, it's amazing to think that the entire valley was once populated. It was only in 1919 that this isolated valley was finally abandoned as people sought the life available to them in Lihu'e and other towns. This is as far as you can go. A half mile farther down the coast is the most beautiful beach in all the islands, maybe in all the Pacific—Honopu Beach. There is none finer. Period. The only legal way to visit the beach is to swim there. If you do this, beware that the current is against you coming back. Only during calm seas, only with fins and only if you're a strong swimmer. In late summer Kalalau Beach snakes its way closer to Honopu, and people walk on the rocks and sand most of the way. Beware of unexpectedly large waves if you do this. For more information on Honopu, see NA PALI KAYAK TRIP above.

With clear water that drops so quickly, it's easy to see why Ni'ihau dives can be so compelling.

Kalalau has portable toilets. The waterfall provides fresh water, which should be treated before drinking. In fact, all fresh water in nature should be treated to avoid possible bacteriological contamination from animals or people polluting the stream.

If you want the security of a guide, **Kayak Kaua'i** at 826–9844 has a six-day guided hike into Kalalau for $1,550.

NI'IHAU SCUBA DIVE

For SCUBA divers looking for clean, clear, virgin waters, several dive operators offer three-tank dives near the privately owned island of Ni'ihau, mostly off Lehua Rock north of the island. (For more information on Ni'ihau, see INTRODUCTION.) Since this island is in the rain shadow of Kaua'i, there are no permanent streams on the island (and consequently no runoff). So visibility is often *well* over a hundred feet. This is possibly the best diving in the state. Between dives we've found ourselves snorkeling with dolphins. *Very* cool.

The waters are rich in critters, arches, caves and pelagics. There's a good chance you will share the water with sharks, so be prepared. The dive requires a 70-mile round trip (if you leave from Port Allen) boat ride and involves drop-offs, currents and sometimes rough seas. This is not for the inexperienced diver. Dives are usually deeper here. The table in the SCUBA section of ACTIVITIES tells which companies offer Ni'ihau trips, mostly around the summer months. We like **Bubbles Below** the best. It's a very good idea to book a month in advance to insure space.

'OPAEKA'A FALLS HIKE

This one eluded us. For years we couldn't find a way down the to bottom of 'Opaeka'a Falls. Then a friend showed us this way, and we feel like fools for not finding it earlier.

First things first. This is *not* a maintained trail. It's pure wilderness on state

land. The state isn't encouraging you to go and they don't maintain anything here. It's simply a faint, vague pig trail that's steep and slippery in spots. If you go, you're practically trailblazing, so if things don't work out well, blame the pigs, *not* the state.

To get there, drive past the 'Opaeka'a Falls lookout on Hwy 580 in Kapa'a. (See map on page 59.) Near the 2 mile marker is a dirt turnout after the guard-rail stops. A trail leads through the jungle to

Oh, how grand it will be—when you see 'Opaeka'a from below. Just ask the swimmer in the pool.

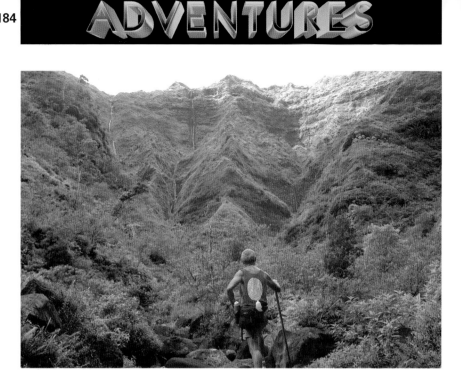

Hike through bamboo, cross the stream several times, step in mud, walk on wet rocks. All this just to marvel at Makaleha. It works for our hiker friend pictured here.

the stream below. After crossing the usually knee-deep stream, you want to head downstream at roughly a 45° angle away from the stream. You go through trees, up a short hill and end up on an odd-looking barren plateau. Walk across the plateau, and there's a hard-to-find path through the spindly strawberry guava trees. It's on a side of a hill, and you're glad that the trees are there to hold on to.

The "trail" leads down to the stream below, but there are several dicey parts that allow you an opportunity to take a bad tumble if you're not careful. We'd avoid this path if it's muddy.

The bottom is a lovely oasis of ti plants, ginger and trees. The falls are *much* larger than they appear from the lookout. (151 feet high—we measured it.) It probably took you a half hour or more to get to the bottom, and you need to remember your path for the way back up.

MAKALEHA HIKE

This hike is in the Adventures section because it is only for the advanced hiker. The trail goes along a beautiful stream, through a bamboo grove and offers lush scenery. There are a number of places along the way to bathe in the stream, which can be deep in spots. Past the end of the trail is a waterfall just for you, if you have the gumption to walk in the stream for a third of a mile. The problem is that the trail is a trail-of-use and is not an officially maintained. As a result, it is splendid in some parts, wretched in others. Some big steps up and down and mud spots keep it interesting. You will have to walk in the stream in some places, so we usually bring tabis (fuzzy mittens for your feet that work well on slippery rocks). Even without the waterfall, you will get a real Indiana Jones feel for this part of God's country.

The trail starts at the end of Kahuna road in northern Kapa'a. (See top of map on page 58 to get there.) From here you walk past the water tank to the trail. At one point, the trail on the right (northern) bank veers away to a water tunnel. Don't go there, but instead cross the main stream at the remains of an old concrete dam. (The area just below the dam makes a dandy swimming hole.) You won't go far through the bamboo grove when the trail goes up steeply. *Bypass* that part and instead walk in and up the stream for about 40 feet, past the rock face, and pick up the trail, still on the left (southern) bank. From here it can be muddy if it's been raining (and it probably has been). This is the real Kaua'i—lush, wet and beautiful. There are places all along here to visit the stream; watch for them. At one point the trail dumps into the stream, and you'll have to cross it onto an island in the river. More upstream walking and eventually you'll have to cross and pick it up on the opposite side of the stream.

The trail's more faint there. You should always be able to hear the stream, but if you get into trouble, there probably won't be anyone along to help. Bring mosquito repellent or don't go. Footwear should include hiking sandals or boots and tabis for stream walking. Bring water. When you come to a fork (where three streams converge at a stunning vista), the waterfall is up the leftmost stream. Allow ample time to get back. In all, it's only 1½ miles each way, but the going is pretty slow in many spots, and it *can* take much of the day.

THE BLUE ROOM

Located in the upper wet cave near Ha'ena, shortly before the end of the road on Kaua'i's north shore, is a phenomenon unknown even to most locals. It's called the Blue Room. It's a separate chamber where light, filtered through the cold fresh water, turns everything blue. We put it in this section because accessing it requires swimming in the cold cave water to the back of the cave, going through a triangular shaped opening (see photo on next page) and swimming about 10 feet to your left until you enter the chamber. Once inside, there's barely anything to hold onto, so you will probably have to tread water until your eyes adjust. The chamber is about 7–8 feet in diameter and 5–6 feet overhead.

The water level varies slowly over time, but we haven't determined if it's due to rainfall variations or tide changes as the fresh water bumps up against the seawater through the ground. Even after stationing a nephew there for a long, boring day to observe the level, we're at a loss to say why it varies. (Thanks anyway, Ryan.)

Makaleha Hike Map

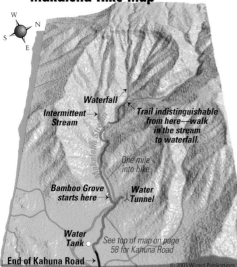

W N S E

Waterfall

Intermittent → Stream

Trail indistinguishable from here—walk in the stream to waterfall.

One mile into hike

Bamboo Grove starts here →

Water Tunnel

Water Tank

See top of map on page 58 for Kahuna Road

End of Kahuna Road →

© 2003 Wizard Publications, Inc.

Low water levels bring too much light, making it less remarkable. High water is better, but the opening to the chamber is shorter. You may have to duck your head before the chamber if the level is really high. If enclosed places aren't your thing, neither is this. If you have trouble negotiating your way, don't blame us. Most have no trouble, some do. Any freshwater anywhere in nature can have bacteria such as lepto—see page 34. The county has erected a sign to point this out. The county may not *want* you to swim here, but you *are* allowed, and it's hard to imagine lepto existing in this particular water that is *so* filtered by nature. All in all, if the light is cooperating, it should be fun. If the light is not cooperating—at least you got a chance to cool off. Besides, the cave looks kind of cool even if you stay dry.

To get there, park at the lot on the ocean side of the highway ²/₁₀ mile before the end of the road at Ke'e. There is a short trail up to the wet cave on the mauka side. Be careful walking down into the cave; it's slippery. Reef shoes and a snorkel make cave exploration easier. You're on your own from here.

The entrance to the Blue Room when the opening's very high.

HONOPU RIDGE TO A DROP DEAD VIEW

Imagine a trail that cuts through forest, ventures down a ridge and culminates in perhaps the most inspirational view on the island. Until recently that's exactly what you had to do...*imagine* it. Back in 1982 one of Kaua'i's most delicious trails was damaged by a hurricane. The State Park, ever grumbling about budgets, decided not to put in the effort to reopen it. Over the course of two decades it became unrecognizable. But recently volunteers have spent the time to bring it back to life. Today Honopu Trail is available to ambitious hikers. Why ambitious? Because, although it's only about 2 miles each way, there's opportunity to wander off the trail if you're not careful. Most of the trail is obvious, but there are a few hunter trails that might lead you astray. (See maps on pages 143 and 138.)

Located on the west side, you take Hwy 50 to Waimea Canyon Road (550). At ⁴/₁₀ mile past the 17 mile marker (not far from the end of the road at Kalalau) there's a turnout on the curve about 100 feet past a telephone pole. Park there and the trail heads left toward the coast. After 5–10 minutes is your first confusing intersection. The right fork is the correct one. (The incorrect left fork leads down to a stream bed.) From here you'll be grateful for long pants because the native Pacific false staghorn ferns tend to claw at your legs. (Jeans can feel heavy—we've become fond of light pants with zip-off legs.) Soon most of your 1,000 feet of elevation loss will occur. (You actually climbed a bit until now.) Always stay on the path most worn. About 1 mile into the trail (it will seem

Sometimes it's hard to capture the immensity of what you're seeing on film. The boat offshore and the helicopter (the light blip above our friend's hat) are testament to the grandness of what awaits you on the Honopu Ridge.

like more) you'll be on a wide ridge that will eventually get narrow enough to see Honopu on one side and Awa-'awapuhi on the other. Eventually the trail comes to a glorious lookout presided over by an 'ohi'a tree on a dirt bluff. The vista into Honopu Valley is so magnificent that it defies description. The entire heavenly valley is before you. Honopu Beach and the Pacific are to your left 3,000 feet below. The scene is so intense that it literally looks unreal. If clouds are in the valley, wait a while. They tend to come and go. The trail continues another 15 minutes, terminating at a point where the ridge takes a drop down to a razorback spine (which you *don't* want to visit). From the end you're treated to a tasty view of Na Pali coast.

At press time there were orange paint marks on some of the trees leading the way. While on the trail, if you take a wrong turn, keep track of where you've been and backtrack. Nothing's worse than being lost in the forest. Our first time in (before someone put up the paint marks) we made two wrong turns, realized our mistakes, and returned to the intersection to find the right way. *Very* old chainsaw cuts tell you you're on the old, correct trail, and a couple of times you'll have to get on your knees through a tunnel of ferns. Also, make sure you're back at your car *at least* 1½ hours before sunset. It will take most people 1½–2½ hours each way, and the trip back up is fairly strenuous. Bring gobs of water down, suck 'em up at the overlook, and bring only what you need back up. The trail has a few areas where there's opportunity to fall or twist an ankle. One short stretch is on the side of a dirt hill that may make some nervous. It's in the ADVENTURE section because of the poor trail conditions in a few scattered areas and because of the potential to get off the trail.

MOUNTAIN BIKE/HIKE THE OTHER SIDE OF WAIMEA CANYON

There's a trail in Koke'e called Kohua Ridge Trail that leads 2½ miles to a dazzling view of Waimea Canyon *from the other side*. Problem is, the trailhead is 3⁶/10 miles from where most cars can go. But bring along a mountain bike to get you there, and you have an afternoon adventure. See map on page 138 and take Mohihi Camp 10 Road to where the map indicates 4WD only (1⁶/10 miles from Hwy 550). The ride to the trailhead is along a dirt road through the forest. The sights are beautiful along the way. The biking is fairly strenuous due to the rolling nature of the road. Get a decent bike with shocks and low gears.

At the trailhead, stash your bike in some bushes and proceed. (Be sure to repeatedly refer to the map so you can anticipate the easy-to-miss sign.) The trail crosses Mohihi Ditch via a small bridge, then heads down to Mohihi Stream. It's usually a boulder hop across the stream. (Don't cross if it's raging.) Then comes the toughest part—¼ mile of steep trail, a slight leveling and then a shorter steep part before the saddle where it veers southwest. (Remember this point for your return.) At the end of the trail is a stunning view of Po'omau Canyon to your right, Koai'e Canyon to your left, with Waimea Canyon in front of you. You're at the apex of all of them. Across the canyon is the Waimea Canyon Lookout, where mere mortals view the spectacular canyon. *You,* on the other hand, have earned the right to see it from a more exclusive perspective. It's been pretty strenuous getting to this point, but it's soon forgotten in the glory of your own personal overlook.

Take your time, but be back to your car before dark.

SECRET TUNNEL TO THE NORTH SHORE

Imagine that you're in an east shore valley. You come upon a tunnel that's a *mile* long. From the moment you enter, you can see the light at the other end. When you emerge, you're in the nearly inaccessible back of the north shore's Hanalei Valley, surrounded by nearly vertical mountains, a perfect river and no people. Aside from a few hunters (who call it Ka'apoko Tunnel), almost no one on Kaua'i had even *heard* of this tunnel until we revealed it. Those who had heard of it considered it one of those urban legends, a myth. Well, it's no myth. And until recently it has been a surprisingly well-kept secret.

In the 1920s a sugar company was seriously coveting the abundant water flowing out the Hanalei River. They needed the water for their east shore sugar. So for $300,000 they carved this tunnel and diverted 28 million gallons of water a day under the mountain and into a series of ditches to quench their thirsty crops. But times change. As sugar production dwindled on the east shore, they found that they no longer needed the north shore's water. So years ago they stopped diverting the water and abandoned the dam. The flume to divert the water is no longer there. They couldn't divert water into this tunnel even if they wanted to without doing major reconstruction on the dam. But the tunnel, blasted out of solid rock, remains.

Getting there can be a sloppy affair. It involves walking 2½ miles along a trail through fairly muddy conditions. (It rains about 160 inches annually here, spread fairly evenly throughout the year.) Once in the tunnel you notice that there's water standing in it. That's from the small amount of water that occasionally drips from the ceiling. It's just the right

A hiker marvels at the richness of Kaua'i, which is ever-present on this hike.

ancient Hawaiians used to walk on to reach the summit of Wai'ale'ale where their altar, at the wettest spot on Earth, still remains. As you approach what appears to be the the the end, you see an odd sight: railroad tracks in the shallow water, probably used to haul the debris out of the tunnel during construction. At the light at the not-quite-end of the tunnel, you can step outside momentarily to visit a small waterfall waiting for you. Then it's back in the tunnel for the remaining ¼ mile. That latter portion is partially lined with cement and shorings, making anyone 6 feet tall duck for a bit. At the real end you need to get up on the dike and take the overgrown trail near the tunnel exit. It goes down for about a minute to the Hanalei River. During good weather the scenery is magnificent. The mountains tower all around you. Wai'ale'ale plateau is above and to your left, its side etched with waterfalls. The river, with some impossibly large boulders, makes a perfect place for lunch.

Most will be more than satisfied with this destination. But if you started early (hiking by 7 or 7:30 a.m.), there is one more challenge for the intrepid. You've been through a mile of tunnel already and are at the river. There's a *very* faint trail on the other side of the river that leads 5–10 minutes upstream to *another* ⁷⁄₁₀ mile-long tunnel. It's more dicey. The

amount to keep about four inches of water fresh. The tunnel is about 6 feet wide and 7–10 feet high with an occasional need for a head duck on the straight portion. The bottom is flat and lined with small rocks, which makes for fairly straightforward walking. You'll notice occasional round holes where dynamite was going to be placed, but wasn't. The tunnel reverberates with the ever-constant sound of the splashing of your feet in the ankle-high water. About 900 feet above you is the ridge that the

Hikers entering the tunnel.

unbelievable and worth all the effort you went through to get here.

A Few Basics

Driving to the trailhead means taking a dirt road (see map). There's a gate on the road *just past* the trail. Hiking boots are recommended on this trail. Tabis (described on page 135), water socks or old tennis shoes work best *in* the tunnel. (The latter cushion the bottoms of your feet the best.) Tabis the whole way might be desirable if it's real muddy. Long pants are also recommended. Ferns have a habit of sticking out in the trail, scratching at your legs. Jeans are OK, but they get heavy and stick to your legs, making it harder. Lighter pants are preferred. Look for delicious red thimbleberries along the way. (The redder, the better.) Bring a flashlight (or two) for the tunnel. Also bring water and snacks.

The trail to the tunnel is a hunters' trail and is usually muddy. The first 100 feet are the muddiest with a permanent puddle near the place where you park. Several short stretches are on uneven terrain and caution needs to be taken. In the first 5 minutes you'll have to cross the Wailua River. *Usually* it's done by hopping across a couple of rocks. If it's too deep and you aren't comfortable, don't go. If it's been raining a lot, don't go. During very heavy rains you may find that the river isn't crossable coming back, presenting you with a dilemma. Just after the crossing, walk upstream, then pick up the trail. Soon there's a large bamboo grove. Bamboo is the best material there is for walking sticks, and it's a good idea to have one on this hike. (It makes a good spider stick in case there are webs across the trail, as any trail can have.) Cut it so that a knuckle is near the bottom, acting as a natural stopper, preventing dirt or

trail's reasonably close but hard to find. Once inside the tunnel, there's lots of head ducking, and it has a more rickety feel. Finding this additional tunnel means working your way through the brush staying inland a ways. An alternate way to find that final tunnel is to stay in the Hanalei River, head upstream past a dam, veer to the right when the river forks, and look for a hard-to-see opening where the tunnel starts. If you find it, go to the end. When the tunnel ends, there's an offshoot to the left. Not far from there, you come to an incline with water gurgling down. Scoot up and you'll emerge in a Shangri-La that will make you giddy with joy—a cathedral of 200-foot sheer walls so steep they actually lean *inward*. Water drips from above, creating an exotic backdrop. To the left is a pounding waterfall. The setting is

mud from filling the hollow tube.

The trail is intermittently "paved" with 'ohi'a logs from long ago. Avoid false trails, like the one on the left 30 minutes into the trail after a long triangular-shaped hedge. Remember, you'll never go more than 15 minutes without seeing the 'ohi'a logs. You'll cross a couple of smaller streams (a foot wide) and a slightly larger stream.

After 1½ hours or so, when the trail encounters a large stream again and seems to end, it angles back through the grass for several minutes before parallel-ing the stream again. It crosses the stream when the stream makes a left turn near a wire. It's the only part of the trail that's not easy to see and seems to confuse people the most. Once you cross the river again, it's not far before you walk on old boards over a ditch, go past an old collapsed ditchman's shack, and to the

gauging station and tunnel. It takes us 1¾–2½ hours *to* the first tunnel, and about 45 minutes *in* the tunnel. Coming back is a bit faster. You'll gain about 600 feet with all the ups and downs.

Needless to say, you'll have the opportunity to get muddy, slip on your 'okole, bump your head, twist your ankle, etc. on this adventure. Use your best judgment. This tunnel is not maintained for this purpose, so please don't complain to *anybody* if you have any problems. This is a strenuous (when muddy), exciting and memorable adventure with absolutely *no* guarantees. *That's* why it's an adventure.

The map tells you how to get to the trailhead. A regular car can usually go past the sign that says 4WD only but *may* have trouble on the last part of the road. You'll have to see. This road is sporadically improved. 4WDS are a sure thing.

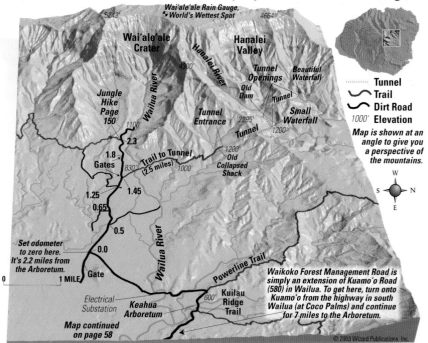

Tunnel & Jungle Hikes Map

RESTAURANT INDEX

No jacket required.

ISLAND DINING

By their very nature, restaurant reviews are the most subjective part of any guidebook. Nothing strains the credibility of a guidebook more. No matter what we say, if you eat at enough restaurants here, you will eventually have a dining experience directly in conflict with what this book leads you to believe. All it takes is one person to wreck what is usually a good meal. You've probably had an experience where a friend referred you to a restaurant using reverent terms, indicating that you were about to experience dining ecstasy. And, of course, when you go there, the food is awful and the waiter is a jerk. There are many variables involved in getting a good or bad meal. Is the chef new? Was the place sold last month? Was the waitress just released from prison for mauling a customer? We truly hope that our reviews match your experience. If they don't (or even if they do),

please drop us a line. Readers help us tremendously in keeping tabs on the restaurants.

We often leave out restaurant hours of operation because they change so frequently that the information would be immediately out of date. These decisions are usually made quite capriciously in Hawai'i. If you're going to drive a long way to eat at an establishment, it's best to call first. Restaurants that stand out from the others in some way are highlighted with the ONO symbol.

In some restaurants around the island you'll see guidebook recommendation plaques, guidebook door stickers and signed guidebooks, but you won't see ours. The reason? We *never* tell them when we're there. We review everything on the island *anonymously*. We're more interested in being treated like everyone else than in copping a free meal. How could you trust our opinion if the restaurant *knew* who we were?

By their reviews, many guidebooks lead you to believe that every meal you eat in Hawai'i will be a feast, the best food in the free world. Frankly, that's not our style. Kaua'i, like anywhere else, has ample opportunity to have lousy food served in a rotten ambiance by uncaring waiters. In the interest of space, we've left out some of the dives. We did, however, leave in some of the turkeys just to demonstrate that we live in the real world.

For each restaurant, we list the price *per person* you can expect to pay. It ranges from the least expensive entrées to the most expensive plus a beverage and usually an appetizer. You can spend more if you try, but this is a good guideline. *The price excludes alcoholic beverages since this component of a meal can be so variable.* Obviously, everyone's ordering pattern is different, but we thought that it would be easier to compare restaurants using actual prices, than if we used symbols like different numbers of dollar signs or drawings of forks or whatever to differentiate prices between restaurants.

When we give directions to a restaurant, *mauka side* of highway means "toward the mountain" (or away from the ocean). The shopping centers we mention are on the maps to that area.

Very few restaurants care how you dress. A few discourage tank tops and bathing suits. Some of the fancy resorts like the Princeville Hotel, Sheraton or Hyatt have dress codes. Their dress codes require **resort wear**, meaning covered shoes and collared shirts for men (nice shorts are *usually* OK), dressy sportswear or dresses for women.

It's legal to bring your own alcohol to restaurants in Hawai'i, and many restaurants, especially inexpensive ones, have no objections to letting you B.Y.O.B.

Local food can be difficult to classify. Basically, local food combines Hawaiian, American, Japanese, Chinese, Filipino and several other types and is (not surprisingly) eaten mainly by locals.

Pacific Rim is sort of a fusion of American and various countries around the Pacific, including Hawaiian and Asian. It's a fine (and subjective) line between American and Pacific Rim. We don't have a separate **Seafood** section because nearly every restaurant on Kaua'i serves some kind of fish.

Below are descriptions of various island foods. Not all are Hawaiian, but this might help if you encounter dishes unfamiliar to you.

ISLAND FISH/SEAFOOD

Ahi–Tuna; raw in sashimi or poke, also seared, blackened, baked or grilled; good in fish sandwiches. Try painting ahi steaks with mayonnaise, which *completely* burns off when BBQ'd but seals in the moisture. You end up tasting only the moist ocean steak. Generally most plentiful April through September.

Hapu'upu'u–A grouper not usually available during the summer; best served baked or steamed.

Kona Crab–An elusive sand burrowing crab that can reach 8" and can only be caught by baited nets and traps; sometimes sold on the side of the road.

Lobster–Hawaiian spiny lobster is quite good; also called "bugs" by lobster hunters. Maine lobster kept alive on the Big Island are also available.

Mahimahi–Deep ocean fish also known as a dolphinfish; served at luaus; very common in restaurants. Sometimes tastes fishy, which can be offset in the preparation.

Marlin–Tasty when smoked, otherwise can be tough; the Pacific Blue Marlin (kajiki) is available almost year round.

Monchong–Excellent tasting deepwater fish, available year round. Usually served marinated and grilled.

Onaga–Also known as a ruby snapper; excellent eating in many preparations.

Ono–(Wahoo); *awesome* eating fish and can be prepared many ways; most plentiful May through October. Ono is also the Hawaiian word for delicious.

Opah–(Moonfish); excellent eating in many different preparations; generally available April through August.

'Opakapaka–(Crimson snapper); great tasting fish generally cooked several ways. Common Oct.–Feb.

'Opihi–Using a specialized knife, these must be pried off rocks at the shoreline, which can be hazardous. Best eaten raw mixed with salt.

Poke–Fresh raw fish or octopus mixed with seaweed (limu), sesame seed and other seasonings and oil.

Shutome–Swordfish; dense meat that can be cooked several ways. Most plentiful March through July.

Shrimp–Kekaha shrimp or prawns are farm raised on Kaua'i and are excellent.

Hanalei Dolphin (826–6113) buys from the fishing boats and has a fish market that sells fresh locally caught fish. Other places include **Cost-U-Less** (823–6803), **Foodland** (822–7271) and **Safeway** (822–2464) in Kapa'a, **Fish Express** (across from Wal-mart) in Lihu'e and the **Koloa Fish Market** in Koloa.

Lu'au Foods

Chicken lu'au–Chicken cooked in coconut milk and taro leaves.

Haupia–Coconut milk custard.

Hawaiian sweet potatoes–Purple inside; not as sweet as mainland sweet potatoes but very flavorful.

Kalua pig–Pig cooked in an underground oven called an imu, shredded and mixed with Hawaiian sea salt (outstanding!).

Lomi salmon–Chilled salad consisting of raw, salted salmon, tomatoes and two kinds of onions.

Poi–Steamed taro root pounded into a paste. It's a starch that will take on the taste of other foods mixed with it. Consider dipping your pipi kaula in it. Visitors are encouraged to try it at least once so they can badmouth it with authority.

Poke–See Island Fish above.

Other Island Foods

Apple bananas–A smaller, denser, smoother texture than regular (Williams) bananas.

Barbecue sticks–Teriyaki-marinated pork, chicken or beef pieces barbecued and served on bamboo sticks.

Bento–Japanese box lunch.

Breadfruit–Melon-sized starchy fruit; served baked, deep fried, steamed or boiled. Definitely an acquired taste.

Crackseed–Chinese-style spicy preserved fruits and seeds.

Guava–About the size of an apricot or plum. The inside is full of seeds, so it is rarely eaten raw. Used primarily for juice, jelly or jam.

Hawaiian supersweet corn–The finest corn you ever had, even raw. We'll lie, cheat, steal or maim to get it fresh.

Huli huli chicken–Hawaiian BBQ style.

Ka'u oranges–Big Island oranges. Usually, the uglier the orange, the better it tastes.

Kim chee–A Korean relish consisting of pickled cabbage, onions, radishes, garlic and chilies.

Kona coffee–Grown on the Kona coast of the Big Island. Smooth, mild flavor; available everywhere.

Kulolo–Steamed taro pudding. (Tasty.)

Laulau–Pork, beef or fish wrapped in taro and ti leaves, then steamed. (You don't eat the ti leaf wrapping.)

Liliko'i–Passion fruit.

Loco moco–Rice, meat patty, egg and gravy. A hit with cholesterol lovers.

Lychee–A reddish, woody peel that is discarded for the sweet, white fruit inside. Be careful of the pit. Good, small seed (or chicken-tongue) lychees are so good, they should be illegal.

Macadamia nut–A large, round nut.

Malassada–Portuguese donut dipped in sugar.

Manapua–Steamed or baked bun filled with meat.

Mango–Bright orange fruit with yellow pink skin. Distinct, tasty flavor.

Manju–Cookie filled with a sweet center.

Methley plums–A wild fruit harvested with a permit at Koke'e State Park during the summer months.

Musubi–Cold steamed rice, sliced Spam rolled in black seaweed wrappers.

'Opihi–Limpets found on ocean rocks. Eaten raw mixed with salt. Texture is similar to clams or mussels.

Papaya–Melon-like, pear-shaped fruit with yellow skin, best eaten chilled. Good at breakfast. Kaua'i has a variety called sunrise or strawberry papaya.

Pipi Kaula–Hawaiian-style beef jerky. Excellent when dipped in poi. (Even if you don't like poi, this combo works.)

Plate lunch–An island favorite as an inexpensive, filling lunch. Consists of "two-scoop rice," a scoop of macaroni salad and some type of meat, either beef, chicken or fish. Sometimes called a box lunch. Great for picnics.

Portuguese sausage–Pork sausage, highly seasoned with red pepper.

Pupu–Appetizer, finger foods or snacks.

Saimin–Noodles cooked in either chicken, pork or fish broth. Word is peculiar to Hawai'i. Local Japanese say the dish comes from China. Local Chinese say it comes from Japan.

Sea Salt–Excellent (and strong) salt dis-tilled from seawater. Much of our sea salt comes from Salt Pond Beach Park.

Shave ice–A block of ice is "shaved" into a ball with flavored syrup poured over the top. Best served with ice cream on the bottom. Very delicious.

Smoothie–Usually papaya, mango, frozen passion fruit and frozen banana, but almost any fruit can be used to make this milkshake-like drink. Add milk for creaminess.

Taro–Found in everything from enchiladas to breads and rolls to taro chips and fritters. Tends to color foods purple. Has lots of fluoride for your teeth.

NORTH SHORE AMERICAN

BEACH RESTAURANT 826–2900

A fun place to have lunch. Located outdoors next to the pool at the Princeville Hotel commanding an intimate view of the adjacent beach and Hanalei Bay, the service and food are good but *expensive*. ($10 for a *hot dog!*) Sandwiches, burgers, chicken and a few surprises like quesadillas. Full (but pricey) bar available. Only dress code requirement is that you must have at least *something* on. **$10–$20** per person. Their Sinfully Chocolate Cake lives up to its name—*very* good.

BUBBA'S BURGERS 826–7839

ONO Funky place to get decent (but *small*) burgers, chili rice, etc., with a limited choice of burger toppings. Their motto is, "We cheat tourists, drunks and attorneys." So if you are a drunk attorney visiting the island, you're on your own, counselor. **$5–$10**. On Hwy in Hanalei and Hwy in north Kapa'a, can't miss 'em. Nothing stands out individually, but overall the place works.

CHUCK'S STEAK HOUSE 826–6211

The food's good, no doubt about it.

Burgers and sandwiches for lunch, steak and seafood for dinner. But it's *way* overpriced. A 12 oz. NY steak is over $25. A lobster tail is $43. And, pardon us for sounding picky, but if you order steak and lobster for *$50* and want a baked potato instead of rice, don't you think it's tacky to charge an extra $2? Just give us the potato for crying out loud! (Oh, it felt good to get that off my chest.) Lastly, if we have one suggestion for Chuck's, it's this: Slow down and stop rushing people. You get the feeling that they can't *wait* till you're finished. We've seen couples in and out in 30 minutes, but $120 poorer. Efficient service is to be admired, but let us eat *at our own pace.* (Boy, we're just ranting fools on this one, aren't we?) **$7–$12** for lunch, **$25–$75** for dinner. Their senior and kids' menus are cheaper. Reservations recommended. Located in Princeville Shopping Center. If you have money to burn and no time to spare, you'll wonder why we didn't give them an ONO.

FOODLAND DELI 826–9880

Though the Foodland grocery store in Princeville Shopping Center will *never* be considered a bargain (their grocery prices are confiscatory), the deli is a good deal. For **$3–$5** you can pick up a fairly decent sandwich (either packaged or custom made) and be on your merry way to the beach.

HANALEI DOLPHIN RESTAURANT 826–6113

This is a north shore tradition that often has great seafood and steak in a pleasant, open air atmosphere. Their problem is reliability, which is why there's no ONO. Sometimes very good, sometimes not good at all. They have some outdoor tables on a lawn next to the Hanalei River—very nice at lunch or while wait-ing for your indoor table at dinner. They are often busy and don't take reservations—so if waiting bothers you, arrive early or you're out of luck. The seafood chowder is usually great. So's the ceviche. We also like the Haole Chicken. They have a seafood market, a good place to pick up fish for cooking back at the condo. **$8–$12** for lunch, **$20–$30** for dinner. Located on Hwy 560 in Hanalei, can't miss it.

HANALEI GOURMET 826–2524

We used to like and recommend this place—my how things have changed! When Zelo's moved in across the street, this place went downhill. Service is poor and the food average. We'll spare you the other gory details. Unless it's night-time and you're looking for a place to prowl, you'll want to take your business over to Zelo's. Burgers, sandwiches, full bar and a small deli next door. Sometimes it's OK, usually not. **$7–$15**. In the Old Hanalei School across from Ching Young Center, Hanalei. Live music nightly.

JAVA KAI 826–6717

An excellent place to stop for breakfast on the north shore. Good coffee and coffee drink selection (love the chai latte!), tasty food and reasonable prices. Their aloha bars are devastating *when they're fresh.* Indoor and outdoor tables available in this cozy place. Try their desserts and baked goods. **$4–$8**. Across the street from Ching Young Center, Hanalei. Open at 6:30 a.m. Also see review on page 203.

LIGHTHOUSE BISTRO 828–0480

First of all, you can't see the Kilauea Lighthouse from here. (Sorry to burst your bubble.) Lunch is our favorite.

(Dinner is overpriced.) The hummus wraps are good, and they have a decent French dip and a small selection of sandwiches and burgers, fish tacos, seafood, veal and cannelloni. We considered giving them an ONO, but the high dinner prices and an overabundance of flies at lunch scared us off. **$8–$12** for lunch, **$15–$30** for dinner.

PARADISE BAR & GRILL 826–1775

In Princeville Shopping Center. Fish for lunch, steak and seafood for dinner. Nothing special, nothing memorable. **$7–$10** for lunch, **$15–$20** for dinner.

POSTCARDS 826–1191

Overrated. That's the operative word, and our reader feedback seems to concur. Renowned on the island, the food is distinctive and can be fairly well prepared. They use organic ingredients and have creative selections. Ambiance is homey. But the high prices and uneven service hurt 'em. Breakfast incudes offerings such as seven-grain pancakes for $8 (that's more than a buck a grain!) a bagel ($4) or their version of eggs benedict ($13). Coffee is $3, but at least we don't have to beg for refills any more. The food may not be hot all the time. Though they serve fish during dinner, this is a vegetarian restaurant, so don't even think of ordering bacon with your eggs. Dinner, however, works a bit better. (But $26 for fish makes it hard to swallow.) Taro fritters make a good pupu, and the fresh fish or the thai coconut curry are recommended. Vegetarians and vegans *love* Postcards and will probably be dismayed that we didn't give them an ONO, but others may scratch their heads and wonder what they're missing. **$7–$15** for breakfast, **$15–$25** for dinner. On mauka side of the highway in Hanalei.

PRINCEVILLE RESTAURANT/BAR 826–5050

This has been a pretty decent restaurant, and it has been an embarrassing dump. Right now it's simply...OK. It's too large inside, giving it a lonely, echoey feeling, but the food's acceptable and the service friendly. Eggs and pancakes, etc., for breakfast, hot and cold sandwiches for lunch. Golfers need not avoid, others need not bother. **$8–$12** for breakfast and lunch. Located just before Princeville in the Prince Golf Course Clubhouse.

WINDS OF BEAMREACH 826–6143

Known for their steak and seafood. The ono fish is recommended when available. **$20–$30** per person. (Cheaper sunset specials available.) Reservations recommended. Located in Princeville next to Pali Ke Kua condominiums. By the way, *beam reach* is a nautical term for when the wind is coming abeam, or a right angle from the length of the boat. (We didn't actually *know* that. We had to look it up.)

ZELO'S BEACH HOUSE 826–9700

A great place! Though not near the beach (you can't even see the ocean from here), the food and atmosphere make this an easy winner. Lots of different burgers, beef, chicken and fish with different permutations. Also some pasta and sandwiches. *Very* extensive beer list, and the wine selection is well-considered. Excellent portions, good salads, fish sandwich, burritos (with chicken or tofu), veggie items...we could go on but suffice it to say the food and beverages are excellent and the selection vast. The chocolate suicide cake is deep and dark—*very* chocolatey. Lunch is **$8–$15**, **$10–$20** for dinner. Located in Hanalei, can't miss it.

ITALIAN

KILAUEA BAKERY & PAU HANA PIZZA
828-2020

ⓞⓝⓞ The bakery is the best on the north shore. Delicious baked goods and breads. (Try the macaroons or macadamia shortbread cookies.) The pizza is pricey, but the unusual fresh ingredients and the flavor combinations of the whole pizza specials work well. An example: Their island-style pizza is ham, pineapple, roasted garlic and copote peppers—much more interesting than traditional Hawaiian-style. More typical pizzas by the slice. As you'd expect from a bakery, the crust is very good. Service is either very friendly or shamefully indifferent—they sometimes seem to pride themselves on their surliness. But the food outshines the attitude. They have four tables indoors and a half dozen outdoors. **$5–$15** for meals. Bakery is reasonably priced. In Kilauea in Kong Lung Center off Kilauea Road. Open 6:30ish a.m. to 9 p.m.

LA CASCATA 826-2761

ⓞⓝⓞ Fantastic upscale Italian food with some steak, seafood and lamb. The entrées change often. Try the squash ravioli for appetizer. This is a consistently good restaurant with usually (but not always) excellent service. Hard to go wrong here unless, of course, you're on a budget. Dinner only. Reservations recommended. **$25–$45**. In the Princeville Hotel in Princeville. Ask for a table by the windows. Casual resort wear requested.

PIZZA HANALEI 826-9494

Located in Ching Young Center in Hanalei, the pizza is average. No better, no worse. Sesame seeds on the crust are a nice touch, but pizzas can get soggy and the toppings aren't overly flavorful. **$5–$15**.

LOCAL

HANALEI MIXED PLATE 826-7888

ⓞⓝⓞ A good selection of local dishes (mixed plate items like the tasty shoyu ginger chicken, stir fry or kalua pig and cabbage), salads, burgers (love the buffalo) and sandwiches. (Consider the fresh ahi over the cheaper, but frozen, mahi mahi.) Portions are ample on most items, and they'll let you sample. Only a few tables and the flies may annoy you, but you can order as take out. Consider the chef's specials. In all, a pretty good choice. **$6–$11** for lunch and dinner. In Hanalei next to Ching Young Center, closed Sundays.

HANALEI WAKE-UP CAFÉ 826-5551

Hanalei restaurants tend to open late for breakfast, if they open at all. This place opens at 6:30 a.m. Some items are OK, but not many, and service is usually the pits. In short, pass unless they're the only ones open. **$6–$8** for breakfast. In Hanalei on ocean side of road. Can't miss it.

VILLAGE SNACK & BAKERY SHOP 826-6841

ⓞⓝⓞ Their baked goods are *excellent* and very reasonably priced. Ambiance is...well, they don't have any. But if you want a place that sells lunch, cake and sometimes jewelry, this is the place for you. Hearty, cheap food. Try the apple cobbler—*very* ono and under $2. **$3–$7** for breakfast and lunch. Not bad food for the meal price. Simple, homey and cluttered. In Ching Young Center in Hanalei town. Open at 6 a.m.

MEXICAN

NEIDE'S SALSA & SAMBA 826–1851

ONO Possibly the best Mexican food on the island. Though they're Brazilian (with some Brazilian dishes), the Mexican items like the burritos and enchiladas are excellent. If you want a taste of Brazil, consider the muqueca—fish with coconut sauce, shrimp and cilantro. Prices are reasonable, and the service, even through spotty English, is good. In Hanalei Center, Hanalei, at the back of the center. **$9–$15** for lunch and dinner. Oddly, they don't open till noon. When they say the plate's hot, what they *really* mean is that you could bake a raw pizza on it.

TROPICAL TACO 827–8226

ONO Long-time visitors to the island will remember the green truck on the side of the road in Hanalei that had been dishing up tasty Mexican food since 1978. It was an island fixture. In 2000, owner Roger Kennedy finally moved indoors (and brought a likeness of his truck with him) into the green Halele'a Building on the ocean side of the highway in Hanalei (and finally got a phone!). Roger's food is still excellent (though a bit expensive and the portions could be bigger), and it's a good place to grab a bite when you're on the run on the north shore. The Fat Jacks and fish burritos are delicious. Polish it off with some shave ice from either Wishing Well or Paradise Shave Ice, or head over to Village Snack and Bakery Shop. Lunch and dinner are **$7–$12.**

PACIFIC RIM

BALI HAI 826–6522

The large open dining room has *beautiful* views of Hanalei Bay and Bali Hai (hence the name). Railing tables are best. Steak and seafood, as well as lamb. The food is too variable to qualify for an ONO. They have some exceptional recipes, but they tend to overcook things. When it's good, it's very good. With their awesome views this can be a good restaurant—just not always. And service is definitely not commensurate with the price. **$8–$15** for breakfast, **$10–$20** for lunch, **$25–$40** for dinner. Located at the Hanalei Bay Resort in Princeville.

CAFÉ HANALEI 826–2760

ONO This is a hard restaurant to classify. The menu is vast with entrées from all over the world. Not just Pacific Rim but Mediterranean, as well. In general, it falls in the Pacific Rim category with lots of American, Japanese and some local entrées. It's expensive. For breakfast you can have oatmeal for almost $5, a buffet for about $23, and many things in between. Menus are long and change often. Lunch is generally **$15–$25** featuring hamburgers, steak, seafood and numerous Japanese entrées. If *$15* cheeseburgers bug you, go elsewhere. (This is the kind of restaurant where if you have to ask...you can't afford it.) Dinner includes lamb, shrimp, Hawaiian snapper and a host of others. Expect to pay **$30–$45** for dinner. Quality and service are superb. Located in the Princeville Hotel in Princeville. Nice view of Hanalei Bay. Casual resort wear requested, meaning nix the bathing suits. Open at 6:30 a.m.

TREATS

SHAVE ICE PARADISE 826–6659

Adequate shave ice, but sometimes a bit

too coarse (need to keep the blade sharper, guys) and too much syrup that's too sweet. On expensive side. Across from Ching Young Center in Hanalei. Try Wishing Well instead.

WISHING WELL SHAVE ICE

 In a truck on the ocean side of the road in Hanalei, their shave ice is excellent; get it with ice cream on the bottom. Service is strangely moody—sometimes nice as can be, sometimes amazingly snippy—but the quality of the shave ice is excellent. Squirrely, seemingly random hours. Closed Monday.

EAST SHORE AMERICAN

AL AND DON'S 822–4221

We're really uncomfortable giving them an ONO. There is only one reason to eat here, but frankly it's a pretty compelling reason. From the window booths, you can hear, see and smell the ocean 100 feet away. Too bad they don't clean the windows more often so you can appreciate the view. Just open the jalousie slats. With regards to the food, the quality is marginally adequate (avoid the tasteless biscuits) and the price is quite reasonable. If you're looking for an obsequious staff, go elsewhere. Indifference will no doubt be the special of the day. Breakfast is **$5**–**$9**, it's **$10**–**$15** for dinner. Just want coffee? They have a minimum breakfast order of **$3** and **$7** for dinner. (You won't spend that little, but it's annoying nonetheless.) Located in the Kaua'i Sands Hotel in Kapa'a. They stop serving breakfast just after 9 a.m., so don't sleep too late.

BUBBA'S BURGERS 823–0069

On the highway in northern Kapa'a. See Bubba's review under North Shore.

BULL SHED 822–3791

Dinner only, quite popular with both locals and tourists, known for good, hearty beef and seafood and moderate portions. The scallops are delicious. All entrées come with a choice of salad or…salad. Sorry, no soup. (With a dependably pathetic salad bar, too.) The window seats are particularly close to the water and the main reason for the ONO (we've been there when the waves actually splashed against the glass), but arrive 10–15 minutes before they open (they start serving dinner at 5:30 p.m.) to get one. The service can be slow and decidedly unenthusiastic. And if I may rant, you only get rice with entrées. If you pay extra and get a baked potato, they take the rice away. Hey, I'm paying for it. Leave it alone! (Whew, I feel better already.) **$15**–**$25**. Limited desserts such as mud pie and a pretty good and reasonably priced wine list. In Kapa'a on the ocean side of highway across from Kaua'i Village. Reservations only for six or more.

CAFFÉ COCO 822–7990

Tucked away and hard to find, they serve some very delicious food along with some unusual recipes. Sort of a vegetarian/Pacific Rim/fish menu with other items as well. Specials and regular items change on a whim—you may hear them debate or invent what to fix on the spot. But many items are clever and tasty like the fish with a guava grilling sauce on organic greens and spaghetti noodles with killer potstickers filled with tofu and chutney. Or try the various vegetarian items or the pizza with feta cheese, olives and spicy marinara. Flavor combinations seem well-chosen here. Relaxing ambiance with tables sprinkled about on gravel under various

umbrellas and awnings with plants all around. (Sometimes mosquitoes are a problem.) Service is so relaxed that it's easy to feel ignored or unwelcome at first. You're not; it's just that they're profoundly laid back. But once you order your food, you are served well. **$7–$17** for dinner. Try the pumpkin spice cake. Across the street from Kintaro Restaurant on Hwy 56 in Wailua (north of 6 mile marker); head toward the back.

COUNTRY MOON JUICE BAR 821–1905

 They make very good sandwiches, handy to grab on the run. Salads, fresh cookies, they also have good juices, frosties and smoothies. On the ocean side of Hwy 56 at 4-1586 in north Kapa'a shortly before you leave town. **$3–$7**.

DELI AND BREAD CONNECTION 245–7115

An absolutely dandy place to get sandwiches (although you'll often have to wait a while at lunch time). Large selection of traditional meats and veggies, plus some extras. **$5–$8**. In Kukui Grove next to Liberty House. Some effective baked goods (though sometimes stale).

DUANE'S ONO-CHAR BURGER 822–9181

Duane's Ono-Char Burger is an institution on Kaua'i. Now into their third decade, Duane's still serves some of the best burgers on the island (though the burgers seem smaller than they were a few years ago). Though a bit too pricey, their specialty burgers, such as the teriyaki burger and the mushroom burger, are delicious. Their milkshakes (especially the marionberry shake) are outstanding. Most opt to eat at the cement outdoor tables, complete with shade from a large tree. Marauding wild chickens usually compete for your jetti-

soned french fries. Or consider taking your food down Anahola Road (south of Duane's) to Anahola Beach Park, where picnic tables at the beach make for a pleasant atmosphere. (Weekends at that beach, however, are a bit crowded.) **$7–$14** for lunch till 6 p.m. On the highway in Anahola; can't miss it.

DUKE'S CANOE CLUB 246–9599

Before we talk about the food, we should mention that this is one of the better places on the island to have a cocktail, downstairs bathed in the sound of rushing water, or outdoors overlooking Kalapaki Bay. We like the table by the small indoor waterfall. The pupu (hors d'oeuvre) selection includes pizzas, ribs, burgers and sandwiches and can easily serve as a meal and is not as overpriced as most resort foods. Service there is only fair. Now as for the restaurant upstairs, the beef and seafood are very good. Consider the fresh catch prepared Duke-style. The prime rib is huge (it's hard to believe it came from just one cow), and their salad bar is one of the better ones on the island. Lanai tables at the railing are best, offering a nice view of the bay. **$15–$28**, which is fairly reasonable for the quality of the surroundings. Service could be a bit warmer and more patient. Located at the Marriott. (You can park in their lot or next to Anchor Cove at the beach parking lot.)

EGGBERT'S 822–3787

Breakfast (served till 3 p.m.) is the specialty but they do have lunch and dinner items. Service can be unresponsive. (At least you don't have to beg for coffee refills as much anymore.) The signature item, eggs benedict, may not live up to your expectations, but the banana pancakes are the fluffiest you'll find. All in

all, it's an OK pick for breakfast, unnecessary for lunch or dinner. $6–$10 for breakfast and lunch (the latter is burgers and sandwiches), $10–$17 for dinner. Located in the Coconut Marketplace by the movie theater in Kapa'a off Hwy 56. Park in the part of the lot closest to the highway.

FLYING LOBSTER 822-6652

Located in the Kaua'i Coconut Beach Resort, this restaurant is called **THE VOYAGE ROOM** during breakfast and lunch. This open-air restaurant has views of the ocean and mediocre food. Their breakfast buffets are a decent value at $11. The service bites. Be sure to take a walk along the beach after dinner. If sand is not your thing, there is a paved path going south, interrupted for a bit. $10–$30 for dinner (which is too much).

GAYLORD'S RESTAURANT 245-9593

This has historically been an excellent restaurant, but they've dropped the ball too often lately for us to give them an ONO. Tables are arranged around a courtyard, and evenings can be very romantic. Lots of specials plus an eclectic assortment of entrées, including fish, pasta, venison, lamb, prime rib, etc. $10–$15 for lunch, $20–$35 for dinner. Reservations recommended. Located in Kilohana just south of Lihu'e on your way toward Po'ipu.

HARLEY'S RIBS-N-CHICKEN 822-2505

Chicken and ribs are the specialty (*boy, that's a surprise*) in this little stand in the Coconut Marketplace in Kapa'a. Ribs are pathetic and served with unnecessary surliness. Chicken strips are passable. Lunch/dinner $5–$10.

HULA GIRL 822-4422

Also called **KAUA'I HULA GIRL**, they started out as a great place for steak, seafood, lamb and other items but have slipped lately and we've had to strip their ONO. For appetizers consider the smoked fish or the crab cakes. $18–$35 for dinner. Lunch is sandwiches and plate lunches for $8–$13. At the northern end of Coconut Marketplace Shopping Center near Hwy 56 between the 6 and 7 mile markers.

JAVA KAI 823-6887

A small coffee place on the ocean side of Highway 56 in northern Kapa'a that serves lots of tasty coffee concoctions and other drinks. (Good chai latte; ask them not to make it too sweet.) Breakfast is bagels, waffles or a breakfast sandwich. Coffee by the pound. $3–$6. At 4-1384 Kuhio Hwy.

JJ'S BROILER 246-4422

A longtime steak and seafood landmark. The menu selection is good, but the food is only a bit above average and portions on some of the items are inexcusably small. So why the ONO? Their location adjacent to Kalapaki Beach makes lunch (which is downstairs) at the outdoor/ indoor tables taste better. (Locations can do that.) Lunch features sandwiches, burgers and several pretty good salads. Their specialty at dinner (which is upstairs) is Slavonic steak (dipped in butter, wine and garlic sauce), but it has slipped a bit. Many of the other dinner items are good, if a bit overpriced. (Stay away from the Broiled Scallops with Crisp Taro.) The ice cream pie is wonderful. With a grand view of Kalapaki Bay, large glass windows (upstairs) and sailboats hanging from the ceiling, JJ's sports a nice atmosphere. The lounge/ lunch area downstairs often has live music and weak drinks at night. (Sometimes it's a bit loud.) $8–$15 for lunch, $20–$35 for dinner. In Anchor Cove, Nawiliwili. All in all, JJ's is best for lunch, average at dinner.

JOLLY ROGER 822-3451

Part of a chain, this is a good place to get cheap meals. Popular with locals for their bargain breakfasts under $4. Some outdoor tables. No reservations. The place is looking a bit shabby. They also have a bad bird problem. Somehow seeing birds (and once a rooster) leap onto a table and eat leftovers (leftover chicken, no less!) is not a sight we wish to see again. $4–$15. Located behind Coconut Marketplace, Kapa'a. Open at 6:30 a.m.

KALAPAKI BEACH HUT 246-6330

Gourmet burgers such as buffalo, mahi-mahi, ostrich, veggie burgers...*even beef*. The buffalo is leaner and more loosely packed, making for delicious eating, and the ostrich is tasty and distinct. (Surprisingly, ostrich is a *red* meat even though it's a bird.) This roadside stand has a counter and some upstairs tables. $4–$7 for breakfast, $5–$10 for lunch or early dinner. They're friendly and do it well. Next to Anchor Cove Shopping Center in Nawiliwili. Open at 7 a.m.

KOUNTRY KITCHEN 822-3511

Dandy place to get breakfast (served till 2 p.m.) with quality food at reasonable prices. Hence the ONO. Lunch also available. You may have to wait during peak times. Large selection of omelette ingredients. (Omelettes are hit or miss; the pancakes are very fluffy.) Be sure to check the board for specials (which, strangely, *never* seem to change). Simple American and local food in a small, diner-style atmosphere. $5–$12 for breakfast, $7–$12 for

lunch. On mauka side of Hwy in northern Kapa'a. Open at 6 a.m.

KUKUI'S 246-5171

Buffets are the specialty here, and they do them very well. Breakfast is about $17. Dinner is $25–$40. (Lunch is off the menu.) Menu items available as well. Their pricier Sunday brunch ($27—add $2 for champagne) is wonderful. In addition to the usual suspects, they have prime rib, Japanese dishes, muffins, omelettes and an outrageous roster of desserts. This is a good place to experience the old Hawaiian adage, "Don't eat till you're full; eat till you're tired." Next to the pool at the Marriott in Lihu'e. Service is only fair, but it's a buffet so it's no big deal.

LIHU'E BARBECUE INN 245-2921

Steak, seafood and sandwiches with some Asian dishes served in a simple, clean atmosphere. Very popular with locals who appreciate the good food and usually large portions. Tasty homemade bread and pies. Teriyaki pork chops, sandwiches, fish, great kalua pig and cabbage— they do most things well. (Avoid the ribs, though. Local style and very fatty.) Love their coconut shrimp, but they don't serve it often because "Mom says it's too much work," according to our waitress. A good value all around. How nice when you find out your beverages and desserts are included with many meals for $7–$9. An *excellent* deal. Located on Kress Street in Lihu'e. $7–$12 for lunch, $10–$25 for dinner.

ONO FAMILY RESTAURANT 822-1710

A wonderful breakfast selection and fairly reasonable prices. One of the reasons for reviewing a restaurant multiple times is

to discern patterns. This is a good example. We may come here one day and be seated by a grumpy greeter and receive bad food. Another three times we'll arrive and get good food (but with the same grumpy greeter). Most of the breakfasts are good (though the hash browns need work, as does the sausage—consider the sweet Chinese sausage for a different experience). The tropical stack of pancakes is also good and their ono breakfast burrito, when they have it, is great. Lunch is average burgers. **$5–$10** for breakfast and lunch. They've changed their name several times, but if the name ono is in it, you're probably at the right place. On ocean side of Hwy 56 in Kapa'a south of 581 at 4–1292.

Papaya's Natural Foods 823-0190

A good health food store that also serves mostly veggie items such as veggie lasagna, tofu and falafels. Several garden burgers. Results are mixed. We've had some good meals here...and we've walked away with our inedible plates still full. Hard to say what you'll get. They have a pretty good breakfast, however. **$5–$9** all day. If you eat at the tables, be forewarned that you are likely to be dining with individuals who consider bathing an unnecessary and decadent ritual. Located in Kaua'i Village in Kapa'a.

Paradise Seafood and Grill 246-4884

Don't you hate it when a place you always loved changes...and not for the better? This used to be Fisherman's Galley, and they had the best fish and chips on the island. Though they claim that it's the same recipe and chef, the quality has slipped. If you get the fish and chips, spend the extra buck or two and have them use ono or ahi instead of the marlin that comes with it. Also chick-

en, steak and pasta. Though service can be achingly long, they put the tip in your bill anyway. We're hoping they tighten the operation a bit so we can return the ONO rating. **$8–$11** for lunch, **$10–$25** (which is overpriced) for dinner. On Hwy 50 in Puhi, can't miss it.

Portal's Blossoming Lotus 822-7678

The food and ambiance are impossible to classify. Think of it as Krishna meets the cosmos. This is a vegan restaurant (absolutely no animal products used). Might want to leave your nice leather jacket at home. Everything's organic here. Items from all over include Greek spanakopitta (tofu spinach filling in a pastry dough crust), Indian mung dahl (a curried legume dish) and American wraps. Tons of teas (hot and cold) are available. Try the lotus blossoms for an appetizer—excellent. Avoid the Om Great Spirit—too watery. The food's hit or miss, mostly pretty good, however, and they seem to use very good quality of vegetables without overdoing it with the oil. Desserts, too, are not a sure thing. They claim that the food has been "blessed and sanctified." That's comforting, but we'd also like to see a greater use of hair nets in the kitchen. **$10–$15** for lunch and dinner. At 1384–4 Kuhio Hwy (56) just north of Hwy 581.

Tip Top Café 245-2333

 This place is recognized by locals as an outstanding bargain for breakfast and lunch. The menu includes some non-traditional breakfast items such as beef stew (except for Wed. and Fri. for some reason) and oxtail soup served first thing in the morning. Banana and macadamia nut pancakes come large, fluffy and light, but hardy and filling. Or try the pineapple pancakes—very tasty. Good coffee. Eggs

are their weak spot. **$5–$7**, no entrées are more than $6. A lunch example would be pork chops, veggies and mashed potatoes for $6. Clean, unpretentious hardiness, less-than-bubbly service. Pick up some of their homemade jam, like the pineapple-papaya. On Akahi Street in Lihuʻe. Japanese menu at dinner with sushi. Closed Mondays.

WAILUA FAMILY RESTAURANT 822–3325

Not a bad place for breakfast, but avoid lunch and dinner, especially the buffet. Usually pretty insipid, but somewhat affordable—especially the combinations—if you're nearing the end of your budget. Burgers for lunch; steak, chicken and shrimp for dinner. **$4–$10** for breakfast, **$7–$10** for lunch, **$11–$25** for dinner. In south Wailua on Hwy 56. Open at 6:30 a.m.

CHINESE

GARDEN ISLAND BARBECUE 245–8868

(ONO) Despite the name it's a Chinese restaurant with a local twist, *not* a BBQ. The selection is dizzying—over 150 items! (And no, we haven't tried *every* one of them.) Portions are good and the price is reasonable. There will almost certainly be something that interests you. Service is lightning fast. Although the food's not the greatest, you ain't paying for the greatest. You're paying for a large selection, large portions, and you want to get in and out fast. So, you're getting what you pay for, hence the ONO. **$4–$10** for lunch and dinner. 4252 Rice St. in Lihuʻe. Closed Sunday.

HONG KONG CAFÉ 822–3288

Fairly typical Chinese menu with plate lunch combos the least expensive option. Quality of food is about right for the price. Not great, not bad. (Tasty duck.) Very clean and tidy inside. **$5–$10** for lunch and dinner. In Wailua Shopping Plaza near Wailua Family Restaurant in south Wailua off Hwy 56.

HO'S CHINESE KITCHEN 245–5255

Hideous Chinese food in unclean surroundings. Any questions? **$7–$15** per person. In Kukui Grove Center, Lihuʻe.

KAUAʻI CHOP SUEY 245–8790

This historically has offered good Cantonese food in reasonably pleasant surroundings. Lately, the food's been way too oily, and the service seems lacking. Portions are still large, and we're hoping they'll straighten things up. They specialize in sizzling platters (where food is placed on a metal plate hot enough to ignite upholstery from 3 feet away). Located in Harbor Mall (formerly Pacific Ocean Plaza) in Nawiliwili. Lunch and dinner are **$9–$18**.

PANDA GARDEN 822–0092

Average Chinese restaurant with pleasant, light surroundings. The food is good and fresh. The hot and spicy is not much of either. The portions are a bit small, so order with this in mind. Located in Kauaʻi Village Shopping Center in Kapaʻa. Lunch is **$8–$12** (plate lunches), dinner is **$10–$20**.

ITALIAN

ALOHA KAUAʻI PIZZA 822–4511

In the Coconut Marketplace. In the past we've said it was strikingly average. But upon further review we feel we may have been a bit too generous (their comment book notwithstanding). We think it's a bit wet and greasy and lacking taste. Their menu says "Kauaʻi's Best Kept Secret." That's comforting. **$5–$10**.

Café Portofino 245-2121

Upscale Italian food with a nice open-air ambiance and lanai with partial view of Kalapaki Bay. Located in the Harbor Mall (formerly Pacific Ocean Plaza) in Nawiliwili. Adequate wine list. The food is good and the portions fair. They do well with the veal, cannelloni and the pasta. Love their minestrone soup. Service could use some improvement. Very popular, reservations recommended. $20–$30 for dinner.

Japanese

Hanama'ulu Café, Tea House & Sushi Bar 245-2511

Japanese and Chinese served in a delightful atmosphere. There are gardens out back, a koi pond, individual tea rooms (if you reserve one) and relaxed but attentive service. Oh, did we mention that the food is consistently great and well presented? You'll almost certainly like this place. Sushi bar. On the main highway (56) just outside of Lihu'e in Hanama'ulu. Hours can be squirrely; call to verify. $7–$11 for lunch, $10–$25 for dinner. Reservations recommended. Mosquitoes can be a problem at times.

Kintaro Restaurant 822-3341

You will be happy with this selection. *Excellent* sushi bar (try the Hanalei rolls), large teppan yaki section (that's where the food is prepared in front of you by a talented, knife-wielding chef), full bar and a very pleasant atmosphere. The food is expertly prepared using only the freshest ingredients. The service is outstanding. Fun but not stuffy. Filet mignon for those who don't want Japanese food. In fact, they have the best steak and lobster on the island. It's cubed and cooked in front of you and it melts in your mouth. A bit pricier than others, but worth it. Just north of Kinipopo Shopping Center not too far from the Wailua River mouth on ocean side of Hwy 56. Dinner only, $15–$30.

Tokyo Lobby 245-8989

Located in the Harbor Mall (formerly Pacific Ocean Plaza) in Nawiliwili. Clean, pleasant and comfortable Japanese restaurant with a gracious and attentive staff. Good food, good sushi bar, good restaurant. $10–$15 for lunch, $10–$25 for dinner. Reservations rec. for dinner.

Korean

Korean Bar-B-Q 823-6744

A good place to try some Korean food with a local twist. The combo plates are the best deal. One or more meats like teriyaki beef, BBQ chicken, kalbi (short ribs), etc., plus plenty of side dishes like rice, mac salad, kim chee and Japanese miso soup, which is excellent, but make *sure* you finish it before the meats arrive. Miso tastes terrible if you eat it with the meats. $5–$10 for lunch and dinner. Located in the Kinipopo Shopping Village in the south part of Wailua on Hwy 56.

Local

Aloha Diner 822-3851

This tiny diner is a decent place to try simple, hearty Hawaiian food without shelling out the money you pay for a lu'au. The kalua pig is acceptable, but not as good as at a lu'au. They also have lomi salmon, poi, laulau and 'opihi when available. $7–$10 for lunch, 10–$15 for dinner. In the Waipouli Complex, mauka side of Hwy in Kapaʻa. Closed Sunday.

DANI'S 245–4991

Clean, cheap and reasonably good. Breakfast is very popular and your best bet here. Lunch is kalua pig, tripe stew, lau lau, pork chops, etc. Service is totally dependent on who your waitress is. It's *very* loud inside and crowded, but this isn't a bad choice if price is important. **$4–$7** for breakfast (coffee is included with meal), **$6–$9** for lunch. At 4201 Rice Street, Lihuʻe. Open at 5 a.m.

HAMURA'S SAIMIN STAND 245–3271

ONO Universally loved by locals and forewarned visitors a-like, they have *some of the best saimin on Kauaʻi.* (See page 196 for definition of saimin.) It is wildly popular, and people come from other parts of the island to eat here. Their selection is scant, but the food is excellent and cheap. Consider the "special" saimin, which has more ingredients and is tastier. Served lunch counter style. Though dumpy, it'll be here forever unless the sodium police raid the place. Makes for good take out, but it's so hot that transporting it almost qualifies as hazardous materials. (Spill any on you, and you may burst into flames.) They have good shave ice. (That part of the business is called **HALO HALO SHAVE ICE**, and they sometimes don't want to serve it. Go figure!) Make sure to get the shave ice with ice cream on the bottom. **$3–$6** for lunch and dinner. On Kress St. in Lihuʻe (off Rice St.); see map on page 63.

KAWAYAN 245–8823

A hard-to-find place that serves good local/Filipino/American food. They have a take-out window and several covered tables around the side. Try one of the curries—tasty, but they skimp on the meat. Or the sweet chili chicken. They also have several sausages (but they run out), hot dogs and burgers. Service can take a while, and the food will never be confused with health food. But if you want a blend of local flavors, you could do a lot worse. In Puhi, take Puhi Road, right on Hanalima, left on Haleukama. It's on the right side at 1543 Haleukama. Food is noticeably better at peak eating times. Lunch and dinner are **$3–$9**.

MARK'S PLACE 245–2722

ONO One of those places that you'd never know was here if someone didn't tell you about it. The food is better than Kawayan mentioned above. In fact, they probably serve the best local food on the island. The prices are reasonable and the portions ample. Consider the mixed plate with chicken katsu, teriyaki beef and beef stew for around $6. That's the most expensive meal. Or try the loco moco, Korean chicken, or one of the specials, like the occasional kalua pig and cabbage. This is local-style food, so don't expect low calorie or low cholesterol. And don't expect to eat in; everything's to go. But if you want to eat what many locals eat and don't want to spend much, this is the place for you. **$4–$7** for lunch and dinner. From Hwy 50 in Puhi, take Puhi Road, right on Hanalima. It's on the corner of Hanalima and Haleukama Street. Closed weekends.

MA'S FAMILY RESTAURANT 245–3142

A little hole in the wall on rarely visited Halenani Street in Lihuʻe (Rice to Kress to Halenani). Ma is in her late 80s and is beloved on Kauaʻi. The most expensive item is steak and eggs at $6. The restaurant is like walking into someone's

kitchen. Maybe they'll sit next to you and talk story; maybe they're too busy and it's just the facts. Either way it's a relaxed, old-time feel. The food's not always the best, but hey—even our *own* moms didn't always make the best of everything. $4–$6 for breakfast (where coffee is free) and lunch, which is *way* cheap for Kaua'i. Open at 5 a.m. (Ma must be an early riser.)

OKI DINER 245-5899

Tasty local food and an extensive selection. Everything from pork chops with mushroom gravy to spaghetti to tripe stew. Chicken katsu, loco moco, teri beef, burgers—the large menu has a little something for everyone (except cholesterol counters). Pretty good pastries and pies. (Though on the heavy side, they're very flavorful but a bit expensive, all things considered.) A good place for breakfast. $4–$10. In Lihu'e at 3125 Kuhio Hwy near McDonalds. Open from 6 a.m. to 3 a.m.

WAIPOULI RESTAURANT 822-9311

A good place to have some reasonably priced and flavorful (if not particularly healthy) food. Lunch features items like teriyaki steak, shrimp tempura (which is good), beef sukiyaki, liver & onions, chopped steak, tofu or burgers. Portions are large, and the place is simple but utilitarian. $4–$8 for breakfast, $5–$10 for lunch. In Waipouli Town Center, Kapa'a, near Foodland on Hwy 56. If they don't bring you your check, take your money to the counter. They're *real* informal here.

MEXICAN

LA BAMBA 245-5972

In the Kukui Grove Shopping Center. The food's bland and the service is poor,

but the price is cheap. So, there you have it. Avoid the vegetarian burrito at all costs. The chile relleno is their best bet. $7–$15 for lunch and dinner. B.Y.O.B.

LA PLAYITA AZUL 821-2323

When we first reviewed this restaurant they hadn't been open very long and our opinion was mixed at best. Since then they've developed into a good restaurant with mostly excellent food (with some exceptions). Great seafood fajitas, great enchiladas with mole sauce. We recommend against anything with the green sauce, however and the refried beans are too thin. Those caveats aside, you'll almost certainly like the food here. The dining room is small and often full. In Kaua'i Village Shopping Center in the corner near the Subway. Lunch and dinner are $9–$17.

MARIA'S 246-9122

One of those places where they do what they do well...we just don't like what they do. It's not Mexican food as most people know. It's lighter with minimal spices and odd sauces. For instance, a chicken enchilada has a bland chicken filling and a green sauce poured over it that doesn't work for us, but some seem to love it. Service can be light as well since understaffing is common. $7–$15 for lunch and dinner. No credit cards. On highway in Lihu'e near the 7/Eleven. Good salsa.

NORBERTO'S EL CAFÉ 822-3362

This used to be the best Mexican food on the island, but no more. What happened? All items come as a meal or à la carte, regular or vegetarian. Consider the taro leaf enchiladas (different than taro-filled), perhaps with some chicken tossed in. Top it off with some of their chocolate cream pie. Funky Spanish decor. $10–$20, dinner only. Located on the main highway in downtown Kapaʻa near 581. Closed Sunday.

PACIFIC RIM

A PACIFIC CAFÉ 822-0013

ONO Hard to classify this one. Sort of the best from many places around the world. Since it opened in 1990, chef Jean-Marie Josselin has won numerous accolades for his world-class food and exquisite attention to details. Prices are high but they food's historically been very good. They've had a few rough patches lately, and we're hoping they don't disappoint us for giving them an ONO. Presentation is good and the setting is pleasant with numerous little touches (but no view, and it's a bit busy). You won't get huge portions here. (Remember Einstein's theory of dining relativity: At expensive restaurants, portions are inversely proportional to the price of the entrée.) Portions notwithstanding, the food you get will probably be awesome. **$25–$40** for dinner. Reservations strongly recommended. Located in Kauaʻi Village in Kapaʻa.

COCONUTS 823-8777

ONO True to the name, nearly everything is made from ultra-heavy coconut wood. Tables, chairs, floor, lamps etc. (Enough about the furniture, *how's the food?*) Good...*very* good. It's a combination of Pacific Rim, pasta, seafood and fowl. The price is relatively reasonable for the quality, and the dishes are very well prepared. Wonderful potato-stuffed sea bass, crispy skin chicken, awesome calamari, and we love their shrimp cakes. Portions on some items are wanting, but they make up for it with tasty bread. Drink selection is admirable, though their preparation is probably their

weakest link. The atmosphere is effective. Desserts seem hit or miss. Overall, a great place. Dinner is **$12–$30**. On Hwy 56 in Kapaʻa, mauka side just north of Safeway.

LEMONGRASS 821-2888

ONO An interesting and eclectic menu featuring Asian, local and American items plus sushi, pasta, fresh fish and steak. Odds are something will appeal to you. Most items are well-conceived. Service has been choppy but usually good. Overall, a pretty good choice. **$18–$30** for dinner. On Hwy 56 in Kapaʻa north of Kauaʻi Village.

WHALERS BREWPUB 245-2000

With their excellent location overlooking Kalapaki Bay, Whalers has amazing potential but their execution seems consistently flawed. The beer is brewed on the spot, and beer lovers should consider getting the sampler—six small mugs ranging from light to very stout. But the beer is often less than stellar. Also, they advertise that they have the "coldest beer on Kauaʻi," which is ironic since one complaint we have is that it's not cold enough. *Go figga!* The food is usually marginal at best (unless you already drank all the samplers, in which case it'll taste just fine) and is overpriced. (Pass on the oysters.) Consider it a place to go for beer and pupus (appetizers). Dinner should be early enough to appreciate the view. Dinner is **$16–$25**, and service can be slow. Located behind the Marriott in Lihuʻe. Take their Rice Street entrance and drive till the end.

THAI

KING AND I THAI CUISINE 822-1642

ONO Owned by the same family that owns Lemongrass, the food, service and value are excellent,

though the ambiance is better at Lemongrass. Try the porcupine shrimp for an appetizer, if they have it, or the killer mango fish, which was a recurring special that they were thinking of making permanent. Nearly all dishes are delicious. Located in the Waipouli Plaza, mauka side of highway in Kapa'a. **$10–$20** for dinner. They burn incense as an offering to Buddha when they open, so wait a bit longer if the smell of *strong* incense bothers you.

MEMA THAI CHINESE 823–0899
A great selection of Thai and some Chinese dishes. This used to be really good Thai and Chinese food but they've slipped enough lately to strip their ONO. Consider the Pad Thai, house curry or one of the vegetable items. On mauka side of Hwy 56 just north of Haleilio Road at 4–369 Kuhio Hwy. **$10–$25** for lunch and dinner.

SUKHOTHAI 821–1224
It's listed under Thai, but they also serve Chinese, Vietnamese, vegetarian and Asian BBQ. The food *can be* well prepared, the restaurant pleasing and service friendly. But not always… Their posted hours are "10:30 a.m. to Closing." Gee, that's helpful. **$8–$20** for lunch and dinner. In Kapa'a Shopping Center near Big Save on mauka side of highway, Kapa'a.

TREATS

BEEZER'S ICE CREAM 822–4411
(ONO) Small, '50s/'60s-inspired ice cream shop. The ice cream itself is nothing special (Dryers), but they do really great things with it. Also a few homemade pies, fudge, etc. Good (but expensive at $7) banana splits. The shave ice needs work. In all, undoubtedly overpriced…but we like it anyway. In Kapa'a on Hwy 56 across from the Hwy 581 intersection.

HALO HALO SHAVE ICE 245–5094
(ONO) Good shave ice, poor service. Located in Hamura's Saimin on Kress Street in Lihu'e; see map on page 63. For some reason they sometimes won't serve it. If that's the case, don't take it personally.

HANALIMA BAKING CO. 246–8816
On the corner of Puhi Road and Hwy 50 in Puhi, they serve pretty tasty malasadas (a Portuguese donut) 3 or 4 for $1, depending on their whims. They also have decent blueberry scones and cocoa puffs. **$2–$3**. Open at 6:30 a.m.

HAWAIIAN BLIZZARD
(ONO) This is simply a shave ice stand in front of Big Save in Kapa'a at the Kapa'a Shopping Center on Hwy 56 near the 8 mile marker. Though selection is limited and they don't offer ice cream on the bottom (our preferred way), they keep their ice blade especially sharp, creating extraordinarily fine shave ice. **$2**. Flexible hours means they're not always there.

KAUA'I BAKERY & CINNAMONS 246–4765
(ONO) Located in Lihu'e's Kukui Grove Shopping Center, they have a sparse selection but outstanding quality. Their apple turnovers are the best on the planet. *(Pretty strong words, Andy!)* They open at 7 a.m. and run out of many things by 11. You won't find bubbly service, *but da grinds broke da mouf, brah.*

KAUA'I FRUIT AND FLOWER 245–1814
Most items are confiscatorily priced ($5 for 8 oz. of banana butter, which is just

bananas and sugar!), but their smoothies are unusual and quite refreshing. On Hwy 56 near Hwy 51 north of Lihu'e.

SOUTH SHORE AMERICAN

BEACH HOUSE RESTAURANT 742-1424

ono A long-time south shore landmark. Steak and seafood with exceptional ocean views— they are right next to the water. Nice sunsets from here. Tables are reasonably spaced. The food quality is usually very good. Vast wine list. Dinner, with entrées like lamb, fresh fish, prime rib and the like, will run you **$25–$40**. On Lawai Road in Po'ipu on way to Spouting Horn. Almost always a memorable meal, this is one of the best restaurants on the south shore. Reservations *strongly* recommended days in advance.

BRENNECKE'S BEACH BROILER 742-7588

This is the first edition we've done where Brennecke's didn't get an ONO. Their view overlooking Po'ipu Beach Park is still awesome, and this is a good place for an early sunset meal. The problem is that someone seems to have gotten complacent. Food and service have slipped to mediocre. You have to beg for water and bread, and the bread rolls are downright terrible. Food prices aren't cheap, and the appetizers are *way* too expensive. (C'mon, over $9 for simple nachos with beans?!) Brennecke's is still capable of great seafood and steak memories, but they need to stop resting on their laurels. They still pour some of the better drinks on the south shore (with legendary mai tais). **$10–$15** for lunch, **$20–$35** for dinner. On Hoonani Road next to Po'ipu Beach Park.

Downstairs and next door, their **BRENNECKE'S DELI** has sandwiches and hot dogs. Though the food's certainly not gourmet, it's amazing how much better it'll taste if you take it across the street to one of the beach park tables and gaze at the delicious scenery. **$4–$7**. Their shave ice needs work.

CAMP HOUSE GRILL 332-9755

ono This is the place to get ribs, steak, seafood, veggie items, chicken, salads, or ⅓ lb. burgers (with tasty spicy fries) at reasonable prices. Food is good, service is usually fast, and the value is definitely good (though the salad bar needs a boost). Their wicked pies will keep you smiling. Kids will like it here. Good place for breakfast. On the mauka side of the main highway in Kalaheo; can't miss it. Open at 6:30 a.m. **$5–$10** for breakfast (with cheaper early bird specials), **$5–$15** for lunch and dinner. They have another location in Kaua'i Village in Kapa'a which isn't as good, so the ONO applies *only* for Kalaheo location.

DALI DELI AND CAFÉ 742-8824

ono A neat little deli in Koloa (to the east of most shops across from the Post Office) featuring tasty deli sandwiches and limited but delicious desserts and breads. Corned beef sandwiches, Italian subs, vegetarian sandwiches and salads. Bagels are a bit chewy, but on the whole you'll like the quality here, and they obviously aim to please. Try their desserts if you are scared off by Lappert's prices. 8 a.m to 4 p.m. **$4–$8**. Closed Sunday. At night they change their name to **CAFÉ CARA**, an Italian restaurant.

ILIMA TERRACE 742-1234

ono Located at the Hyatt in Po'ipu, they offer good food in a beautiful, open-air setting near

a Hyatt waterfall. Although breakfast is a bit overpriced at **$10–$20** ($19 for the buffet), lunch and dinner are fairly reasonable. Dinners are all buffets for around **$30** with different theme nights: seafood night, prime rib or Italian; they are all delicious, offering a great selection of well-prepared choices and tasty desserts. The setting is fantastic—ask for the table next to the waterfall. Reservations recommended. Note to management: You gotta do something about your bold bird problem.

JOE'S ON THE GREEN 742-9696

On the Kiahuna Golf Course next to the driving range, the open-air feel and views of mountains give it a pretty good atmosphere. But the prices are too high and food too mediocre. For instance, the continental breakfast is $7.25 and two eggs, meat and toast is $7.50. Expected at a resort, perhaps, but not here. Service is friendly, but less than attentive. **$8–$11** for breakfast and lunch. From Po'ipu Road take the road into Po'ipu Shopping Village, drive past it, and go into the Kiahuna Golf Course.

KALAHEO COFFEE CO. & CAFÉ 332-5858

A more than acceptable place to stop on your way to Waimea Canyon in the morning. Only three coffees to choose from to go with your breakfast, and the breakfast menu is small. The standard breakfast could use some work, but the breakfast "bonzo" tortilla wrap is a winner. Baked goods aren't numerous, but the cinnamon knuckles are delicious and tilted us toward giving them an ONO. Sandwiches and salads at lunch. Coffee by the pound to take back home. **$4–$8** for breakfast, **$5–$9** for lunch. On highway in Kalaheo. Open at 6 a.m.

KALAHEO STEAK HOUSE 332-9780

Located on Papalina Road in Kalaheo. It's good enough for an ONO—*usually*. When it's good, the steak is *really* good. The seafood isn't their best work—stick with the beef. You can get a whopping 24 ounces of prime rib for **$25**. The Cornish game hen can be very good. No reservations. Dinner only, **$20–$30**.

KEOKI'S PARADISE 742-7534

This is a special sort of place that people either love or hate (we love it). The ambiance is the story here with plants everywhere, a large fish lagoon, waterfalls and thatched roof booths (try to say *that* three times fast). It's the South Pacific that never really existed except in movies. The exotic bar area serves burgers, sandwiches and ribs at lunch and dinner for **$8–$13**. Some people wait there for a table while others make a meal of it to save money. The tables in the main area are arranged in several levels. Purists will sniff that the ambiance is not real—so what?! It is still exotic inside. If you are in the right mood, this is the sort of place you will remember for a long time to come. As for the food, it's a steak and seafood restaurant with above average food and service. Quite good, but not great. Several of the entrées, such as the prime rib and the lasagna, are only served as long as they last. They have a 26-ounce prime rib for those who swam here from O'ahu. The hula pie is equally large. The place can get pretty busy, which can have an effect on the service. Reservations strongly recommended. **$20–$35** for dinner. Located in the Po'ipu Shopping Village in Po'ipu.

PLANTATION GARDEN 742-2216

Here's a perfect example of how difficult it is to classify some restaurants. Veal,

steak, Italian dishes, local items like lau lau, shrimp wonton appetizers (which are awesome)...the menu is all over the place. Some portions are small (four raviolis for $20!), some are fine. If you walk in when they first open, even if there's not a soul at any table, you may still be made to wait (they point you to the bar) for a long time. So make reservations. In all, good but overpriced. $20–$35 for dinner. In Kiahuna Plantation Resort overlooking the pretty cactus garden.

SHELLS 742-1661

The most delicious thing about this restaurant is the view, one of the best you will find on the south shore. It's at the water's edge overlooking the beach with lots of windows and some outdoor tables. The breakfast buffet, though pricey at $16, is memorable for this reason. Off the menu also available. Dinner features fish, pasta, lamb, beef with lobster tail, etc., most prepared very well. Since part of the price you are paying is for the view, dinner, especially late dinners, aren't a very good deal since it's too dark to see. $15–$20 for breakfast, $20–$35 for dinner. At the Sheraton Po'ipu.

SHIPWRECK'S SANDWICH SHOP 742-7467

A good place to go when you're in the area, in your bathing suit and want something simple to eat. Good sub sandwiches, and their ice cream is the delicious Tropical Dreams from the Big Island (which puts Lappert's to shame.) Delivery to Koloa and Po'ipu. In Po'ipu Shopping Village toward the back. $5–$10 for lunch and dinner.

TIDEPOOLS 742-1234

Located at the Hyatt Po'ipu, their best feature is a very romantic atmosphere. A thatched roof, a stocked freshwater lagoon next to your table and flickering tiki torches outside provide a calm, quiet dinner environment. The limited menu concentrates on fresh fish, with some beef and vegetarian items. (Good ahi sashimi.) $25–$45. Service is adequate. Reservations recommended. Dinner only.

TOMKATS GRILLE 742-8887

This is an easy place to recommend. Tasty and well prepared burgers, ka-bobs, sandwiches (love the French dip with the delicious fries), chicken and salads for lunch with a little steak and seafood thrown in at dinner. All served in a decidedly feline atmosphere. (Though, ironically, the *real* cats seem to hang out down the street at Pizzetta.) The kids' menu has peanut butter and jelly sandwiches, among others. The ambiance is relaxing with an open-air feel next to a small fish pond and garden. Fast, efficient service. Some of their specialties are rather inventive. Good place to bring the kittens, though they also feature a full bar and a huge selection of catnips (beer and tropical drinks) for the adult cats. Our only complaint is that it can get a bit warm under the hot tin roof. If you're looking for a nice, relatively inexpensive place to eat your cat chow, Tomkats will keep you purring. (Oops—I promised myself I wouldn't use any moronic puns in this review. Feel free to hiss now.) $7–$12 for lunch, $7–$20 for dinner. In Koloa town. Look for the sign near Pizzetta.

ITALIAN

BRICK OVEN PIZZA 332-8561

We have a lot of affection for this place and we eat here often, but we have to admit that it's a bit overpriced. The pizza is the best on

Kaua'i, bar none. Though not baked in a real brick oven, they pride themselves on making their own sauce, sausage and other ingredients. (Inexplicably, though, the mushrooms are canned.) In the more traditional Italian vein, the sauce takes on less importance. The crust is thin with scalloped edges and brushed with garlic butter with tasty results. Simple Italian atmosphere, attentive, friendly service and excellent pizza. But the prices. It's high enough to qualify them as expensive. Over $28 for a 15-inch combo. To make matters worse, they seem to have structured it so that mostly visitors will pay inflated prices. That's because pizzas eaten there, which most visitors do, are about 10% higher. Those taken out, which most residents do, are cheaper. We consider that a tourist tax on the pizza, and if you want hold that against them, we'll understand. It's still a great place for pizza and sandwiches, but they *are* a bit pricey. Prices are $8–$18. No reservations. Kids are given a wad of pizza dough to play with—nice touch. (And fitting, since adults will *spend* a wad of dough.) Located on mauka side of highway as you enter Kalaheo; can't miss it. Closed Monday.

DONDERO'S 742-1234

Regional Italian food. Entrées change too often to recommend a specific one here. Pastas, veal, fresh fish and lamb, usually expertly prepared. Outstanding wine list. Elegant dining; their dress code requires casual resort wear, meaning covered shoes, collared shirts for men, etc. Dinner is $25–$40. In the Hyatt Po'ipu. Reservations recommended.

PIZZETTA 742-8881

The pizza is not great, not bad. Their spicy sauce is marginally interesting as a novelty—basically the normal red sauce mixed with Tabasco. You're better off heading to Brick Oven in Kalaheo. They also have lots of pastas and other Italian items. Pizzetta is occasionally good, but not often enough. $10–$15, lunch and dinner. Free delivery in Po'ipu.

POMODORO 332-5945

Upscale Italian food in small, pleasing surroundings. The owners of the former Casa Italia opened this place when their restaurant in Lihu'e literally blew away. Excellent food quality, attention to detail and great service. The lasagna is *highly* recommended. So are the raviolis. The baked penne is a bit too cheesy, but overall, this is the best Italian food on the island. Dinner is $13–$25. In the Rainbow Plaza in Kalaheo. (Ocean side of highway.)

JAPANESE

NANIWA 742-1661

A beautiful view highlights the wonderful sushi. This is the best on the island (though not authentic Japanese in preparation). Scrupulous attention to freshness and presentation and a good variety. Overlooking Kiahuna Beach in Po'ipu. Tempura and other cooked items for non-sushi lovers. Price is $25 on up to the sky. At the Sheraton Po'ipu. Reservations strongly recommended.

LOCAL

ISLAND TERIYAKI 742-9988

Eclectic mix of local dishes "Asian kine" entrées such as Bangkok chicken (chicken, Thai peanut sauce, tomatoes, ginger slaw and rice all in a tortilla wrap), chicken curry and others, "Latin, Mediterranean, &

Local Kine," as well. Their signature teriyaki (chicken, beef or fish) is good. Also smoothies and shave ice. We almost withheld our ono because of the noticeable difference in service between locals and visitors. Locals get waited on first and receive friendly, cheerful service, and their food is often brought out. Visitors get stone-faced stares, and they'll merely shout your name when it's ready and point to the forks. That's unfair, so feel free to stay away, if necessary. $5–$8 for breakfast, $7–$10 for lunch and dinner. A good value. On Koloa Road in Koloa near the large monkeypod tree.

KOLOA FISH MARKET 742–6199

Simple plate lunches like lau lau, kalua pig, etc. Small selection but decent quality. $6–$7. In Koloa on Koloa Road.

SUEOKA'S SNACK SHOP 742–1112

Probably the cheapest food on the south shore. Prices top out at around $4. Burgers, beef curry, fish burgers, chili rice and plate lunches. It's been popular forever with locals. Remember, since it's local style, items may be different than you think. For instance, the teriyaki burger isn't ground beef—it's strips of teri beef on a bun. On Koloa Road near Po'ipu Road on the side of Sueoka's Market.

MEXICAN

TAQUERIA NORTEÑOS 742–7222

Usually good food, embarrassingly large portions and a small price make this place an excellent choice for Mexican food on the south shore. Their food is fresh and pretty tasty (though not "authentic" Mexican by any stretch). It's literally a hole in the wall located past the 4 mile marker on Po'ipu Road (520) in Po'ipu Plaza. Take-out only, but don't wait too long; it doesn't travel well (gets soggy). There are few places on Kaua'i where two people can eat all the good food they want for about $10. (Prices seem to be by whim. Even though we usually order the same thing, the cost is different each time.) Lunch and dinner. Closed Wednesdays.

PACIFIC RIM

ROY'S PO'IPU BAR & GRILL 742–5000

Well known throughout the islands for having the midas touch, Roy Yamaguchi has a knack for combining flavors very successfully. You won't get huge portions here, but the food is extremely well prepared and well presented with prices commensurate with the quality. Atmosphere is somewhat elegant but busy, with a large, glass, soundproof wall showcasing the kitchen. (Ask for a table in the patio room for a less busy atmosphere.) The service is efficient, attentive and friendly, but they sometimes rush you a bit. If they do, tell them to slow down. Fresh fish, pasta, chicken, beef and a host of nightly specials, all skillfully created. The fish is usually incredible. For appetizers try the wood fired pizzas— Outstanding! The signature dessert, baked chocolate soufflé, is obscenely delicious—order it à la mode to actually *counter* the richness. Located in Po'ipu Shopping Village. Dinner is $20–$35. Reservations strongly recommended.

THAI

PATTAYA ASIAN CAFÉ 742–8818

The same family that owns King and I in Kapa'a opened this restaurant in Po'ipu Shopping Village. It's a *beautiful* outdoor café, and the food is pretty good (though not as good as King and I). It's too pricey for lunch, and the food is a tad

on the oily side. We like the pineapple fried rice, though, and they have good curries. **$10–$25** for lunch and dinner. That's *a lot* for lunch, so no ONO.

TREATS

KOLOA COUNTRY STORE 742-1255

Kind of hard to find, but they make some awesome baked goods plus coffee drinks. Consider the cinnamon rolls with flavored frosting. They open at 8 a.m., but sometimes the baker is late with the baked goods. They also have some PCs for surfing. In Koloa behind Crazy Shirts in the courtyard.

LAPPERT'S ICE CREAM 742-1272

They have locations in Koloa, Princeville and Hanapepe. All offer locally-made Lappert's Ice Cream, which has slipped over the years. It's also gotten too expensive. Two people can get one scoop each and a chocolate cone and spend over *$7.* Open at 6 a.m. for pastries and coffee. In Po'ipu consider Shipwreck Sub's ice cream instead. *Mo betta!*

WEST SHORE AMERICAN

GRINDS 335-6027

Standard breakfast fare, hot and cold sandwiches plus pizza for lunch at this former Dairy Queen. Pretty ordinary stuff except for the mean cinnamon rolls. Service can be oddly inept. **$5–$8** for breakfast, **$6–$13** for lunch. In 'Ele'ele Shopping Center on Hwy 50 near Hanapepe. Open at 5:30 a.m.; good if you're doing a boat trip nearby.

KOKE'E LODGE 335-6061

Hearty. That's the word that comes to mind. They classify themselves as local

soul food. We particularly like the cornbread and chili or the BBQ beef. Their coconut pie is excellent. Lunch only for the most part. **$5–$10**. Located *waaaay* up the road in Koke'e on Waimea Canyon Road past the 15 mile marker. This is the road you take to get to Waimea Canyon and the Kalalau Lookout. Open 9 a.m. to 3:30 p.m.

WAIMEA BREWING COMPANY 338-9733

The beer isn't very good; it has a funny taste. And the food is...well, who cares? It's a brewpub with bad beer. Anyway the food's passable, nothing more. Burgers, sandwiches, etc. **$10–$20**. At Waimea Plantation Cottages, Waimea.

WRANGLER'S STEAKHOUSE 338-1218

Well, with a name like Wrangler's, you ain't a' lookin' for no Mongolian food, and you ain't a' gonna find it here. (Cowboy accents are hard to do in print.) The dinner menu is steak (which they do *very* well) and seafood. Lunch is burgers, steak and some specials. (Try the Kau Kau Tin.) Some outdoor tables in sunny Waimea can make for a pleasant meal. Good food with reasonable service. **$8–$15** for lunch, **$20–$35** for dinner. On the ocean side of the highway in Waimea, can't miss it.

ITALIAN

HANAPEPE CAFÉ 335-5011

They classify themselves gourmet vegetarian Italian. The ono is for dinner only; we find the breakfast and lunch just so-so. Waffles, eggs, etc., for breakfast. Soups, sandwiches, pasta and several kinds of garden burgers for lunch. Dinner works better. Tasty and creative entrées such as lasagna, crepes a la asparagi, etc.

$5–$10 for breakfast and lunch (but they don't open till 9 a.m.). $20–$25 for dinner. Reservations recommended for dinner. Closed Monday.

PACIFIC PIZZA & DELI 338–1020

A surprisingly good pizza place on the ocean side of Hwy 50 in Waimea next to Wrangler's. In addition to the typical ingredients, they have innovations such as teriyaki chicken, shrimp, spicy Thai sauce, salmon, etc. The crust is crunchy on the bottom—very tasty—and their sauce complements things well. They could use a bit more toppings on some, but the pizza is very flavorful. Consider having them go easy on the cheese—sometimes they use too much. Other items such as calzone; but we've stuck with the pizza. Your options are limited on the west side. It gets a bit warm inside, but this is probably the best food you'll find out there. $6–$15 for lunch and dinner.

LOCAL

GREEN GARDEN 335–5422

Very diverse menu. From meatloaf to lobster to spaghetti to Chinese dishes to omelettes (for dinner). Our classification as a local restaurant is a cop-out on our part; it's a little of everything. (Wait, that *is* the definition of a local restaurant.) Call it quasi-upscale local food. They have been here since 1948, so they must be doing *something* right. That *something* is serving quality food at a reasonable price—*most of the time*. But they do disappoint on occasion. Be sure to ask about the specials. The homemade pies are great, especially the liliko'i pie. Ask for a table away from the main road. $5–$10 for lunch, $12–$25 for dinner. (Lobster is more.) Closed Tuesdays.

THAI

TOI'S THAI KITCHEN 335–3111

Amazingly good Thai food. Prices are probably too high, but Toi's food is excellent. Try it with cold Thai tea. Their curries are quite memorable. Their signature dish is Toi's Temptation. On mauka side of highway in 'Ele'ele Shopping Center, just before Hanapepe. $10–$25 for dinner.

TREATS

HAWAIIAN HUT 335–3781

In Hanapepe on Hanapepe Road. Their specialty is shave ice. They often pour a cream sauce on top, which, combined with their *ultra*-sweet syrup, makes for an overly rich shave ice. $2–$4.

JO-JO'S CLUBHOUSE 635–7615

Unquestionably the best shave ice on the island. Expertly prepared, large portions (piled twice as high as the cup), very reasonable prices and an outrageous selection of over 60 flavors, possibly the best selection we've ever encountered. What else is there? Their shave ice alone is worth the drive to Waimea. Across from the 23 mile marker. Great place to stop on your way to or from Waimea Canyon (we *always* do). If you want, take your shave ice around the corner on Pokole Street and eat it near the pier, which has a shaded picnic area. Only problem is that it's sometimes too crowded and understaffed, so there may be a wait. And the service can be poor at times. Also, we wish they had a way to keep the syrup chilled before pouring onto the ice. When this is done, it keeps hard ice from forming on the bottom of the shave ice.

ISLAND LU'AUS

If you've ever seen a movie that takes place in Hawai'i, odds are there was a lu'au scene. This is where everyone stands around with a mai tai in one hand and a plate of kalua pig in the other. There's always a show where someone is twirling a torch lit at both ends, and, of course, the obligatory hula dancers. And the truth is, that's not far from reality. The pig is baked in the ground (called an imu) all day and is absolutely delicious. Shows are usually exciting and fast moving. Although the lu'aus on O'ahu can make you feel like cattle being led to slaughter, Kaua'i's lu'aus are smaller and much more pleasant.

The best lu'au on the island is at **SMITH'S TROPICAL PARADISE** (821–6895). Lu'aus are Mon, Wed and Fri. The food is pretty good (not great) and the setting is marvelous. (They need more desserts, though.) It's surrounded by a huge garden area. Though the garden could use a little polishing, the site works perfectly for a lu'au. After dinner, you move to a separate show area where the stage is separated from you by a small pond. The show is the most dazzling on the island. While not authentic by any means, it's well choreographed, very disciplined and is quite entertaining, complete with an erupting volcano. **$52**. ($1 more for a tram ride of the gardens, which strikes us as pretty chintzy on their part.) Free open bar, but it closes at 7:30. Allow 30 minutes for a garden tour before the imu ceremony. You can also attend the show alone, without the food, for $14.

Other lu'aus include **DRUMS OF PARADISE HYATT LUAU** (742–1234). The food is well-prepared (though they must not like serving dessert—their system creates a bottleneck there that's almost endless). They suffer a bit from location. Often indoors, the stage is too low and close to the front tables, so many people end up with partially obstructed views. Performances, however, are good (with some notable exceptions). Free open bar all night, and there's no annoying lounge lizard hogging the stage. No imu ceremony (where you watch them take the pig out of the ground), but they make a wicked kalua pig anyway. **$65**.

PRINCEVILLE HOTEL (826–9644) has fairly good food and location, but the show is pretty weak. The north shore setting is excellent, adjacent to the beach at the Princeville pool area. Get a seat near and facing the pool, which allows you to see the sun setting over the ocean and Bali Hai. There is a good variety of food. They also don't skimp on desserts. Though you probably won't be told, your ticket includes free well drinks at the poolside bar in addition to the standard beer, wine and mai tais. The show needs improvement. Thursdays and some Mondays. **$60**. Acceptable, but you're better off at Smith's.

KAUA'I COCONUT BEACH HOTEL (822–3455) has lu'aus every night. **$55**, one kid admitted free some nights. The lu'au is surprisingly mediocre considering that they do it more than anyone else. Marginal food, talented but under-utilized performers, cramped—hey, at least the drinks are free all night. Good seats are an extra $5. Perhaps because they do it every single night, there's no search for excellence, just satisfaction with the way things are. Their motto is "Best Lu'au on Kaua'i." Well, not in our book.

The **RADISSON KAUA'I** (335–5828) holds their lu'au near the pool. At least they're supposed to. But they seem skittish about passing rain showers and often hold it indoors, even on beautiful evenings. The food's average. Nothing more. As for the show, it's the homiest of any on the island, for all the good and bad that that implies. Good because they'll never be accused of being slick. It seems to come from the heart and their use of percussion at times is admirable. Bad because there are moments of such clumsiness that you'll have to work to hide your smirk. Their bar offers only a few exceptionally weak drinks, so you'll have to have them season it if you're looking for something other than glorified mai tai punch. $55.

KILOHANA (245–9595) in Lihu'e has a lu'au every Tuesday and Thursday for $58.

All in all, lu'aus can be a real blast. If your time allows for one, it is highly recommended.

DINNER ON A BEACH

How about a secluded romantic dinner on a beach? For around $270 per couple (depending on what you want) **HEAVENLY CREATIONS** (828–1700) will serve you at the beach of your choosing. You decide the menu, they provide everything else. What a perfect way to make up for forgetting your anniversary. **PRINCEVILLE HOTEL** (826–9644) offers a romantic catered dinner for two on its beach for $395 per couple. Available to non-guests as well. **HYATT HOTEL** offers it for $290 per couple.

ISLAND NIGHTLIFE

I know what you're thinking. "Gee, this section sure is small." True. Let's face it—Kaua'i won't be confused with Las Vegas when it comes to nightlife. That's part of our charm. But hey, it's not like we spend *all* of our nights rearranging our sock drawer. (Usually just Fridays, and *oh,* what a crazy time *that* is!) Besides, if you did most of the things in the previous two sections, you're too pooped to party.

That said, there is probably enough nightlife on Kaua'i to satisfy *most* people's needs. Many of the restaurants feature entertainment at night, but the schedules are always changing. You can call the restaurant you choose from the listings above and inquire as to their entertainment.

People have different desires when it comes to nightlife. Here we simply try to describe what's available and let you pick what you want.

PO'IPU

STEVENSON'S LIBRARY at the Hyatt is designed to appeal to anyone who ever wanted to visit the private library of one of the Rockefellers. Richly decorated, bookcases filled with the classics, pool tables (not billiards), large aquarium, chess tables and a terrace. The bar is the center attraction and is beautifully crafted out of strips of koa and monkeypod. Some of the staff can be a bit snotty, but otherwise, it's a nice place to have a drink. Things can get surprisingly lively. The **SEAVIEW TERRACE** commands a fabulous view of the resort and can be a relaxing place to have a drink after a long day. Nightly music.

Sheraton's **POINT** is a smashing place for an early evening cocktail overlooking the beach. Live music some nights.

KEOKI'S PARADISE at 742-7534 in the Po'ipu Shopping Village has entertainment in the lounge most nights. Hula demonstrations in the shopping center's courtyard many nights.

LIHU'E

DUKE'S BAREFOOT BAR at the Marriott is a great place for a drink; sporadic music offered. **ROB'S GOOD TIMES GRILL** (246-

0311) on Rice St. offers entertainment every night. Mostly a local spot.

Moviegoers can call **KUKUI GROVE CINEMAS** at 245-5055 for a listing of their features.

KAPA'A

ROYAL COCONUT GROVE LOUNGE at the Kaua'i Coconut Beach Resort (822-3455) is a decent place for a beverage while you listen to music near the pool. Some like to grab a drink here and stroll along the beach. The **JOLLY ROGER** behind the Coconut Marketplace usually distinguishes itself by having cheap mai tais. They're weak, but what do you expect for three bucks? **TRADEWINDS, A SOUTH SEAS BAR** *in* the Coconut Marketplace is a small but lively little bar. Dancing some nights. Hula shows are held nearby several nights a week. **LIZARD LOUNGE** in Waipouli Town Center has music and dancing some nights and is open till 2 a.m. for all you late night reptiles.

Movie goers should check the **COCONUT MARKETPLACE CINEMA** at 821-2324 to see what's showing. (Lihu'e's Kuku'i Grove Cinema is better.)

Call about live community theatre at **KAUA'I INTERNATIONAL THEATRE** (832-6768).

The **POOLSIDE BAR** at Islander on the Beach is a favorite place to pick up a mai tai before walking over to the beach, plopping down and watching the waves.

NORTH SHORE

HANALEI GOURMET (826-2524) across from Ching Young Village usually has music but is only recommended for those on the prowl. It's a bit seedy there. **SUSHI BLUES** (826-9701) is as the name implies with lots of cigarette smoke. **AMELIA'S** (826-6211) at the Princeville Airport has local bands on weekends.

THE HAPPY TALK LOUNGE in the Hanalei Bay Resort has always been one of the best places in Princeville to have a drink and appreciate the night air. The Princeville Hotel (826-9644) has the **LIVING ROOM**. A bit subdued with great views of Hanalei Bay. Sushi at 5 p.m. Both offer different types of music.

WEST SHORE

Find a bright light bulb and watch the geckos eat the mosquitoes.

DINING BEST BETS

Best Pizza—Brick Oven Pizza
Best Dessert—Chocolate Suicide Cake at Zelo's
Best Cheap Mexican Food—Taqueria Norteños
Best View—Beach House Rest., Po'ipu
Best Phony but Exotic Ambiance— Keoki's Paradise
Best Shave Ice—Jo-Jo's Clubhouse
Best Saimin—Hamura's Saimin
Best Hamburger—Zelo's, Kalapaki Beach Hut, or Duane's Ono-Char Burger
Best Beer List—Zelo's
Best Lu'au—Smith's Tropical Paradise
Best Pancakes—Tip Top Café
Best Sushi—Kintaro or Naniwa
Best Vegetarian Dishes—Caffé Coco
Best Sandwich—Deli & Bread Connect
Best Sunday Morning Buffet—Kukui's
Best Inexpensive Baked Goods—Village Snack Shop
Best Lasagna—Pomodoro's
Best Price Gouge—Chuck's Baked Potato
Best Place for a Romantic Dinner— Tidepools or Dinner on a Beach
Best Local Food—Mark's Place
Best Place on South Shore for Drinks and Pupus—Point at the Sheraton
Best Ice Cream—Shipwreck's Sub

WHERE TO STAY INDEX

Wanted: Visitor seeking room with a view. Must be willing to burn your return airline ticket.

WHERE TO STAY

Your selection of where to stay is one of the more important decisions you'll make in planning your Kaua'i vacation. To some, it's just a place to sleep and rather meaningless. To others, it's the difference between a good vacation and a bad one.

There are four main types of lodging on the island: hotels, condominiums, bed and breakfasts, and single family homes. The vast majority of you will stay in one of the first two types. But B&Bs and single family homes are often overlooked and can be very good values. If your group or family is large, you should strongly consider renting a house for privacy, roominess and plain ol' value. There is a list of rental agents in the WHERE TO STAY INDEX, each willing and happy to send you a list of homes they represent. We also have a B&B referral service there.

We have *brilliantly* labeled the four main sections of Kaua'i as North Shore, South Shore, East Shore and West Shore. **Hotels are in green** and **condominiums are in blue**. Hotels usually offer more services, but smaller spaces and no kitchens. Condos usually have full kitchens, but you won't get the kind of attention you would from a hotel, including daily maid service. There are exceptions, of course, and we will point them out when they come up. You can find their locations on the various maps.

All prices given are RACK rates, meaning *without any discounts*. Tour packages and travel agents can often get better rates. Most resorts offer discounts for stays of a week or more, and some will negotiate price with you. Some won't budge at all, while others told us *no one* pays RACK rates. Also, these prices are subject to taxes of over 11%.

The gold bar indicates that the property is exceptionally well priced for what you get. **SOLID GOLD VALUE**

The gem means that this hotel or condominium offers something *particularly* special, not *necessarily* related to the price. **A REAL GEM**

Experienced visitors to Kaua'i often stay on the north shore in the summer and the south shore in the winter for optimum weather and surf conditions during those times.

These are subjective reviews. If we say that rooms are small, we mean that we've been in them, and they feel small or cramped to us. If we say that maintenance is poor, we mean that the paint might be peeling, or the carpets are dingy or it otherwise felt worn to us.

WHERE ARE THE REST?

You'll notice that some of the resorts listed here don't have full reviews. That's because when we went to press, we found that the rest of the book had increased by *32 pages* (to accommodate all the new stuff we found).

Also, we wanted to include aerial photos of the resorts. After all, a picture speaks a thousand words (and a thousand words takes too long to read, anyway).

So we had a choice. Give you less info on *all* of them or do detailed reviews on only a *portion* of them. Neither choice seemed palatable.

So we came up with a *third* way: List minimal info on all (including if they are GEMS or SOLID GOLD VALUES), print detailed reviews on *most* and post full reviews of all on our Web site, **www.wizardpub.com**. After all, most people use this section before they come to the islands. And with the Web (which has infinite space available), we could do more, like post larger aerial photos of the resorts with specific buildings labeled when appropriate, provide constant updates when necessary and put links to the various rental agents or hotels right in the review, allowing you to go to their sites and get more photos of the rooms. You should remember, however, that resorts post photos to lure you in, and some aren't above posting modified or overly flattering shots when they were new and sparkling. Our aerials don't lie and are designed to give you a feel for

their ocean proximity (does oceanfront *really* mean oceanfront?), so you'll know what kind of view to expect from a given location within the resort. Resorts whose review is posted on our Web site are identified with **WEB REVIEW**

Though most of our Web site is available to anyone, we thought that these extra reviews should only be available to our readers. So when you get to the page with the reviews, you'll have to enter the following password:

uk2442

You'll only have to enter this once and from then on, you can look at all of them.

Please remember that all these reviews are *relative to each other*. This is important. Even staying at a dump right on the ocean is still a *golly gee!* experience. In other words, *Hey, you're on the ocean on Kaua'i!* So if we sound whiny or picky when critiquing a resort, it's only because their next door neighbor might be such a better experience. It doesn't mean you'll be miserable, it just means that *compared to another resort*, you can do better.

HOTELS

All hotel rooms described **(shown in this color)** have air conditioning, an activity or travel desk, telephones, small refrigerators, lanais (verandas), cable TV and have cribs available upon request. None have room service unless otherwise noted.

CONDOMINIUMS

One of the confusing aspects to renting a condo **(shown in this color)**, cottage or house on Kaua'i is the fact that there's no central rental source for many individual properties. Most condo complexes, whether large or small, consist of individually owned condominiums. An individual owner has the prerogative of renting his or her unit through any rental agent they so choose. Consequently, a

50-unit condo resort might be represented by many rental agents. Usually (but not always), prices for comparable units within a given resort are equivalent through different agents. When we describe a particular resort, we will often give the names or phone numbers of one or two companies that dominate the rental pool. But realize that this does not always do justice to the *entire* property. When we describe rates, it is for the larger rental agents. Different agents have different policies for the same complex.

Once you have decided where you want to stay, you can contact the resort. You may also want to contact some of the rental agents on page 222 to determine if they represent any units from the property you have chosen.

Also realize that condominium owners usually have complete autonomy in how they furnish their individual units. Consequently, a resort that we describe as a good deal might have individual units that are not as hot. (Notice how we neatly cover our 'okoles, so that if you get a less-than-charming condo in a resort we recommend, we can always say you got one of the few duds there.)

Many condos have minimum stays—usually three nights. We don't always list this because it changes with different rental companies. More and more rental agents are also requiring you to pay *all* of your condo rental costs before you arrive. It may make you nervous, but you might not have a choice if you're intent on staying at a particular place.

Three bedroom/two bath units are described as 3/2, two bedroom/one bath units are described as 2/1, etc. Differentiation between half baths and full baths is not made. The price spread for rooms of a given size is due to different views, different locations within the resort and seasonal fluctuations. So when you see that a 2/2 unit rents for $140–$180, you should figure that

$180 units have a better view or are closer to the water. The terms Oceanfront, Ocean View and Garden View are used rather capriciously in Hawai'i, so you should be skeptical of them. **Unless otherwise noted,** all rooms come with telephones, complete kitchens, coffee makers, lanais (verandas), cable TV, ceiling fans and have cribs available upon request. Maid service is usually every few days or less at condos unless otherwise noted. None have air conditioning unless otherwise noted. (On Kaua'i, trade winds usually make a/c unnecessary, and few opt for it.)

North Shore Accommodations

THE CLIFFS
(800) 367–7052 or (808) 826–6219
(800) 222–5541 or (808) 826–6585

196 units, tennis courts, pool and spa. Most units are timeshares, but many are not. Clean, nicely furnished 1,000 sq. ft. interiors. The room layout is pleasing, especially the 1,500 sq. ft. units with

Web address for all accommodation reviews is www.wizardpub.com

lofts and high ceilings. Buildings 8 and *maybe* 9 are worth the upgrade to ocean view; otherwise, stick with garden views since other ocean views are pretty distant. 1/2 units are $200–$225, 1/2 units with loft (quasi second bedroom) are $250–$275. The second set of numbers are for Oceanfront Realty whose rates can be substantially cheaper but they have fewer services. With those cheaper rates, it's a SOLID GOLD VALUE

HALE MOI
(800) 535–0085 or (808) 826–9602

40 units. Cheap. No, not the price, but the quality. Duplex units share a lanai. Inside, the construction feels...cheap. The sound of passing traffic is a given if you leave the jalousie windows open (which you'll want to do). And the mountain views are mixed but generally poor. Top this off with Marc Resort's ridiculous rates of $155–$219, depending on if you want both sides (one of which has a kitchen). Either way, the bed is in the main (only) room. In short, you can do better almost anywhere.

HANALEI BAY RESORT AND SUITES
(800) 827–4427 or (808) 826–6522
(800) 826–7782 or (808) 826–9775
WEB REVIEW

HANALEI BAY VILLAS
(800) 222–5541 or (808) 826–6585
37 units. What a surprise. From the outside you'd expect poor views from these

pole houses. The ocean is mostly blocked and the quality of the construction doesn't seem high. But the builders catered to the *mountain* views behind you, which are quite excellent. Two-story units are spacious at 1,300 sq. ft. with the living area upstairs. In all, a decent value for $175.

HANALEI COLONY RESORT
(800) 628–3004 or (808) 826–6235

52 units, pool and spa, BBQS. No telephones, no TV. Kitchens lack dishwashers. Only beachfront resort on the north shore. Some of their units are as close to the water as you will get on Kaua'i *(25 feet)*. We especially like units in A, F, G, I and the front J units. The resort is secluded and somewhat isolated. All units are two bedroom (although the bedrooms aren't completely walled off and second rooms have twins). Rooms are nicely kept. Their location on Kepuhi Beach is outstanding, and the attention to detail is admirable. (Like how they clean the windows between

A REAL GEM

guests.) While the lack of room telephones might make arranging your day slightly awkward, others will welcome it. Restaurant next door. 2/1 units (850 sq. ft.) are $160–$320. Garden views are quite nice. Seventh night free and other packages.

HANALEI INN
(808) 826–9333
WEB REVIEW

KAMAHANA
(800) 222–5541 or (808) 826–6585
WEB REVIEW

MAUNA KAI
(800) 826–7782 or (808) 826–9775
WEB REVIEW

PALI KE KUA
(800) 535–0085 OR (808) 826–9066

98 units, pool and spa. Nicely furnished units, private path to eastern part of Hideaways Beach below the cliffs (which is otherwise only reachable by swimming from the western part of the beach). Many units have very fine ocean bluff views, but it's a bit pricey at these rates. Try to get an upstairs unit. Also, avoid units 5–16 whose poor views demand a steep discount. Restaurant on premises (Winds of Beamreach). Nicely tucked away offering quiet privacy. 1/1 units (763–993 sq. ft.) are $219–$269, 2/2 units (1,100 sq. ft.) are $275–$345. That's too much. You

can do much better with other rental agents, such as Hanalei Aloha, than the on-site agent, Marc Resorts.

PALIULI COTTAGES
(800) 222–5541 or (808) 826–6585

¼ Mile to ocean

8 units, fireplace, microscopic pool in each unit. Each unit is a stand-alone condo, so you will get lots of privacy. Pleasant valley views and reasonably spacious split level interiors make this a decent bargain. The pools are a joke— probably looked good on paper. 2/2 units are $75 and up plus cleaning fee. A good deal as long as you don't mind sharing the place with centipedes. They seem particularly fond of this place.

PRINCEVILLE HOTEL
(800) 826–4400 or (808) 826–9644

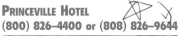

252 rooms, 6 tennis courts, 3 restaurants, 24 hour room service, cocktail lounge, fitness center, in-the-pool bar, several shops, ballroom, conference room, valet parking, keiki program, wedding coordinator, pool with three spas and a keiki pool, lu'au and a free 60-seat cinema. About a third of the rooms have lanais. Casual luxuriance is

A REAL GEM

Web address for all accommodation reviews is www.wizardpub.com

the overall feel here. The hotel is richly furnished with a fabulous lobby featuring 18,000 square feet of marble, a marble fireplace, clamshell fountain and a drop-dead view of Hanalei Bay through the glass walls. The lobby is *so* richly furnished that it's easy to miss little things...like the $100,000 19th-century Erard piano near the Café Hanalei restaurant. The valet parking area has Princeville's trademark serene fountains. The rooms are more expensively furnished than the other resorts on the island and are quite comfortable. They even have a unique feature (on Kaua'i, anyway). The bathrooms have windows with liquid crystal panes. The result? Instant opaqueness at the flip of a switch. In regular rooms these windows overlook the main part of the hotel room; in Jr. suites they overlook the outside. Private dinners on the beach are available for $395 a couple. Expensive, but very romantic. They also give massages near the ocean.

The hotel is designed in a series of tiers, stepping their way down a mountain. The payoff is great ocean views from most rooms. Rather than gaze upon ugly roofs below you, they've thoughtfully planted grass on them. At the bottom is the pool area. The swimming pool is near the beach and is filled all the way to ground level without the usual lip. (Called an infinity pool, in case you're thinking about getting one.) Have a beverage in the pool from the swim-up bar, or walk across the pool bridge and take a few steps across the grass to Pu'u Poa Beach, an easily accessible and relatively user-friendly beach. In comparing the Princeville Hotel to the Hyatt in Po'ipu, the Hyatt has a more exotic, tropical feel, while the Princeville has a richer and more expensive feel (and a better beach). Both are outstanding; it just depends on what you're looking for. The Marriott is somewhere in between, and the Sheraton Po'ipu rooms aren't as nice but

are closer to the water. Because of common ownership, guests here get deeper discounts at the two golf courses.

Rooms 101–119 are avoidable because the hallway in front of them is the main route used by most pool and beach goers. We'd also recommend Mountain View or Ocean View rooms. The interim "Partial Ocean View" units we've seen only show the ocean from the lanai. Parking is an offensive *$15*, valet or self, so you may as well let *them* do it. Local calls are $1.50 and 800 calls are *$2!*

Their Seamless Check-in is a wonderful perk. Go straight to your room and avoid the check-in desk. (Coming and going, if you want.)

Here's a magic code word: Sheraton offers 30%–35% discounts on most rooms if you ask for a *Suresaver Discount* or if you join their *Starwood Preferred* (which is free) when you reserve. Without these significant discounts, rooms (547 sq. ft.) are $405–$615. Prince Jr. Suites (which are nice but a bit on the small side for suites at 821 sq. ft.) are $705. Other suites range from $1,800 up to $4,500 for the Royal Suite. That price includes complimentary everything (as it *darn* well should).

PUAMANA
(800) 222–5541 OR (808) 826–6585
WEB REVIEW

PU'U POA
(800) 222–5541 or (808) 826–6585
(800) 535–0085 or (808) 826–9602
WEB REVIEW

SEALODGE II
(800) 585–6101
86 units, pool. Most units have incredible ocean bluff views at *extremely* reasonable **SOLID GOLD VALUE** prices. You'll never get tired of gazing at the extensive offshore reef. 1/1 units are around 500 sq. ft.

and are a bargain at $105, 2/2 units (second bedroom is a loft) are $135. Even at $135 (from some agents) it's an easy place to like due to the location. The listed phone number has a dozen units; other rental agents include Hanalei North Shore, Hanalei Aloha and Oceanfront. (See list on page 222.) Three night minimum.

East Shore Accommodations

ALOHA BEACH RESORT KAUA'I
(888) 823–5111 or (808) 823–6000

228 rooms, 2 pools, spa, 2 lighted tennis courts, room service, fitness center, free valet parking, volleyball court. This used to be a pretty gloomy resort, but the current owners (who paid less than 10% of what the former owners paid into it) have turned it around nicely. They called it the Holiday Inn SunSpree Resort until 2002. Located adjacent to Lydgate Park (the safest place to swim on the island—they also have a playground), this resort actively pursues families with children. (Sometimes they even catch 'em.) From the Sony PlayStations in every room to

SOLID GOLD VALUE

the keiki room service to the pancakes with peanut butter on them (tastier than you'd think) in the restaurant where kids under 12 can eat free, this place exudes a family feel. Rooms in Pikake Wing are larger (402 sq. ft.) than the Maile Wing (327). Some rooms have bathtubs. They also have 13 cottages that are 510 sq. ft. These are a good value since they have a kitchenette, are very close to the Kamalani Playground and can often be had for $182. Some cottages face the ocean and are the same price as the garden view (if you ask).

This resort's RACK rates are *ridiculous*, but few pay them. Ask for the "Aloha Rate" (which we'll list in parenthesis) and it's this rate that makes them a SOLID GOLD VALUE. Garden views are $239 ($110), Ocean Views are $309 ($130), cottages are $379 ($280 includes buffet breakfast for two). The Jr. Suites are $329 ($160).

BANYAN HARBOR
(800) 422–6926 or (808) 245–7333
(800) 767–4707 or (808) 245–4711

148 units, tennis court, pool. Some have a/c. Lots of improvements here have made this a better deal than it used to be. Many of the units are long-term rentals and some are timeshares, but there are still lots of vacation rentals. Few pay the RACK rate we list, so check for packages.

Web address for all accommodation reviews is www.wizardpub.com

For instance, they often have room/car packages that are cheaper than rooms alone. And the second set of numbers is Prosser Realty, which has cheaper rates than below. 1/1 units (a smallish 460 sq. ft.) are $110, 2/2 units (around 900 sq. ft.) are $140. Of the 2/2s the single level layouts are better. Their brochure is a little misleading. It claims, among other things, that Banyan Harbor is "just steps" from the Kiele Golf Course, as well as Poʻipu's course. So we figured it out. At 2½ feet per step "just steps" means 2,100 steps to Kiele and *33,600* steps to Poʻipu. Better start strolling now...

COCO PALMS RESORT

As we went to press, historic Coco Palms Resort was still closed. It *literally* took the better part of a decade for them to get their insurance check after Hurricane ʻIniki vandalized the place in 1992. (Hmm, next time use FedEx.)

GARDEN ISLAND INN
(800) 648–0154 OR (808) 245–7227

21 rooms. This inn, located near Kalapaki Beach in Nawiliwili, is spotlessly clean with lots of nice touches from the husband/wife owners, such as fresh flowers, free use of their boogie boards and snorkel gear, microwave, fridge and daily maid service. Some have a/c. This is a good choice for those seeking a nice, simple place to sleep, without the exotic grounds of a resort. Rooms are $75–$125.

HALE LIHUʻE MOTEL
(808) 245–2751

21 rooms. A gross, cheap dump. Simple as that. $34. Cash only "in advance."

HOTEL CORAL REEF
(800) 843–4659 or (808) 822–4481

24 rooms, no phones, no air conditioning, refrigerators in some. This is one of those I'm-just-looking-for-a-place-to-sleep types. Good oceanfront location and clean rooms. The Ocean View rooms for $59 are the best value. Rooms are $59–$89.

ISLANDER ON THE BEACH
(800) 922–7866 or (808) 822–7417

198 rooms, pool and spa, poolside bar. Open, plantation style setting adjacent to Wailua **SOLID GOLD VALUE** Beach. Each building has a name. The Kauaʻi and Niʻihau buildings are fairly close to the ocean, allow-

*Password for all Web site accommodation reviews is **uk2442** (you only have to enter it once)*

ing you to fall asleep to the sound of the surf. Rooms are smallish at 365 sq. ft. and go for $145–$198. Jr. Suite (with full kitchen) is $240. The front desk crew tends to be pretty snippy, but you won't have to deal with them too much, and their resident rooster population needs to be thinned a bit. The SOLID GOLD VALUE was sort of a leap of faith. They have lots of specials, and few ever pay the price we listed (and we're assuming you won't either). Grab a beverage from the poolside bar and have a sip at the adjacent beach.

KAHA LANI
(800) 922–7866 or (808) 822–9331

WEB REVIEW

KAPA'A SANDS RESORT
(800) 222–4901 or (808) 822–4901

24 units, pool. This is an excellent bargain. Their small oceanfront studios (some have a pull down Murphy bed—these are recommended for more living space) **SOLID GOLD VALUE** are very clean and cost $117. Small, but

they make good use of space. For this price you are as close as 75 feet from the water on a pretty beach. What a deal! Resident offshore turtles will keep you entertained at dusk. Quiet and private. 3 or 7 night minimum. The aerial photo makes it look like some of the oceanfront units are blocked by trees but the crowns of the trees are above the ocean's horizon, so your ocean views are fine. Studios are $100–$117 (definitely spring for the oceanfront), 2/2 units are $134–$154.

KAUA'I BEACH VILLAS
(800) 822–4409 or (808) 245–7711

150 units, air conditioning in bedrooms, pool and spa, 4 tennis courts (2 lighted), daily maid service. You can also use Radisson's pools next door. Units vary tremendously depending on the condo's owners, creating many overpriced rooms and some reasonable rooms. For instance, the dreamy oceanfront G16 is worth every penny, whereas E18 is horrendously overpriced. Buildings G and H are the best. Most of the resort is timeshare, so be careful not to get mauled by one of the salesmen. Located on a less swimmable part of Nukoli'i Beach. Their rates dropped a lot recently, but then they added an annoying $25 "reservation fee." 1/1 units (684 sq. ft.) are $135–$205, 2/2 units (1,185 sq. ft.) are $180–$260.

Web address for all accommodation reviews is www.wizardpub.com

KAUA'I COCONUT BEACH RESORT
(800) 222-5642 or (808) 822-3455

307 rooms, tennis courts, room service, restaurant, conference room, cocktail lounge, pool and spa and a lu'au on the premises. A tired, neglected resort owned by the Pleasant Hawaiian Holiday people. It was for sale at press time and had been for almost *20 years,* according to the staff. Morale, maintenance and the overall look displayed a lack of commitment. The RACK rates are beyond ridiculous, but few pay them. (Most guests have packages.) In short—get a good bargain or go elsewhere. Their beach isn't very swimmable. Rooms (384 sq. ft) are $140–$280 (oceanfront rooms are larger).

KAUA'I INN
(800) 808-2330 or (808) 245-9000
WEB REVIEW

KAUA'I INTERNATIONAL HOSTEL
(808) 823-6142

They can accommodate 30 people in their dorms or private rooms (just a bed).

Not a bad place to stay. They also have a bulletin board with lots of off-site rooms for rent with descriptions like, ROOM FOR RENT—MUST LIKE PURPLE. $20 for the dorm, $50 for the private rooms. Laundry facilities, pool table, shared bath and kitchen and a pay phone. The TV room was a drive-in once, but not on purpose. We hope they keep the tire tracks as a memento.

KAUA'I MARRIOTT RESORT & BEACH CLUB
(800) 220-2925 or (808) 245-5050
WEB REVIEW ◆

KAUA'I SANDS HOTEL
(800) 367-7000 or (808) 822-4951

203 rooms, 2 pools, conference room, restaurant (Al and Don's). Oceanfront location next to the Coconut Marketplace and reasonable prices make this a very popular hotel with tour package promoters. Many visitors are seniors who take advantage of the generous senior discounts. Buildings are old but exceptionally clean. (They could use more electrical outlets, though.) Overall, a solid, simple place to stay. Rooms are $98–$110 for studios, $110 for kitchenette. Add $29 and you get a car. Lots of packages, so ask.

*Password for all Web site accommodation reviews is **uk2442** (you only have to enter it once)*

LAE NANI
(800) 367–7052 or (808) 245–8864
(800) 688–7444 or (808) 822–4938

84 units, lighted tennis court, pool, daily
maid service. We almost
withheld our GEM this time.
Since Outrigger took over,
prices have gone up too
much and service has come
way down. Too bad. It's still a gem,
just one whose retail price has crept
too high. Pleasant grounds and a very
nice oceanfront location. They have a
Hawaiian heiau on the premises, as well
as a wonderful boulder–enclosed ocean
pond for the keikis (kids). Building 5 has
oceanfront units. Premier Resorts (the
first set of numbers listed) has fewer but
less expensive rooms; call them before
Outrigger. 1/2 units (around 900 sq. ft.)
are $220–$270, 2/2 units (around
1,100 sq. ft.) are $240–$330.

A REAL GEM

LANIKAI
(800) 367–5004 or (808) 822–7700
WEB REVIEW

MOTEL LANI
(808) 245–2965
9 rooms. They claim this "was probably
the first hotel built on the island."
It's...disheveled but reasonably clean (for
the money). Rooms are small—most
under 200 sq. ft.—but have bathrooms
and fridges. Some have a/c. Best view is
of the dumpster. $32–$50. Cash only. If

you only stay one night, there's a *$2*
cleaning fee. (Don't worry, you get your
money's worth.)

PLANTATION HALE (BEST WESTERN)
(800) 775–4253 or (808) 822–4941

160 units, a/c, 3 pools, 2 spas. This
used to be a fairly dreary place, but it's
fared well as a Best Western. No views
(except of the highway from some
rooms), but it's clean and most people
get good rates (cheaper than our printed
RACK rates). Ask for their "Best Rate,"
which is $105. At that price it would
definitely be a SOLID GOLD VALUE. 1/1
units (770 sq. ft.) are $165–$195.

PONO KAI
(800) 456–0009 or (808) 822–9831
(800) 535–0085 or (808) 823–8427
241 units, 2 lighted tennis courts, pool
and spa, 2 saunas. Although it's a fairly
old resort, it's relatively well cared for.
Part timeshare, part vacation rental. They
still sell timeshares here. If you're not
interested, practice saying, "I don't speak
English," in your best Hungarian accent.

Web address for all accommodation reviews is www.wizardpub.com

Rates are quite reasonable (especially the oceanfront), and the price spread between garden view and oceanfront is smaller than most, so spring for the oceanfront if you can. The top phone number doesn't distinguish between ocean *view* and *front,* so grab the fronts. (Bldgs. A–D.) 2-bedroom units have exceptionally large master bedrooms. The lower phone number has similar RACK rates and they have lots of discounts. 1/1 units (740 sq. ft.) are $189–$239, 2/2 units (1,132 sq. ft.) are $209–$279.

RADISSON KAUA'I BEACH RESORT
(888) 805–3843 or (808) 245–1955
WEB REVIEW

TIP TOP MOTEL
(808) 245–2333

34 units, air conditioning, some with TVs, (no refrigerators). Let's face it, the name Tip Top Motel does not exactly instill confidence. But if you are looking for a clean, simple place to stay, this is the place for you. The rooms are very basic and usually immaculate. Each room has two single beds. The restaurant downstairs is a great bargain (see review under DINING). Owned by the

same family since 1916. Price per room is $45 (includes tax). Can't beat that. Located on Akahi Street on Lihu'e.

WAILUA BAYVIEW
(800) 882–9007
(800) 767–4707 or (808) 245–4711

45 units, pool, a/c in most bedrooms. This is probably the best bargain on Kaua'i. Very **SOLID GOLD VALUE** clean inside and out, nicely furnished for the money, excellent elevated oceanfront location. 1/1 units are $99–$121. What a deal! The only problem you'll run into is an awkward payment method. The agent at the second number requires prepayment of all nights *plus* the security deposit one month prior to arrival. But they're on the island. The first number is a mainland-based rental agent so you'll have to arrange getting your key by mail. Either way, to hear the roar of the ocean (and be *so* close to the beach) is worth whatever it takes. Units ending in 01–03 don't have *quite* as good a view. Higher floors are better.

South Shore Accommodations

The **STOUFFER WAI'OHAI BEACH RESORT** and the **PO'IPU BEACH HOTEL** have both been closed since the early '90s courtesy of Hurricane 'Iniki. Wai'ohai's new owners will open it as **MARRIOTT'S WAI'OHAI BEACH**

*Password for all Web site accommodation reviews is **uk2442** (you only have to enter it once)*

CLUB, a timeshare resort. Much to neighboring Kiahuna's horror, construction won't be finished until late 2004 in a start/stop fashion. (Like an annoying neighbor forever working on a room addition.) As for the decaying Po'ipu Beach Hotel…at press time nobody wanted it. (How sad.)

ALIHI LANI
(800) 742–2260 or (808) 742–2233
WEB REVIEW

EMBASSY VACATION RESORT, PO'IPU POINT
(800) 535–0085 or (808) 742–1888

219 units, a/c, fitness center, pool and keiki pool, 2 spas, daily maid service, child care, 22 acres of landscaped grounds and a beautiful stair-step lily pond. This is a hard resort to review because it's such a mixed bag. We were really excited about this property when it was being built and thought that this would be the new *in* place on Kaua'i. All the ingredients were there. In the end it seems that they sweated all the big stuff but not enough of the small stuff. For instance, their pool is a marvelous half sand-lined, half regular pool, so you can gently wade in. Rooms are large with huge master baths. Grounds are nicely landscaped. Child programs are free. That's the big stuff. But nearly all the lights have gobs of dead bugs in them, the lawns have large dead spots, lots of stuff seems worn or broken, and the breakfast area (where you get your "island orientation" as local activity vendors make their pitch to you) is dreary. If you don't want to hear it, go behind a wood lattice divider where a few tables await.

This is probably the last time we'll review this resort. All its rooms are being sold as timeshares, and we don't review full timeshare resorts since they are owned outright…sort of. (At press time it was a little more than 50% sold).

We don't want to sound like we're picking the Embassy apart. It's a fine resort. It's just that compared to other large south shore resorts, they come up short. The RACK rates are too high, but most who stay here do so through a discounter. 1/1 units are $349–$419, 2/2 units are $389–$529.

GARDEN ISLE COTTAGES
(800) 742–6711 or (808) 742–6717
WEB REVIEW

HYATT REGENCY KAUA'I RESORT & SPA
(800) 633–7313 or (808) 742–1234

A REAL GEM

602 rooms, 4 tennis courts with pro shop, golf course, room service, 5 restaurants, cocktail lounges, Camp Hyatt child care service, 5 conference rooms, valet parking, multiple pools and spas, health club, extra refrigerators upon request, lu'au and complete business services. It was hard for us to review this resort without sounding like a couple of drooling sycophants. But the reality of the Hyatt is that they did almost everything right. Put simply, it's our favorite big resort on the island. As you walk into the lobby

Web address for all accommodation reviews is www.wizardpub.com

and see the ocean framed by the entrance, you realize that here, they really sweated the details. The grounds are as exotic as any you will find in all the islands. Their pools are incredible. Gallon for gallon they're more fun than any we've seen. The upper swimming pool seems to meander forever. It even has a slight current and hides such goodies as caves tucked behind small waterfalls (they're easy to miss). Take your time exploring it as it winds through lush vegetation. At the end of the upper pool, you can take the "elevator" (a free and respectably fast waterslide) to the bottom. There you will find what they call the action pool, complete with a volleyball net, waterfalls, spas and an area for children. An island there hides a hot tub. One of our few complaints is that the sidewalk material they use around the pool is quite slippery when wet—and, of course, it's always wet. Above is the adult pool. Across from the lower pool are several *acres* of saltwater lagoon. If you want saltwater without the waves, here it is. The "sand" is actually gravel imported from San Juan Capistrano. (And it's hard on tender tootsies.) Inside the lagoon are several landscaped islands. The grounds are lush and very well maintained and feature a smashing waterfall below the Seaview Terrace Lounge. The resort is located on a so-so beach called Shipwreck Beach. They have covered cabana chairs on the beach. (They're coveted, and the Hyatt could use more.) If you're lucky enough to be under a cabana in the evening during a passing shower, it's something you will long remember. Large hammocks are scattered throughout the grounds. Their nine shops run the gamut from fine art to footwear. Their activity desk by the pool has lots of freebies such as kites, Walkmans, croquet sets, etc. They have a wedding coordinator on site. Guest services are good.

Opened in 1990, the Hyatt has matured into a fairly smooth resort. Occupancy rates are high and perhaps they're not as hungry as they once were. If we have a complaint, it's that service isn't quite as crisp as in the past. Also, items like the $6 per day *self*-parking fee ($8 for valet) in place of the formerly free valet parking are disappointing. (And that valet fee is *per day*, even if you don't leave the resort.) Local calls are a buck. The Hyatt's still an easy gem, just not quite as shiny. (Their awesome grounds still keep them in a class by themselves.)

If your intention is to come to Kaua'i and never leave the resort (which we hope you *won't* do), the Hyatt is the place to come. You'll never get bored here. This is a *great* place to bring the kids, but it doesn't feel overrun with them. Camp Hyatt provides extensive child care service for kids age 3 and up (if potty-trained). Anara Spa is 25,000 square feet and the finest spa on the island. So, what's the catch? Well, amenities like this don't come cheap, but they are not as expensive as you might expect. Spacious rooms (600 sq. ft.) are $395–$600. Suites are $1,000–$3,600. Garden view rooms have the most bang for the buck. Be aware that they have an early departure fee if you opt to trim some days off your stay.

KALAHEO INN
(888) 332–6023 or (808) 332–6023
WEB REVIEW

KIAHUNA PLANTATION RESORT
(800) 688–7444 or (808) 742–6411
(800) 367–5004 or (808) 742–2200
333 units, daily maid service, restaurant. Kiahuna is popular with repeat visitors to Kaua'i. They are grandfathered into their cozy beach location. (Newer resorts have to build farther from the water.)

*Password for all Web site accommodation reviews is **uk2442** (you only have to enter it once)*

Each building labeled on larger shot on Web site.

Buildings 2, 30 and 31 *really are* beach-front. (Our favorite rooms are 7 and 4 in building 2.)

A REAL GEM

The resort lacks a swimming pool, but you're free to use the one next door at the Sheraton Garden Wing. (You can also use their tennis courts.) There are two separate on-site management companies: Outrigger and Castle. We recommend Outrigger; they're easier to work with.

Kiahuna exudes a relaxed, old world, plantation feel. The grounds are lush, well groomed and mature. You'll see ancient monkeypod trees with huge bromeliads as well as lots of orchids. (Not to mention Kiahuna's trademark cactus garden.) Kiahuna is also blessed by its location on a world-class beach (Kiahuna Beach). It's backed by a huge lawn. (The entire resort is paved with bountiful grass.)

Here's the negative. Kiahuna has rotten neighbors. Specifically, the abandoned Po'ipu Beach Hotel and the construction-prone former Wai'ohai (now called Marriott's Wai'ohai Beach Club). The latter is undergoing complete reconstruction, and the building will take place in a start/stop fashion until *2004!* Buildings 40–42 are horribly located behind the pounding construction zone. We'd avoid those rooms. The only exceptions are the occasional "Wai'ohai Specials" that rental agents run for around $100. You have to ask for it and it's not always available. Also poorly located are Bldgs. 9, 10, 11 and 15.

All rooms are decorated differently. An example: Room 6 has an amazing ocean-front location, but its owners used a smelly seagrass floor that's uncomfortable to walk on. So it's hard to say how you'll fare with a specific room. But Kiahuna's calm charms permeate the entire resort.

There is a larger than usual spread in prices depending on proximity to, and view of, the ocean without substantial differences in quality of rooms. 1/1 units are $215–$450, 2/2 units are $345–$700. The top phone numbers listed are for Outrigger management, which has most of the rentals; the bottom numbers are for Castle Resorts.

KUHIO SHORES
(800) 367–8022 or (808) 742–1391
(206) 938–5802

75 units. Exceptional shoreline location.

SOLID GOLD VALUE

You're right on or above the water. Clean units, minimal grounds. And you'll never get tired of their dreamy views. Corner units have particularly tasty vistas. 1/1 units (854 sq. ft.) are $125–$150, 2/2 units (around 1,100 sq. ft.) are $225. 4-night minimum or pay a $75 cleaning fee. The (206) number is for a group of owners who rent units. Credit cards pay an extra 3½%.

MAKAHUENA
(800) 367–5004 or (808) 742–2482
(800) 367–8022 or (808) 742–7555
78 units, small pool, spa, lighted tennis court. The developer seems to have

Web address for all accommodation reviews is www.wizardpub.com

spared…well, lots of expenses, actually. Like the endless concrete stairs at every turn, cheap-looking fixtures, etc. Some of the units are fairly nice inside, many are not. And the resort's not as clean as your other options. We've never been real warm toward Makahuena, and with other south shore resorts improving lately, this resort seems even less compelling. The location out on the point will expose you to *lots* of sea spray-laden wind, so don't expect the windows to stay clean. Those winds, however, tend to keep the units cool. There are 8 different floor plans, so it's hard to say if you'll get a good one. 2nd floor units are better. 1/1 units are $180–$250, 2/2 units are $190–$390, 3/2 units are $290–$345. Prices are lower at the second set of phone numbers.

Nihi Kai Villas
(800) 325–5701 or (808) 742–1412

WEB REVIEW

Po'ipu Crater Resort
(800) 367–8020 or (808) 742–7400
30 units, pool, saunas, tennis court. Located in the bottom of a small crater, the grounds are pleasant and well maintained, but there is no view. (Technically speaking, you're in a hole.) When the trade winds aren't blowing, it can get pretty hot in there, and sounds bounce around in an odd way. Lots of rental agents have units here, not just the number listed. 2/2 units are a pretty good deal at $119–$139.

Po'ipu Kai Resort
(800) 367–8020 or (808) 742–6464
(800) 922–7866 or (808) 742–7424

Poipu Kai's 6 regions identified on larger Web site shot.

350 units, 9 tennis courts with pro shop, 6 pools and spas. This sprawling 110-acre resort sports lots of open ground, widely varied units and close proximity to the Hyatt, its restaurants and shops. Although many rental agents represent Po'ipu Kai, **Suite Paradise** and **Aston** have the most units. **Suite Paradise** has the better rooms and at lower RACK rates, but **Aston** deals with most of the tour package companies that sometimes get good rates for you. If you book it yourself, do it through **Suite Paradise** (their numbers are the ones listed first). The resort is so varied it's hard to sum it up. Po'ipu Kai is broken into six regions with the Po'ipu Sands region having the best

beach access (Building 5 is particularly good). In some ocean view units, the ocean is only visible if you break your neck in two places and hang it out the window. House of Seafood is the on-site restaurant and is a winner. Prices are all over the place and gave us blinding headaches trying to figure it out. In general, **Suite Paradise** 1/1 units are $86–$263, 2/2 units are $129–$300, 3/2 units are $157–$243, 4/4 units are $295–$326. Price increases if you only stay one night. **Aston** 1/1 units are $210–$365, 2/2 units are $290–$445. **Grantham Resorts (800) 325–5701** also has some units at Po'ipu Kai at good prices.

Po'ipu Kapili
(800) 443–7714 or (808) 742–6449

60 units, 2 lighted tennis courts, pool.

A REAL GEM

Well maintained and sculpted grounds, very spacious rooms for the money, and a second-home atmosphere make this an easy recommendation. Buildings 1, 2, 6 and 7 (all 2/3s) have very nice ocean views. You can pick herbs from their garden if you choose to cook. 1/2 units (1,120 sq. ft.) are $210–$275, 2/3 units (1,820) are $280–$395 (more at Christmas). They also have 2,600 sq. ft. penthouses for $500–$550. 5 night minimum.

Po'ipu Makai
(800) 367–5025 or (808) 245–8841

15 units, *very* small pool. The grounds are cramped, the tiny pool's a joke. But the **SOLID GOLD VALUE** views, especially from the third floor rooms, are *excellent*. Right on the rocky shoreline! 2/2 units are $210–$235. The gold bar is for second and third floors. 5 night minimum.

Po'ipu Palms
(800) 742–2260 or (808) 742–2233
WEB REVIEW

Po'ipu Plantation
(800) 634–0263 or (808) 742–6757

¹⁄₁₀ Mile to Ocean

9 units, a/c, spa, BBQ. Not really a condo, nor a hotel. More like a plantation. (Oh…I get it!) Formerly a pretty cozy place, but things change. It doesn't seem as well-tended as it used to be. And it's annoying to see signs telling you that towel changes are $3 and to change your

Web address for all accommodation reviews is www.wizardpub.com

sheets is a ridiculous *$12*. In short, you can do better elsewhere. 1/1 units are $105–$130, 2/2 units are $150–$168. The adjacent "main house" is available for weddings and as a B&B.

Po'ipu Shores
(800) 367–5004 or (808) 742–7700

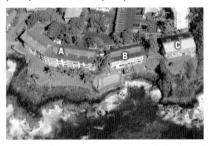

39 units, swimming pool, daily maid service. The rooms feel small, and the grounds aren't much to speak of. You're paying for the extraordinary proximity to, and sound of, the ocean, not the size of the rooms (which are unremarkable and tired). This makes them a relatively decent value. The higher the floor, the better. You might want to avoid the annoying townhouse-style layouts of building C. 1/1 units (which actually have a second bedroom) are $225–$270, 2/2 units are $265–348. Check for discounts. Square footages are all over the place but generally smallish. Their $1 per local call is the sort of steep hit you'd expect at a higher end resort, not here. The $395–$430 penthouse, originally built personally for the developer, is huge and glass-walled (though spartan) and has one of the grandest views on the south shore.

Prince Kuhio
(800) 367–8022 or (808) 742–7555
(800) 367–5025 or (808) 245–8841

72 units, pool. This is a *much* improved property. Built in 1962, the resort's clean for its

SOLID GOLD VALUE age. Grounds are very

well-tended. Located across the road from the ocean, this was a hotel at one time and was later converted to condos, so expect some bizarre room layouts. Some long-term rentals here. Studios are $75, 1/1 units are $90. 5 night minimum.

Sheraton Kaua'i Resort
(800) 782–9488 or (808) 742–1661

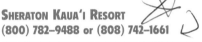

413 rooms, 2 pools, 2 keiki pools, spa, 6 shops, 3 restaurants, 3 tennis courts (2 lighted), valet parking, 3 conference rooms, fitness center (with an inspiring view), 2 massage rooms. The Sheraton is the perfect complement to the Hyatt. While the Hyatt excels at gorgeous and exotic grounds, the Sheraton boldly embraces the ocean. The Ocean and Beach wings are closer to the ocean than at any other major Kaua'i hotel. The sound of the surf hitting the rocks below the Ocean Wing is soothing. Kiahuna Beach, in front of the Beach Wing, is wonderfully close and easy to access. The Garden

A REAL GEM

Wing is generally lacking but is cheaper. All rooms are on the small side (410 sq. ft. for the garden view, 510 sq. ft. for Ocean and Beach), but the resort makes up for it with its cozy relationship with the water. Most rooms are connected to others by a lock-off—good for families needing more than one room. Their restarants—Shells, Naniwa and Amore—have incredible beach views. Kids (under 12) eat free at Shells, and they have a child care program for $30 per half day. The Point lounge is a smashing place for an afternoon cocktail with light fare, and the sunsets from fall to spring are excellent.

The beachside pool is nice and they have a small waterslide. Cabana chairs are a steep $25 per day. Sheraton has a "resort fee" of $20 per day, which includes parking (a long walk), *full buffet breakfast for two*, tennis courts and a few other doodads. Their seamless check-in is wonderful—just head to your room with the bellman, no hanging around at the registration desk. When picking a room, this is one of those places where it's worth the extra money to spring for an ocean view room, if you can swing it. Ask about an "escape to Hawai'i" discount when you reserve. Rates are $320–$500. Suites $900–$1,100.

SUNSET KAHILI
(800) 827–6478 or (808) 742–7434

36 units, pool. Built in 1968 (you'd swear

it was the '50s), it's old but well-kept. All units have nice ocean views, with the fifth floor being particularly good. It used to be popular with seniors, but they said they're "trying to get away from that"—whatever that means. Average value. 1/1 units are $125–$150, 2/2 units are $225.

WAIKOMO STREAM VILLAS
(800) 325–5701 or (808) 742–7220

60 units, tennis court, pool. Pretty and well-kept grounds and large rooms (all garden **SOLID GOLD VALUE** views). Lots of privacy, very good value here. 1/1 units (1,100 sq. ft.) are $79–$125, the 1,500 sq. ft. 2/2 units (2nd bedrooms are a loft with limited privacy) are $125–$155. (More at Christmas.) Repeats get 10% off.

WHALERS COVE
(800) 367–7052 or (808) 742–7571
WEB REVIEW ◆

West Shore Accommodations

KOKE'E LODGE
(808) 335–6061
WEB REVIEW

PMRF BEACH COTTAGES
(808) 335–4752
12 cottages (6 more planned), 3 lighted tennis courts, driving range, fitness center, pool, racketball, handball, restau-

Web address for all accommodation reviews is www.wizardpub.com

rant. Adjacent to Barking Sands Beach, this place is a steal—if you're in any branch of **SOLID GOLD VALUE** the military or retired. (Having seen *Saving Private Ryan* won't qualify.) Each cottage is a self-contained 1,000 sq. ft. 2/1, and you can have 'em for only $55–$75. (It's almost worth a stint just for that perk alone.) We considered trying to bounce a quarter off the bed but thought better of it.

WAIMEA PLANTATION COTTAGES
(800) 922–7866 or (808) 338–1625

Note the muddy ocean water here.

50 units, stereos, pool and keiki pool, conference room. These cottages were once plantation workers' homes, and each is as different as their former owner's tastes. We had a hard time coming up with adjectives to describe the rooms. They have old-style floors and furniture, just like from the plantation days. Units have been refurbished with modern amenities, but they retain the old-style feel inside, *usually* without feeling *too* old and worn. They are very clean. At this former plantation, peace and privacy are yours—the trade-off is relative isolation given the location on the extreme west side. There is much feeling of 'ohana (family) here, and you will definitely experience the aloha spirit. With their location so close to the mouth of the very reddish Waimea River, swimming in the murky ocean water is pretty poor at this marginal beach. The coconut grove and banyan trees add to the quiet charm of this property, and this is a good place to watch the sunset over the private island of Ni'ihau. The on-site restaurant, Waimea Brewing Company, is fair, though the beer needs help. Units vary tremendously from $175 for some 1/1 cottages, to $650 for a 6/3 oceanfront cottage. Contact them for a complete list.

YWCA CAMP SLOGGETT
(808) 245–5959 or 335–6060
WEB REVIEW

Rental Agents

Nearly all the rental agents on the list on page 222 also represent private home vacation rentals, as well as condominiums in various resorts. Contact them in advance to obtain lists of rentals available or hit their Web sites. (We have links to all of them from our site.) Many great bargains can be found this way.

Index

Restaurant index on page 194, Where to Stay index on page 222.

Restaurant index on page 194, Where to Stay index on page 222.

Index

245

Restaurant index on page 194, Where to Stay index on page 222.

Index

Restaurant index on page 194, Where to Stay index on page 222.

Restaurant index on page 194, Where to Stay index on page 222.

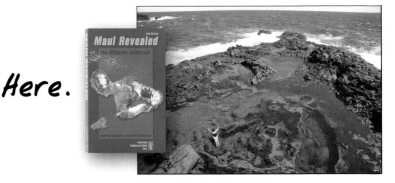